The Railways Marple and District from the earliest days to 2015

By WARWICK R. BURTON M.A.(Cantab.)

Marple in its heyday c.1910. View northwards from Brabyns Brow Bridge. At the Up platform the MSL 2-4-2 tank No.735 takes water on an up Hayfield train, while large numbers of passengers get out. A down goods train can just be seen on the opposite line. Notice the up loop, 'table road' end goods shed to the right.

To commemorate the 150th anniversary of Marple Station in 2015 and dedicated to the memory of my parents, Maurice ('Monty') Burton (1919-2005) and Margaret ('Marjorie') Burton (1922-2011).
Published by M.T. & W.R. BURTON, MARPLE

Introduction

If you go and stand on the Brabyns Brow Bridge and look at Marple Station today, you will see a suburban station served by diesel units shuttling between Manchester, New Mills and Sheffield. If you are lucky you may see a goods train pass through.

But if you had gone to the same spot in the 1890's, you would have looked down upon a busy main line station at the height of its importance. A large, four platform layout with a substantial range of buildings and a fine array of canopies, built to deal with throngs of passengers would confront your eyes. To one side, instead of a car park as now, you would see a small but busy goods yard handling every kind of merchandise. Instead of diesels of uniform appearance, you would be struck by the variety of liveries borne by the locomotives and carriages. For at that time Marple was an important junction on the Midland Railway's route from London to Manchester and Liverpool. For instance, if you went to Marple station at about 9.30 am, you would see all four platforms occupied by no less than seven trains at once, with destinations ranging from London St. Pancras and Nottingham to Liverpool and Sheffield. At various times you would see dining and sleeping car expresses call, trains being divided for Manchester, Liverpool and Blackburn, and yet others being marshalled up. Going to Manchester you had a choice of trains to three different termini- London Road, Central and Victoria by four different routes. On a typical day well over a hundred trains were booked to call; these trains terminated at 22 different places, ranging from Bristol to Blackburn, Southport to Lowestoft and Leicester to Blackpool, linking Marple directly to well over 100 different stations in 13 counties. Including non-stop expresses and goods trains, about 240 trains had to pass through Marple every 24 hours - or an average of one every six minutes day and night!

How did Marple Station come to be such a hive of activity? This book attempts to show how Marple attained such importance, and how it has declined to its present suburban status. The story begins in the last years of the 18th century with the railways' progenitors, the canals, and deals with the early schemes to put Marple on the railway map. Much of the tale is of the cut-throat Victorian railway politics which gave the district its rail network, and of the arrival of the Midland Railway which gave Marple its importance.

But ever since Marple was by-passed by the Midland, to give higher speeds to Liverpool and Manchester in 1902, the tale is one of decline, with rising road competition. In the "Beeching Era" of the 1960's many lines in the district closed, but in Marple the basic network survived. The 1970's however saw a reversal of fortunes, and now our railways seem to have an assured future.

This is a local history, a history of the railways which were built through Marple, a community perched on the edge of the Pennines, once a cotton township, but now largely a pleasant suburb. The area covered centres on Marple Station, but includes the stations at Strines, Rose Hill, High Lane and Middlewood, which serve out-lying parts of the Marple district (this book covers the former Marple Urban District Council area which included Marple, Mellor, Rose Hill, Strines, High Lane and Middlewood). But it is a local history painted against the larger background of railway and national politics, and the dramatic social and economic changes of the past 185 years since the opening of the Liverpool and Manchester Railway in 1830 brought the first modern main line railway in the world to North West England. This edition was prompted by the 150th anniversary of Marple station on 1st July 1865, and the need to update the earlier editions to include events since 1980 up to the present. Chapters I-XII have been re-issued much as written in 1980, though with some corrections, additions and amendments; these first twelve chapters are written from the perspective of 1980. A completely new chapter XIII covers the period 1980-2015.

Warwick R. Burton
Formerly of 69 Bowden Lane
Marple, Cheshire
Now of 3 Fairway, York, YO30 5QA

1st Loco. into Marple station 'RATTLESNAKE' on Sunday 14th June 1863

First published October 1980
Second edition published June 1981
Third edition published February 1983
Fourth expanded edition published June 2015

Harwich Boat Train passes through Marple from the North, 1979 (author).

Acknowledgements

The number of people whose writings, photographs, reminiscences and assistance have helped towards the production of this book is too numerous to recount, but to them all I am very grateful. But I first must acknowledge my debt to my father, who first stimulated my interest in railways, and over the years gave guidance and assistance in my researches. I owe a great deal of the detailed information and reminiscence, which puts the flesh on the bare bones of my book, to the late Mr. "Hughie" Fletcher. He was intimately acquainted with the railways of Marple from the last years of the 19th century until his death in the 1970's, both as a child, then as a joiner in the employment successively of the Midland Railway, L.M.S. and B.R., and subsequently as a Maintenance Foreman, and finally in retirement. This book would be the poorer without his contribution. I wish particularly to acknowledge my debt to George Dow, by whose kind permission I was able to use the information and photographs set out in his monumental trilogy "Great Central" to provide much of the basic material for this book; his "Great Central" provided me with a first class example of a railway history.

I must thank the late Mr. I.R. Smith for kindly permitting me to use some of his photographs to illustrate this book (as well as providing information on the Macclesfield Line and Dieselisation) and also to J.R. Hillier and E. Oldham for the use of their excellent photographs. Specific credits accompany each photograph in the text; photographs taken by the author are so credited. Photographs with no credit are from photographs in the author's collection. I am indebted to all the authors referred to in the Bibliography, whose works have provided much useful information; to the Railway Staff, past and present, of the Marple Area, who have over the years given me assistance and much information of value ; and to various members of the Marple Antiquarian Society, and its successor the Marple Local History Society, for their help and encouragement. I particularly wish to thank Judith Wilshaw, who kept the book 'in print' after the third edition sold out. I am also indebted to Ann and John Hearle, Chris Walters, Hilary Atkinson and Neil Mullineux. I am grateful to the Friends of Rose Hill Station and particularly Craig Wright, who did a lot of proof reading and provided information, and David Sumner. I am also grateful to Chris Taylor, Steve Black, Greg Abell and other members of the Friends of Marple Station for information. Other groups that have contributed are Anne Ryan and the Friends of Strines Station and the Allcards of the Marple Locks Heritage Society. I must thank Network Rail for details of freight trains, Ashley Goddard of the Office of Rail Regulation for passenger figures, Paul Harrison for details of services on the Hazel Grove Chord, the Midland Railway Study Centre at Derby for information on the landslip of 1893, and Peak Rail for information on the Marple area signal boxes. Sue Day of the Horseboating Society provided information on the narrow boat 'Maria'. I would like to thank Josiah Slingsby for editing, typesetting and layout. Finally a big thank you to Arthur Procter for high quality up to date photographs.

Abbreviations (to 1980-for post 1980 abbreviations see Chapter XIII)

B.R.	-	British Railways/Rail
C.L.C.	-	Cheshire Lines Committee (G.C., Mid & G.N. Joint)
d.m.u.	-	diesel multiple unit
G.C./G.C.R.	-	Great Central Railway
G.C. & Mid	-	Great Central and Midland Joint Railway
G.C. & N.S.	-	Great Central and North Staffordshire Joint Railway
G.M.P.T.E.	-	Greater Manchester Passenger Transport Executive
G.N./ G.N.R.	-	Great Northern Railway
L. & M.	-	Liverpool and Manchester Railway
L.M.R.	-	London Midland Region
L.M.S.	-	London, Midland and Scottish Railway
L.N.E.R.	-	London and North Eastern Railway
L.N.W.	-	London and North Western Railway
L. & Y.	-	Lancashire and Yorkshire Railway
M. & B.	-	Manchester and Birmingham Railway
M.B.M.	-	Macclesfield, Bollington and Marple Railway
M.B.M. & M.J.	-	Manchester, Buxton, Matlock and Midlands Junction Railway
M. & L.	-	Manchester and Leeds Railway
M.N.M. & H.J.	-	Marple, New Mills and Hayfield Junction Railway
Mid/M.R.	-	Midland Railway
M.C.C.	-	Marple Community Council
M.S.J.A.	-	Manchester South Junction and Altrincham Railway
M.S.L.	-	Manchester, Sheffield and Lincolnshire Railway
M.U.D.C.	-	Marple Urban District Council
N.S.	-	North Staffordshire Railway
P.T.E.	-	Passenger Transport Executive
S.A. & M.	-	Sheffield, Ashton-under-Lyne and Manchester Railway
S. & M.	-	Sheffield and Midland Joint Railway (M.S.L. & Mid)
S.D. & W.B.	-	Stockport, Disley and Whaley Bridge Railway
S.E.L.N.E.C.	-	South East Lancashire and North East Cheshire (P.T.E.)
T.U.C.C.	-	Transport Users Consultative Committee

'Up' is towards London and away from Manchester; 'Down' is away from London and towards Manchester

Seal of the Sheffield & Midland Joint Committee. (BR)

Monogram of the Sheffield & Midland Joint Committee. (Author)

Contents

Introduction 4
Acknowledgements 5
Abbreviations 5
Contents 6

I. **The Dawn of the Railway Age: 1794-1845**
   1. The Earliest Railways in the District (1794-1830) 7
   2. Some Might Have Beens (1830-6) 7
   3. The Sheffield, Ashton-under-Lyne and Manchester Railway (1836-45) 7

II. **The Railway Comes to Marple: 1845-68**
   1. The Abortive Whaley Bridge Branch (1845-51) 8
   2. L.N.W. "Invasion"- The Stockport, Disley and Whaley Bridge Railway (1854-57) 8
   3. The M.S.L. Reaches "Compstall" (1857-62) 9
   4. The Marple, New Mills and Hayfield Junction Railway (1860) 9
   5. Construction of the M.N.M. & H.J. (1861-5) 9
   6. Opening of the M.N.M. & H.J. (1865-8) 11
   7. The First Marple Station (1865) 11
   8. The Effect of the Railway 12

III. **Enter the Midland: 1845-72**
   1. The Midland Attempts to Reach Manchester (1845-56) 13
   2. The Midland Advance from Rowsley (1857-65).... 14
   3. The Midland Enters Manchester and Marple. (1866-8) 14
   4. The Sheffield and Midland Joint Committee (1868-72) 14
   5. Marple Station in 1872 15

IV. **Marple's Expansion 1872-89**
   1. The Origin of the Cheshire Lines Committee (1859-74) 15
   2. The Manchester and Stockport Railway (1866-75) 16
   3. Marple Rebuilt (1875) 16
   4. Train Services in 1875 17
   5. Manchester Central (1875-88) 18
   6. The Midland Junction Line (1889) 19

V. **The Macclesfield, Bollington and Marple Railway: 1863-1910**
   1. Origins (1849-64) 20
   2. Construction and Opening (1865-73) 20
   3. The Middlewood Curve (1876-85) 21
   4. Description of the Line 21
   5. Train Services 24

VI. **Fin de Siècle: Marple's Heyday 1890-1898**
   1. The Dore and Chinley Line (1888-94) 24
   2. The Marple Landslip of 1893 24
   3. Marple Train Services: August 1898 24
   4. Improvements to Marple Station 27
   5. Operating at Marple... 28
   6. Strines.. 29

VII. **Marple By-passed: 1898-1911**
   1. The Need for the "New Line" 31
   2. Construction and Opening.................................. 31
   3. Train Services in the Early 20th Century 32

VIII. **A Changing World: 1911-1939**
   1. World War I 34
   2. The Aftermath of War and the Grouping (1918-1930) 35
   3. Train Services Between the Wars 36
   4. The Macclesfield Line 37

IX. **World War II and Nationalisation: 1939-61**
   1. World War II (1939-45) 38
   2. Nationalisation (1945-8) 38
   3. The Post War Period (1948-55) 43
   4. The Modernisation Plan (1955-61) 44

X. **The Beeching Era: 1962-70**
   1. The Beeching Report 45
   2. The End of the Midland Main Line 46
   3. Freight Closures 47
   4. The Closure of the Hayfield and Macclesfield Lines 47

XI. **Marple Rebuilt: 1970**
   1. The Decision to Rebuild 50
   2. The Plan for the New Station 50
   3. Demolition and Rebuilding 51
   4. The Official Opening 51
   5. Description of the New Station 52

XII. **The Turn of the Tide: 1970-1980**
   1. Continuing Doubts -The Early 70's 54
   2. SELNEC and the "Picc-Vic" Scheme 55
   3. Greater Manchester Transport (1974-80) 55
   4. Future Prospects 57

XIII. **The Railways of Marple 1980-2015**
   1. Abbreviations since 1980 60
   2. Marple Station 60
   3. Strines Station 62
   4. Rose Hill Station 62
   5. Privatisation and Franchises 64
   6. Train services 1980-2015 65
   7. Rolling Stock 68
   8. Freight Trains 69
   9. Marple-Stockport 70
   10. Tourism 70
   11. The Future 71

Marple Railway album 72

Bradshaw 1910 75
Addendum-The Horseboat 'Maria' 75
Index 76
Bibliography 78
Author's Biography 79

List of Plans and Diagrams
   Marple Station c.1900 33
   Middlewood Station c.1910 23
   Railways around Marple c.1910 30
   Rose Hill Station c.1900 23
   Strines Station c.1900 30

All Diagrams by Author

I. The Dawn of the Railway Age. 1794-1845

1. The Earliest Railways in the District (1794-1830)
The origins of the earliest railways of the district are inextricably bound up with the preceding canal era, and the need to improve transport facilities between Sheffield and Manchester which as manufacturing centres grew enormously in the early 19th Century.

The Peak Forest Canal was incorporated in 1794 to run from Ashton via Marple to Bugsworth and Whaley Bridge, with Samuel Oldknow a leading promoter of the scheme. The main part of the canal was opened in 1796, the exception being the Aqueduct over the Goyt, and the Marple flight of locks, which were not completed until 1800 and 1805 respectively. In the interim, an inclined plane tramway, with horse traction, ran from the base of the Lime Kilns at Top Lock to join the end of the canal from Ashton. This was to take materials to the site of work, and to allow traffic to pass between the separate portions of the canal. This operated from 1798 and was out of use by 1807. I hesitate to say this was the first railway in Marple, as there were probably earlier crude tramways at the numerous small collieries of the district, but it was certainly the first of length and any more than local significance. The immediate aim of the Peak Forest Canal was to carry limestone from the Peak District. To gain access to supplies beyond the easy reach of canals due to the hilly terrain, the Peak Forest Tramway was constructed and opened up in sections 1796-1800. The Tramway ran from Bugsworth via Chapel-en-le-Frith to the various quarries at Peak Forest.

The need was however felt for better communication between Sheffield and Manchester, than was provided by either canal or road at the time. Various schemes were proposed in 1813 and again in 1824 and 1826 to link the two cities by an extension of the Peak Forest Canal from Bugsworth, by various combinations of canals and inclined plane railways. In 1825 the Cromford and High Peak Railway was authorised to link the Peak Forest Canal at Whaley Bridge with the Cromford Canal at Cromford Wharf, and thus link Manchester to the East Midlands. It was opened in 1830-1, a standard gauge (4' 8½") line, like the Liverpool and Manchester, and most British railways since. To pass through the uncompromising terrain of the High Peak, long inclined planes worked by stationary steam engines, and sharp curves were employed. Despite these problems, and those of transshipping goods to and from canal at either end, this railway gave great advantage in the transport of goods over the horse and cart. This, combined with the opening In 1826 of the Macclesfield Canal from Marple Top Lock to the Trent and Mersey Canal near Kidsgrove, formed the most direct route from Manchester to the West Midlands and London, placed Marple on a series of important through routes by canal and tramway for the carriage of goods. Most passengers however still went by road, on foot, horseback or coach. The coming of the canal continued the prosperity brought by the Industrial Revolution, and particularly Oldknow's Mills, and has left its mark on the district; the canal was Marple's economic lifeline until the arrival of the railways in the 1860's. These canals, and both the Peak Forest Tramway and Cromford and High Peak Railway figure again in the railway political battles of the 1840s, 50s and 60s.

2. Some Might-Have-Beens (1830-36)
There was however still no direct route from Manchester to Sheffield. The impending opening of the Liverpool and Manchester Railway however stimulated the promotion in 1830 of a railway to extend right the way between the two cities. George Stephenson, 'The Father of Railways', was the engineer of this line, though there is some doubt whether he actually surveyed the line, or merely acted in a consultative capacity. Certainly, with its numerous inclined planes and heavy gradients, it was a most un-Stephenson-like line. It was to start from a junction in Manchester with the Liverpool and Manchester Railway, and proceed to Stockport, where it turned east, and ran along the banks of the Goyt, via Marple to Whaley Bridge; in Marple the line was to pass beneath the canals, by means of one of the "short tunnels" referred to in the plans.

To surmount Rushop Edge a lengthy series of inclined planes were required. The line then ran down the Hope Valley, and again by inclined planes over Totley Moor and to Sheffield. The course of the tine is remarkably similar to the Midland Railway's much later route from Manchester via Stockport and Marple and the present 'Hope Valley Line' to Sheffield, which however used tunnels not inclined planes to conquer the Pennine Range.

The scheme met with considerable opposition from those who looked askance at a so-called trunk route which contained 6½ miles of tunnels and 6 inclined planes. A particular critic was Henry Sanderson, the promoter of the 1826 scheme, who in 1831, suggested an alternative route via a Woodhead tunnel, Glossopdale, the Valley of the Etherow past Compstall and Marple, and so to Manchester via Stockport.

Both of these schemes would have placed Marple on a through Sheffield-Manchester trunk route, but it is fortunate that the 'Stephenson' scheme with all its inclined planes was not built. It belonged to an earlier, more primitive era of railways, and was more akin to a mineral tramway. The second, Sanderson scheme was very close to the eventual course chosen for the Manchester-Sheffield trunk line, but the route into Manchester via Marple and Stockport was not to be, and the line built took a more direct route via Godley. It is interesting however to briefly speculate what might have happened had the Woodhead route been built via Marple!

3. The Sheffield, Ashton-under-Lyne, and Manchester Railway (1836-45)
The need still remained however for a route from Manchester to Sheffield; the success of the Liverpool and Manchester Railway (L. & M.) whose receipts, particularly from passengers, exceeded all expectations, gave added impetus for a Railway linking the two cities, especially one suitable for passengers, which the Stephenson scheme had manifestly not been. In 1836 such a line was promoted and a route via Penistone, a Woodhead Tunnel, Longendale and Ashton decided on, with branches to Glossop and Stalybridge. This was authorised by Parliament in 1837 as the Sheffield, Ashton-under-Lyne, and Manchester Railway (S.A. & M.).

It had been originally intended to have a separate terminus for the S.A. & M. at Store Street in Manchester but it was soon decided, in order to reduce costs, to make a junction with the so called Manchester and Birmingham Railway (M. & B.) at Ardwick and run into a joint terminus at London Road. The M. & B. was authorised in the same year as the S.A. & M. to run from Manchester to the Grand Junction Railway at Crewe; it was opened in 1842, and included the massive Stockport Viaduct.

But it soon became apparent, even before these lines were constructed, that a great deal of inconvenience was going to be caused by the number of separate terminals in existence or planned in the city - four in all. Accordingly in 1838 the directors of Manchester and Leeds Railway (M. & L.) approached the L. & M. Board and it was agreed to build a line linking the two railways, with a joint station at Hunt's Bank. The L. & M. agreed to this, and work started. The L. & M. however had immediate doubts about the scheme, and proposed to the M. & B. and S.A. & M. that they should jointly build a line from Ordsall Lane, near the L. & M. terminal at Liverpool Road to Store Street, crossing Manchester on a viaduct, with "a great central station for general use at Store Street" and a tunnel connecting with the M. & L. terminus at Oldham Road. Prophetic words, a "great central station"! But the scheme was not to be, and the hope of having one central Manchester station faded. Instead stations proliferated, so that by 1910 Manchester had 7 where trains terminated, if Salford and Mayfield are included; even now there are 3. As it was the M. & L., having already started building the Hunts Bank link, frightened the L. & M. into keeping to its original arrangement, by threatening to ally with the Old River

Company and thus gain independent, albeit watery, access to Liverpool. Accordingly in 1844 the Hunts Bank station opened, and was named Victoria.

A link between L. & M. and Store Street was eventually built and opened in 1849 - the Manchester South Junction (and Altrincham) Railway (M.S.J.A.) -the Altrincham branch was an afterthought; but this was too late, and henceforth the railways of Manchester were irrevocably split into North and South halves. The line eventually built to Marple, being a branch off the successor of the S.A.& M. was therefore inevitably a southern Manchester line. This split continued until the 1980s and early 1990s when cross-Manchester links were finally created. However by 1841, the first section of the S.A. & M. was ready, albeit only single track, and trains began running from the temporary M. & B. terminus at Travis Street in Manchester to 'Godley Toll Bar' near where Godley Junction now is. There were stations at Fairfield, Ashton, Hooley Hill (renamed Guide Bridge in 1845), Dukinfield Dog Lane (closed in 1845; it was about half a mile east of Guide Bridge near where the line crosses the Peak Forest Canal), Newton and Hyde, and Godley Toll Bar. In 1842 the line was extended to "Glossop" (now Dinting) with an intermediate station at Broadbottom. In the same year the new joint terminus with the M. & B. was opened at Store Street, later known as London Road, and stations were opened at Ardwick and Gorton. Ashburys did not open until 1855. Sheffield was finally linked with Manchester to the strains of "See the Conquering Hero Comes" from the band accompanying the first through train in 1845.

Meanwhile the S.A.& M. had already arranged for horse drawn omnibus feeder services to Ashton and in 1842 Mr. James Boulton went into business providing horse drawn passenger boat connections by canal. Early in 1843 he started a service from Dukinfield Dog Lane Station along the Peak Forest and Macclesfield Canals to Marple and Macclesfield. To provide this service he bought 6 or 7 disused boats from the Glasgow and Paisley Canal; each accommodated 100 passengers, and travelled at 8 to 10 m.p.h.

The boats were drawn by 2 horses, on one of which rode a postillion in buckskin trousers. Fares charged were 1½d per mile 'cabin' and 1d per mile 'steerage', with 60 lbs of luggage per person free. These boats took precedence over all other canal traffic. Boulton received 3d from the S.A. & M. for every passenger coming off his boats who bought a full ticket to Manchester. While progress must have been rapid on the level sections of the canal, going up the flight of 16 locks at Marple must have been painfully slow. No doubt many got out to walk, refreshing themselves en route at the Aqueduct, Navigation and Ring 0' Bells public houses. It is not known how long this service lasted. It probably ceased when the Stockport-Macclesfield line opened in 1845, but it marks the first extension of rail based transport interests into Marple, the prelude to the arrival of the railway proper.

II. The Railway Comes to Marple. 1845-1868

1. The Abortive Whaley Bridge Branch (1845-51)

The next fifteen years are a tale of the railway which was coming to Marple, but never actually got there for one reason or another. The year 1845 marked the height of the 'Railway Mania', when a multiplicity of competing and needless schemes were proposed; most of them collapsed when the bubble burst in 1846. Two mania schemes were eventually built however, and had a great effect on our district.

The first was the ponderously titled 'Manchester, Buxton, Matlock and Midlands Junction Railway' (M.B.M. & M.J.), which was to make a line from Cheadle Hulme to Ambergate, and thus provide a route for the M. & B. to Ambergate and so to London independent of the Grand Junction Railway (G.J.R.) with which the M. & B. was in continual dispute. This line would have passed very close to High Lane and the southern end of Marple.

The other line was promoted by the S.A. & M. and was for a line from Hyde Junction via Marple to Whaley Bridge, with a branch to Hayfield; the eventual aim was to reach Buxton and provide an outlet via the C. & H.P. to the Midlands The M.B.M. & M.J. and this branch were obviously therefore in competition in covering much the same ground between Manchester and Buxton, but agreement was reached that neither company would oppose the other. Both were authorised in 1846.

The S.A.& M. in 1846 purchased the Ashton, Macclesfield and Peak Forest Canals, along with the Peak Forest Tramway connecting with the latter. This consolidated their grip on these feeders to the railway, prevented any competition from the canals with their proposed Whaley Bridge branch, and occupying the district they passed through, probably with a view to preventing an invasion by any other company, notably the London and North Western Railway (L.N.W.) recently formed by the amalgamation of the L. & M., M. & B., Grand Junction and London & Birmingham Railways. These canals remained in Railway ownership - S.A. & M. (1846-47), M.S.L. (1847-97), G.C.R. (1897-1923), L.N.E.R. -until nationalisation in 1948 so were owned by the railways -102 years longer than any other organisation. Upon nationalisation they passed to the British Transport Commission, North Western Divisional Waterways of the Docks & Inland Waterways Executive. This in turn became the BTC Board of Management in 1953, the British Transport Waterways in 1955, and the British Waterways Board in 1963. From 2012 the canals were vested in the Canal & River Trust. Meanwhile the S.A.& M. accepted a tender from Miller and Blackie of £238,515. 18s. 8d. for the construction of the line from Hyde Junction to Whaley Bridge; a ceremonial cutting of the first sod was held, and work began. One of the last acts of the S.A.& M. Board was to accept a tender for rails for the line, for on 1st January 1847 the S.A. & M. amalgamated with various lines in Lincolnshire and became the Manchester, Sheffield and Lincolnshire Railway (M.S.L.).

But the mania of 1845 was followed by a slump, and drastic economies were necessary. In November 1848 work on the Whaley Bridge branch was stopped, and in 1851 powers for the line beyond Hyde allowed to lapse and the rails pulled up on that portion which had been finished as far as Hyde, because they were needed elsewhere. Thus Marple, which might have had a railway by 1850, had the finances of the M.S.L. been less shaky, was forced to wait another 15 years to get its line.

2. L.N.W. 'Invasion'- The Stockport, Disley and Whaley Bridge Railway (1854-57)

In the interim the M.S.L. had to countenance an 'invasion' of its 'territory' when in 1854 the nominally independent Stockport, Disley and Whaley Bridge Railway (S.D.& W.B.) was authorised; it was in fact an L.N.W. scheme. And it was perfectly obvious that with a railway to Whaley Bridge, the M.S.L.'s interests would suffer. In particular the traffic then passing from the C.& H.P. onto the Peak Forest Canal at Whaley Bridge would pass onto this new line, thus avoiding transshipment, and the M.S.L. would lose its hold on the territory south east of Manchester and its hopes of reaching Buxton. The L.N.W. Chairman, Lord Chandos, blandly assured his counterpart on the M.S.L., Lord Yarborough, that they would protect the canal traffic of the M.S.L., as far as it could, from the competition of the S.D.& W.B. - though there was plainly no intention of honouring this, as events showed. Had finances not been so shaky, there is little doubt that the M.S.L. would have revived their Whaley Bridge branch, linked it with the Peak Forest Tramway, and made an attempt to get to Buxton first and block the L.N.W.'s schemes. This it prepared to do in 1856, when, on the advice of the Midland, it resurrected the Whaley Bridge branch to run from Hyde Junction, via Romiley, Marple and New Mills to Bugsworth. Here it was to connect with the Peak Forest Tramway to reach Buxton; there was also to be a Hayfield branch. But the M.S.L. was in no financial position to get to Buxton. What is more, the M.S.L. had no wish to break entirely with the L.N.W. which was the only major railway with which it had any physical links.

The M.S.L. was therefore unable to do anything to prevent the S.D. & W.B. which opened in 1857, and was thus the first railway to pass through the area that later became Marple Urban District Council, albeit only the southernmost tip. Soon after a link was made to the C. & H.P. at Whaley Bridge, and this promptly drew off most of the traffic which had previously passed onto the Peak Forest Canal, to the disgust of the M.S.L.

Until 1857 both the Midland Railway and M.S.L. were party with the L.N.W. to an illegal 'common purse' arrangement known as the 'Euston Square Confederacy' designed to strangle the newly built Great Northern Railway, opened in 1850 from London King's Cross to Doncaster. However, the agreement collapsed in 1857 due to double-dealing on the part of the L.N.W. As a result the M.S.L. & G.N. promptly allied themselves to run a service between London King's Cross and Manchester via Retford, thus breaking the L.N.W.'s previous monopoly of all London-Manchester traffic. The L.N.W. was furious and tried to prevent this new service by blocking lines into London Road Station, imprisoning passengers who dared to arrive by G.N. trains from London, and even throwing the M.S.L. Ticket Clerk out of his Booking Office and his tickets after him onto the street!

3. The M.S.L. Reaches 'Compstall' (1857-62)

In this new climate, and with improving receipts, the M.S.L. determined to obtain revenge on the L.N.W. and press on into the Peak District.

In 1858 the only part of the Whaley Bridge line which had been completed was opened to passengers from Hyde Junction to Hyde (now Hyde Central), as a single track branch. In the same year the M.S.L. obtained parliamentary powers to construct a line, following the course of the proposed Whaley Bridge branch, from Hyde, via Woodley and Romiley to 'Compstall'. This terminus was to be perched high above the Goyt Valley near Marple Aqueduct, and was obviously not intended to be permanent, but rather pointed into the Peak District. A tender of £80,000 was accepted from James Taylor and construction began. Work was rapid and the line opened on 5th August 1862. At last the railway had reached Marple - or almost. The line was single track, and the stations had only one platform. Romiley's present Down buildings (i.e. on the Manchester platform) very probably date from the opening of the line or soon after, with the exception of the stair hall which was added in the 1880's. There is no record of what 'Compstall' station looked like. It was probably a temporary wooden affair and no traces are now visible, though the hollow on the South side cutting wall just west of the viaduct may represent a trace of its site.

Bradshaw 1862 shows a service of 7 trains each way between Manchester London Road and 'Marple'. It is interesting that Compstall was called 'Marple' in the timetables as an unpleasant surprise lay in store for anyone who arrived thinking they were at Marple, or 'Compstall', for that matter, as the station was a long way from either! There was also one late evening train each way between 'Marple' and Guide Bridge only giving a total of 8 each way in all. Two trains each way called at all stations to Manchester, but the rest omitted certain stops. The timings were 45-50 minutes for an all stations train, while the fastest took 35 minutes - not bad for 1862 and hardly much worse than the timings of today for the same route!

4. Marple, New Mills and Hayfield Junction Railway (1860)

"Whereas the construction of a railway on a point on the authorised Newton and Compstall line of the Manchester, Sheffield and Lincolnshire Railway at Marple in the County of Chester to New Mills and Hayfield in the County of Derby would be of public and local advantage ...." so ran the formal preamble of Bill for the Marple, New Mills and Hayfield Junction Railway (M.N.M.& H.J.) laid before Parliament in 1860. The L.N.W. however failed to see the "public and local advantage" of the line, but instead saw this ostensibly local line as a thinly disguised M.S.L. attempt to penetrate districts of which the L.N.W. had come to regard itself as sole proprietor. The L.N.W. therefore promoted another 'local' scheme, the Disley and Hayfield Railway, as a branch off its protégé, the still nominally independent S.D.& W.B.

Incredibly both Bills were passed by Parliament and construction began on both lines. But public opinion was in favour of the Marple line, and ultimately the Disley and Hayfield line was abandoned - but not before some earthworks had been constructed in the Hayfield Valley. It is as well this line was abandoned, as it would have been ludicrous to have two separate lines serving the small village of Hayfield.

The M.N.M.& H.J. remained an independent railway company for some years yet, and had its own board of directors, though the M.S.L. was well represented on it. It had its own elegant seal with the title of the company, and the arms of Cheshire and Derbyshire inscribed thereon.

5. Construction of the M.N.M.&H.J. (1861-5)

The engineering works required by the M.N.M. & H.J. were severe, and it must be remembered that all the work was done by pick and shovel, wielded by navvies, with some use of gunpowder to blast rock. Wheelbarrows, horse-drawn carts, primitive hand cranes, and temporary tramways with small contractors steam locomotives were all that were used to shift thousands of tons of earth. The engineer for our line was J.G. Black and the contractors for the Compstall-New Mills section Benton and Woodiwiss, who employed the hundreds of navvies, as well as the more skilled carpenters, stone masons and bricklayers that were required to make a railway line. Most of the men moved about the country, following their contractor to wherever there was work. Some came from Ireland, whence they had fled the 'hungry forties' of the Irish Potato Famine. They were infamous for their hard drinking, foul language, and vicious brawling, but were also capable of superhuman labours in shifting earth all day in all weathers. Their effect on the life of Marple in the brief period from 1861 to 1865 that they were in the district is not recorded. But it must have reminded residents of the construction of the canals earlier that century, during which a judge, when sentencing seven persons to death for murders committed in the disorders accompanying the construction of the canal, said he "hoped there were not many more Marples in this kingdom." The navvies building the Woodhead Tunnel not so long before had been considered so degenerate that it was felt necessary to send a missionary to them, and he found them living in mud huts, and willing to sell their wives for a gallon of beer! One hopes that the construction of the M.N.M. & H.J. was not the scene of such depravity; and in fact many navvies and craftsmen settled down in Marple, thus augmenting the Irish Roman Catholic population which similarly arrived with the canals. A number of old Marple families with Irish names derive from the influx of labour for the construction of canal and railway. This is particularly the case in Marple Bridge, and it is significant that the first Roman Catholic Church in Marple was built in Marple Bridge.

At the northern end of the line is the most impressive structure on the line, Marple Viaduct. On it, the line emerges from a broad cutting where once 'Compstall' station stood, and strides on the viaduct across the valley of the Goyt, 124 feet in the centre above the river on 12 stone arches, 918 feet long in all. Immediately on gaining the Marple side of the valley the line crosses the Peak Forest Canal by a skew girder bridge. The Peak Forest Canal Aqueduct is a remarkable and lofty construction, stupendous when built, but is dwarfed by the railway viaduct beside it, particularly when the aqueduct is viewed from the train. The aqueduct took over five years in building between late 1794 and 1800 but such was the advance in building techniques and organisation in 50 years, that the viaduct only took one year from April 1862 to April 1863 despite being a much larger structure. Seven men lost their lives in building the Aqueduct but none on the Viaduct. The Viaduct Is a simple and yet solid and dignified work, as good now as when built 150 years ago, though carrying trains many times heavier than those of the 1860's.

The Marple Wharf Branch seems to have begun as a temporary contractor's line opened in June 1862 to bring in materials to build the railway line. However it outlived the construction of the railway. It served the pound between locks

Marple Goyt Viaduct from the West in 1906.

Marple Goyt Viaduct with a d.m.u. to Hayfield, July 1968. (I.R. Smith)

2 and 3 but was later extended to serve the pound between locks 1 and 2. In a M.S.L. minute of November 1866 about the Peak Forest Tramway from Bugsworth, Underdown, the General Manager of the M.S.L., recommended the construction of sidings near Dove Holes from the Quarries to the Midland Railway at Peak Forest whence the M.S.L. had running powers northwards. The long term aim of this was to close the upper level and inclines of the Peak Forest Tramway-though in the event the tramway did not close until 1925. Underdown was not seeking the closure of the Peak Forest Canal; rather the Marple Wharf branch was to be retained to allow transshipment of limestone from Dove Holes from the railway to the Peak Forest Canal and onwards by canal to its destination. The cost of the Marple Wharf Branch was £1790 and included a crane. The Horseboat 'Maria' referred to in the Addendum at the end of this book was constructed in 1854 at Jinks boatyard at Top Lock Marple to convey ballast from Bugsworth to Guide Bridge for the M.S.L. The Marple Wharf Branch diverged from the main line just south of the Aqueduct so the signal box controlling this junction was therefore called Marple Wharf Junction - several years before the Macclesfield line joined the line at this point. The Wharf branch consisted of a single track slip off the main line, passing through the cutting bank and Aqueduct Road, which was the probable course of the tramway built in the construction of the canal locks. Immediately beyond this road, there were two sets of sidings each adjoining a wharf beside a canal pound. The northern single siding was at a higher level than the canal, and would be suitable for transshipping from rail wagon to canal barge, while the southern two sidings were below canal level, so that the wagon floors would be about level with the wharf, and the canal barge opposite; this would be suitable for transshipment both ways.

The wharves however fell into disuse as less and less traffic passed by canal as the railways network expanded, and the branch was removed in about 1900. The course of the branch is however quite clear, and the wharves intact if overgrown; the discerning eye could in 1980 even pick out the remains of rotten sleepers and rusty ironwork amid the bushes.

Beyond Marple Wharf Junction, where a signalbox would have been erected in time for the opening of 1865, the line passes through a deep broad cutting, and enters Marple North Tunnel, which passes beneath the same canal that the viaduct crosses over and the same canal that Marple Wharf is on a level with. This if nothing else brings out forcibly the rate of descent of the Marple locks. Marple North Tunnel, according to Midland Railway line diagrams was 99 yards long, but is now shown as 88 yards; this is due to rounding to the nearest chain - a chain is 22 yards - hence the discrepancy. Another cutting through the grounds of Brabyns Hall, and passing under the narrow stone bridge No. 28 carrying the coach drive to the Hall, brings us to the site of Marple station. The station was and is badly sited - it is crammed onto a natural ledge extended by excavation into the hillside. There was no room to expand and access onto Brabyns Brow difficult. But in building the line the engineers had great problems to face.

The line is at about 375 feet above sea level most of the way from Hyde to New Mills. As the line from Romiley approaches the valley of the Goyt the engineers had to either go over or under the Peak Forest Canal to get to Marple - it would be impossible to build a line to the east of the canal as this would have required huge embankments. Going under the Peak Forest Canal at this point would plunge the line into a very long deep tunnel under Marple, and result in heavy gradients to reach New Mills. Going over at a high level, as was in fact done, was the only real choice. Having once gone under the canal it was necessary to get back across its course, to keep to the banks of the Goyt - the alternative would be several miles of tunnel under Marple Ridge. The railway therefore, to cross the canal's path, had to go under it instead of over, which it does passing through Marple North Tunnel. It was quite a feat to drive a tunnel a few yards under the canal. From Marple North Tunnel the line had to cling to the precipitous sides of the Goyt valley - almost sheer cliffs in places - to reach Strines, hemmed in therefore by canal, and steep valley sides. The railway had little choice of course. The line therefore passed along a steep hillside midway between the settlements of Marple Bridge and Marple. That does not explain the present siting of the station, which is highly inconvenient for both places, being approached by very steep hills. It might be argued that a better site would have been just off Arkwright Road near where Stone Row stood, as this was much closer to the then centre of Marple. This is true, and while it would have been possible to get a station in just north of Marple South Tunnel, it would have been very cramped, with no room for platform buildings, very difficult access, and with no room for bay platforms, a goods yard and other extensions which were found necessary. What is more, such a site, while more convenient for Marple would have been very inconvenient for Marple Bridge and Ludworth. It is true that the line could have been carried much closer to the centre of Marple, but only in a tunnel 100 feet or more below the ground - an impossible location for a steam worked passenger and goods station. The site actually chosen, while inconvenient, makes use of a natural ledge to gain some elbow room, and has direct, if hilly, road access. It is also about midway between the settlements of Marple and Marple Bridge. While the stately viaduct was rising, and the cuttings were being hewn from solid rock south of the station, the station itself was rising, built of brick and local stone; no doubt thousands of bricks arrived by rail and canal to make the buildings.

The work on the northern section of the line appears to have been rapid, for soon after the completion of the viaduct in 1863, work was sufficiently advanced for a locomotive to run across the viaduct and into Marple Station. This locomotive which had the honour of being the first to enter Marple Station was a contractor's locomotive called 'Rattlesnake'. It was an 0-4-0 tank engine weighing 8 tons with 4 coupled wheels, 3 feet in diameter, and a boiler pressure of 60 lbs. This little engine had a maximum speed of 10 m.p.h. and had been employed on contractors trains between Hyde and 'Compstall'. It could pull 8-10 full wagons up the 1 in 70 to Romiley, and on a level road as many as 15 to 20. It was however a very 'jumpy' locomotive due to the chain drive, and this probably gave rise to its name. Entering Marple on Sunday June 14th 1863, it made quite an impression on Marple, and a photograph of the locomotive hung in the waiting room of the pre 1970 Marple Station. The locomotive was later used to construct other railways all over the country up to the end of the 19th century. The site of the station was originally crossed by the 'Seven Stiles' footpath, which ran from Bowden Lane to Marple Bridge. The footpath still exists in part today. It was diverted slightly when the canal was built. In 1866 the widowed Ann Hudson inherited the Brabyns Hall Estate from her cousin John Wright. The estate adjoined the line, and was in fact cut by it. The Hudsons being

High Church Tractarians, All Saints, of the Low Church tradition, did not find favour, and in 1869 allocated land adjoining the station site, for a Church, completed in 1870, where they could worship as they wished. Some old residents of Marple used to say that "the Hudsons built St. Martin's not for the Love of God or the Church, but to stop the railway getting any more of their land". Presumably they thought a Church as good a barrier to expansion as any. This is however probably folk myth.

Anyway as a result of the railway and the building of St. Martin's Church, finished in 1870, the 'Seven Stiles' footpath was diverted. On descending from the canal it was carried over the line by a footbridge, on much the same as its previous line, and then instead of carrying straight on as previously, it was turned at right angles to run between station and Church, to emerge on Brabyns Brow at a little gate between the Church Lych Gate and the station goods yard gate. Later the footpath was diverted yet again, when the station was expanded in 1875, and the tall glass and iron canopies erected. It was probably felt not desirable to have a footbridge passing a 'stone's-throw' away from the glass roof, with St. Martin's Church School so close. So the footpath was diverted to its present course, high on the cutting top west of the station.

South of the station a deep rock-hewn cutting led to Marple South Tunnel, originally 270 yards long, passing through a rocky outcrop, with a sheer drop to the Goyt Valley, around which no railway could pass. It used to be said that the construction of this tunnel and the line to the south necessitated the diversion of the dead straight road down to Oldknow's Mill, but this is again folk myth and probably a memory of the 1893 landslip near this point (see the new section 2 in Chapter VI). Beyond the tunnel, the engineers carved a narrow ledge on the almost sheer sides of the Goyt Valley, on one side making a cutting wall 50 feet high, on the other raising a tall embankment on the precipitous slope. Half way along this section passed a footpath ascending out of the valley to Strines Road, which was used every Sunday to conduct the apprentices domiciled at Bottoms Hall to All Saints Church. A footbridge was provided to avoid disturbing so sacred a procession, and it was dubbed 'Arkwright's Bridge' after Oldknow's better known partner, and the name is used in preference to the more prosaic official 'Bridge No. 24' to this day.

Emerging from this ledge, the railway was immediately confronted by the Goyt yet again. The course of the line could have followed the eastern bank of the Goyt to New Mills but a much larger viaduct would have been necessary there, so it was decided to cross the Goyt near Strawberry Hill Farm, where a glacial moraine narrows the valley. Here a five arch viaduct was built with an iron girder spanning the widest point over the Goyt itself to avoid having a pier on the riverbed. The railway was then taken through the succession of cuttings and embankments as it crossed the alternate ridge and fold of the flanks of Mellor Moor to New Mills, though on occasions where the hillside grew steep the railway was forced once again to cling to a ledge on the hillside. At New Mills the station is in the most cramped spot conceivable; it is on a ledge blasted out of rock, with the resulting man-made cliff towering above, the foaming river Goyt below with a vast, vertical retaining wall to support the railway above. Immediately to the east are the mouths of the two tunnels carrying the line under New Mills itself. Strines Station was not so confined, but being on the hillside was not very close to the Strines Village and Textile Works it was meant to serve, which were in the valley bottom. Such were the engineering works on the Marple and New Mills Section, which while heavy and taxing the ingenuity of the engineer to find a relatively level way through such a difficult and varied landscape, were not exceptional so far as railways in the Pennines and Peak were concerned.

6. Opening of the M.N.M. & H.J. (1865-8)

There were great delays in the construction of the line, due to the varied engineering problems, and it was not until 1st July 1865 that the line onwards from Compstall to Marple and New Mills was opened. Though there are no records of the opening day, great must have been the rejoicing in Marple when the first train entered, no doubt to the accompaniment of brass bands, and rounded off by a sumptuous dinner and toasts of "Success to the Marple, New Mills and Hayfield Junction Railway". Strines was not however completed until the following year and first appears in Bradshaw's Guide in August 1866, so the exact date is not known but may be 1st August 1866. The line was originally single throughout, as was the whole branch from Hyde Junction. Platforms were on one side only - the Down or present Manchester platform at Marple, Strines and New Mills; as yet no goods facilities were provided. The line was worked from the outset by the M.S.L. with a train service of 8 trains a day each way. With the extension of services to New Mills, the temporary terminus of 'Compstall' was closed. Four days after the opening, the M.N.M.& H.J. was amalgamated into the M.S.L. At first the M.S.L. showed little enthusiasm for the extension to Hayfield, but was spurred on by reports received that the L.N.W. was surveying for a line from Chapel-en-le-Frith to Sheffield, and was thinking of reviving its moribund Hayfield branch. So late in 1865 the M.S.L. accepted a tender of £27,400 from Rennie and Co. for the construction of the Hayfield branch. Delays however accompanied the construction of this line, not quite 3 miles long. Being in a valley bottom, no very considerable engineering works were required, apart from the 197 yard long tunnel under New Mills (called 'Hayfield Tunnel'). The line was opened to passengers on 1st March 1868. The branch was built wide enough for double track, but when opened was single, and remained so for the whole of its existence. except that a short half mile section out of New Mills was later doubled. As yet there were no goods facilities anywhere on the Hyde Junction-Hayfield branch, and these did not come for some years yet, which is unusual as lines generally opened for goods prior to passengers. A small engine shed was provided at Hayfield.

Meanwhile the M.S.L and L.N.W. had composed their quarrel arising out of the entry of the G.N.R. into Manchester in 1857, and had agreed to the construction of a new joint station at London Road, to replace the old station which had only one arrival and one departure platform. The new station was completed in 1866 and used by the Marple and New Mills services. It was partitioned into two separate halves for M.S.L. and L.N.W. with arrival and departure platform for each, and a large iron railing between the two companies, which also had entirely separate offices in the frontage. The M.S.L. side was where platforms 1-4 now are, and in the adjoining roof span the L.N.W. had the space now platforms 5-8. These two 1866 roof spans remain in use to this day, though with later additions.

7. The First Marple Station (1865)

Marple Station, when the line first opened in 1865, was very different from the large affair which existed until demolition in 1970. The line was as yet single, and as the branch carried only a very light passenger service and no goods trains, there would be no loops or sidings. It is probable therefore that in 1865 the station consisted of a single platform, on the Down side, though land was set aside to the east for further expansion when required. The single platform was probably about 200 feet long, that is less than half its eventual length, and on this platform were erected the station buildings, adjoining Brabyns Brow Bridge.

All the stations on the Hyde Junction-New Mills branch had only one platform as yet, which was on the Down in all cases except Hyde where the original platform appears to have been on the Up, nearer the town. The original buildings at Hyde Junction, Hyde, Woodley, Romiley, Marple, Strines and New Mills are all on this original single platform, and had a very strong family likeness, though none is quite like any other; little motifs, common however, to them all was the use of a carved stone pinnacle in the shape of a trefoil at the apex of gables, dormer windows, porches etc., a distinctive form of corbel supporting the end of the gable, and similar windows and doors. Original buildings now only survive at Romiley, Woodley and New Mills, of which New Mills is in almost original 1865 condition, and Romiley most altered, but these common features can still be seen. New Mills is unusual in that the initials of the Contractor or Mason - 'I.C.B.' and the date - 1864 were carved in the trefoiled apex of the dormer window of the station house, where they are still visible to the discerning eye.

The designer of Marple, and almost certainly of all the others, was the Chief Architect of the M.S.L. at London Road, Louis Edgar Roberts M.I.C.E. This gentleman lived in Victoria Park, Longsight and eventually retired to Chorlton where he died in 1916. The style chosen for all the stations was a mild Tudor which was apparent in the stone mullioned windows, 'four centred' arches above the 'Perpendicular' style doors, the use of gables and dormers and motifs such as the trefoiled and pinnacled gable ends, barge boards and ornamental corbels. This was then a new style in Marple, but very common on railway lines in the 50's and 60's and often quite pleasing, while giving the air of reassuring solidity so dear to Victorian enterprises. The buildings Hyde to Marple inclusive were of red brick with stone ornamentation on door lintels, windows etc. Strines and New Mills were of locally quarried stone, as was Hayfield which was of the same architectural family. For some inexplicable reason Hyde Junction however was also of stone.

Marple was only then a wayside station, but had buildings larger than any other on the branch except Hyde, presumably as it was considered the most important place on the branch. The site for the buildings was very awkward, as the platform where the waiting rooms were required was well below the level of Brabyns Brow and stairs were necessary to link street and platform level. At road level was an entrance hall and porch which led to a square stair hall with five flights of stairs leading down from street level. At the foot of the stairs were two ticket windows, while the door led onto the platform. This arrangement lasted until the 1920s when a passage was made leading out of the stair hall through the ticket office and provided with ticket windows. Adjoining the stair hall there was a one storey range of buildings, all entered from the platform. First was a large general office, with ticket windows to the stair hall, then a Ladies' Room, with frosted glass, and a lavatory at the rear. The next room was used in the 20th century at least, as a parcels and left luggage Office. Next came the Gents' lavatory, and then the General Waiting Room, which subsequently became a First Class waiting room when a larger waiting room was provided further north along the platform, and ended its days as the Station Master's Office. Then came the three storey station house, a very commodious dwelling, and finally there was a room for the Porters and a Store Room. Along the front of the buildings was a fine cast iron canopy, filled with glass, supported on corbels on the wall. This was identical to the one still existing at New Mills. The station was probably gas lit from the start, as gas had by then come to the village.

8. The Effect of the Railway

Before the railway age, the district was dependent on canal and road for transport. The canals were reliable, except in Summer drought and Winter ice, but painfully slow and labour intensive. As we have seen the canal did for a while carry a passenger service, but with a top speed of 10 m.p.h. and a much lower average speed due to the locks, their use was limited for passengers, particularly for long distance travel. There were some turnpike roads in the district but there was no public transport apart from the lumbering common carrier's wagon. One had to be moderately prosperous to own a horse, and only the very rich could afford a carriage. The few stage coaches serving Marple, were a very far cry from the relatively fast mail coaches; even by the best mail coach however it took nearly 24 hours to reach the capital. Travel by coach or horse was hardly comfortable, and in the winter the roads were often impassable. The coming of railways to Manchester, Stockport, Hyde, Hazel Grove and Disley, placed Marple near railway

'Beechwood' the home of Edward Ross. 12th Sept 1978 (Author)

The Grave of Edward Ross, Secretary of the MSL 1850-92, in the churchyard of St. Mary's R.C. Church, Marple Bridge. (Author)

lines, but left it dependent on canal or road to get to and from the stations. When the railway actually reached Marple in 1865 however, Manchester was brought within 35 minutes of Marple by the best trains - a quite creditable timing, even by today's standards, and other towns in the vicinity were also brought within reach. The coming of the railway brought a far wider range of opportunities before the inhabitants of Marple, especially the lower middle and working classes, who hitherto had rarely travelled. Railway fares, though not cheap, were a fraction of stage coach fares - for those who could afford the fare (which could certainly not include more than a proportion of the working class) it was now possible to travel quite easily and visit Manchester or the Pleasure Gardens at Belle Vue. Gradually people's horizons were widened by the ease of transport offered. In particular the professional and mercantile classes found it was possible to reside pleasantly in country districts such as Marple, and travel daily to Manchester, Hyde etc. The opening of the railway placed Marple among the places considered highly desirable to live, especially in view of the beauty of the surroundings. Accordingly, solid mid-Victorian villas begin to appear from 1865 onward on Longhurst Lane, Lower Fold, Church Lane, Hibbert Lane and Station Road, the latter renamed when the railway came, having formerly been Back Lane. One of the most distinguished early 'commuters' was Edward Ross J.P. who was the Secretary of the M.S.L. from 1850 to 1892. He lived in a very large stone house called 'Beechwood' on Stone Row, built on land owned by the M.S.L above the Marple South Tunnel. The garden was across the road and linked to the house by an iron footbridge, said to prevent the family's children coming into contact with low class urchins. He had a private footpath from Stone Row to the station, descending to the line beside the South Tunnel portal by means of steps, and running along the cutting side of Brabyns Brow, which saved him the detour via St. Martins Road: traces of this path can still be seen. Ross was a devout Roman Catholic, and gave many gifts to beautify St. Mary's R.C. Church in Marple Bridge, where he was buried In 1892; his monument still stands in the churchyard.

As the canal age gave Marple the 'Navigation Hotel' so the railway age gave the district the 'Midland' and 'Railway Hotel' in Marple Bridge and the 'Railway Inn' beside Rose Hill station (see Chapter V.4). All three were renaming of older pubs to keep up with the times -the 'Railway Hotel' in Marple Bridge was renamed as early as C.1830, inspired no doubt by the success of the L. & M. but the 'Hare and Hounds' did not become the 'Midland' until the 1870s, when it went up market supplying horses and carriages for ongoing journeys. The 'Railway' at Marple Bridge was bought by

Ian Niven, a Director of Manchester City Football Club and renamed the 'Royal Scot' in 1975.

The trains working the local services to Marple in the 1860s were composed of 1st, 2nd and 3rd class carriages, of wooden construction, and with minimal springs - they were varnished teak and embellished with the company's coat of arms. The 1st Class were upholstered and comfortable up to a point. 2nd class coaches might or might not be upholstered, while 3rd class coaches had 6-a-side compartments, with wooden seats. Lighting was by miserable oil lamps let in through a hole in the roof. The locomotives were painted a pleasant Brunswick green, lined out black and white, with reddish brown under-frames. The locos working Marple services would have most likely been rather old 2-4-0 or 2-2-2 tanks of diminutive proportions, from Gorton or Hayfield Shed. The trains had no automatic brakes, and there were in fact no brakes on the carriages at all. The driver and guard alone had control over rather primitive handbrakes. Though travel by train was by our standards primitive, with rough riding coaches, uneven track and sharp jolts on starting and stopping, no heat and hardly any light, it was a great deal better and quicker than anything before, though modern 'Pacers' are probably equally rough riding!

III. Enter the Midland. 1845-1872

1. The Midland Attempts to Reach Manchester (1845-56)

We must now return to 1845 and the Railway Mania to trace the steps by which the Midland came to play such an important part in the railways of Marple. Do you remember the Manchester, Buxton, Matlock and Midlands Junction Railway (M.B.M. & M.J.)? The line was projected in the 'Railway Mania' of 1845 as a means of providing the M. & B. with an outlet to the south independent of the Grand Junction Railway route via Crewe, Unfortunately as soon as the M.B.M.& M.J. got its Act in 1846, its most enthusiastic supporter, the M. & B., amalgamated with the Grand Junction and other railways to form the L.N.W. and the LN.W. was not interested in a route to London competing with its own. This, combined with the post-Mania slump, made it very difficult to actually obtain finances for the line, and all that was eventually opened was an 11½ mile branch from Ambergate to Rowsley- a short line for such a long title! The line was originally worked by the Midland, but unfortunately the L.N.W. had inherited from the M. & B. a considerable number of shares in the line, so that in 1852 the Midland was forced to agree to a joint Midland/L.N.W. lease of the line for 19 years. The Midland was chiefly interested in the line as a springboard for Manchester. The L.N.W.'s only interest in the line was to prevent it being used as such. Eventually however when the Midland did reach Manchester, the L.N.W. gave up its interest in the line and the M.B.M.& M.J. became part of the Midland in 1871.

Meanwhile the Midland was unable to do much on this front for some years, as it was dependent on the L.N.W. for access to London via Rugby; and both companies were pre-occupied with the newly built Great Northern Railway. In an attempt to strangle this new company, which had broken the L.N.W.'s monopoly of all traffic north out of London, the L.N.W. formed an alliance with the M.S.L., L.&Y. and Midland. 1854 however saw the promotion of a nominally local railway, the Stockport, Disley and Whaley Bridge (S.D. & W.B.) which we have already met, causing agitation to the M.S.L., by invading its 'territory'. But this line also offended the Midland, as it followed the projected course of the M.B.M. & M.J. closely and was rightly seen as an L.N.W. attempt to occupy the territory in between, and so block their route to Manchester; for this nominally local line was in fact heavily subsidised by the L.N.W.

The Midland were however unable to put up parliamentary opposition as they had no direct interest in the area. The L.N.W. assured both Midland and M.S.L. that it had no intention of using the line to reach Buxton. In 1856 however the Midland suggested an extension from Rowsley to Buxton to meet with an extension of the S.D. & W.B. and thus permit through running between Derby and Manchester. The L.N.W. refused to consider through traffic, and would only agree to accommodate local traffic, which clearly

Marple Station in its early days. A M.S.L train headed by a class 68 4-4-0 No. 441 built at Gorton In 1881. The train from Manchester is shunting from the Up main to Up loop ready to depart to Manchester again. Note the footbridge as yet lacks a roof. c.1885 (George Dow)

showed their intention of blocking the Midland. Meanwhile the L.N.W. broke its assurances and secretly promoted a nominally local extension of the S.D. & W.B. to Buxton. The proposed course was extremely sinuous and heavily graded and in this the Midland rightly saw the line as designed to prevent any fast through running, if the Midland ever should reach Buxton. By now both the M.S.L. and Midland were so frustrated by the L.N.W.'s double dealing that they broke up their alliance with the L.N.W. The M.S.L. promptly allied with the G.N. The L.N.W. was initially furious at the G.N./M.S.L. alliance which brought a competitive route from London into Manchester; but in the end they decided to make the best of a bad job and concluded an illegal agreement with the G.N., M.S.L. and L. & Y. to prevent the Midland reaching or sending any traffic to Manchester, an attempt which failed, due to the boundless energy of the Midland.

2. The Midland Advance from Rowsley (1857-65)

The Midland was however by now free from the L.N.W. grip for access to London, having in 1857 concluded an agreement with the G.N. for Midland trains to run into King's Cross via Bedford and Hitchin. Caution was therefore thrown to the winds and the Midland promoted a Bill for a line from Rowsley to Buxton, and requested running powers over the S.D. & W.B. and its Buxton extension to Manchester. The L.N.W. tried to scotch this by proposing a direct route from Whaley Bridge to Buxton, or alternatively by leasing the C. & H.P. and making it into a through route to block the Midland. These attempts however failed, and the Act for the Rowsley and Buxton line was passed in 1860 but the L.N.W. made it quite clear it would not allow any through traffic to pass via Buxton.

The Midland was not put off and decided on an independent line to Manchester, whatever the cost, and commenced surveying. One day, in the Autumn of 1861, took place a chance meeting which was to alter the course of railway history, and have a profound effect on Marple. The Chairman, Deputy Chairman and General Manager of the Midland were driving through the countryside, examining the course of various proposed routes to Manchester. Suddenly in a narrow lane they came face to face with a party of M.S.L. Directors and Officers in a dog cart. "And what are you doing here?" the M.S.L. party good naturedly demanded. The two parties then spent the rest of the day together, and in the course of conversation it was suggested by an M.S.L. Director that the Midland might be able to use the M.S.L. and M.N.M.& H.J. line to reach Manchester. This proposal was eagerly seized by the Midland men who offered terms the M.S.L. could not refuse. Thus the M.S.L. double-crossed its allies the L.N.W. & G.N. For at that very time the M.S.L. was still smarting from the L.N.W. invasion of its territory via the S.D. & W.B. and was at loggerheads with the G.N. over some other issue in South Yorkshire; in addition it had no wish to see yet another competing line in their territory between Manchester and Buxton. This meeting has gone down in railway history as 'Dog-Cart Diplomacy'! A formal agreement was reached later the same year, and in 1862 the Midland's Rowsley and Buxton Extension Line was promoted to run from Blackwell Mill (near Miller's Dale) on the Rowsley and Buxton line under construction, to New Mills on the M.N.M. & H.J. with powers that "the Midland should run its own trains over the railways of the Sheffield Co. (i.e. M.S.L.) to or from Manchester, and every other place in Manchester, in Lancashire, or Cheshire, or beyond". Prophetic words! The L.N.W. in panic offered the Midland "facilities" over their Buxton line, but the Midland counsel at the parliamentary hearing retorted that the Midland knew what "facilities" were where the L.N.W. was concerned. The L.N.W. had what it considered a serious objection to the line, in the plight of gouty patients coming to Buxton to take the waters for the easing of their complaint and forced to change at Millers Dale by reason of the new Midland Main Line's avoidance of Buxton. But the line enjoyed the support of every landowner on its route, Manchester Corporation and numerous manufacturers and merchants, while the City's Chamber of Commerce spoke warmly of the improvement in communication with the Midlands such a line would bring. Notwithstanding the alleged plight of gouty patients, the line was authorised by Parliament, and work began.

Meanwhile work had been progressing since 1860 on the Rowsley and Buxton line, which presented innumerable difficulties to construction through the narrow gorge of the Wye from Bakewell onwards, with numerous tunnels, viaducts as well as underground streams and caverns to contend with, while the ducal estates of Haddon and Chatsworth had to be protected from disturbance. The line was eventually finished, and the official opening to Buxton took place on 30th May 1863. A special train ran from Derby followed by a luncheon in Buxton at 2 p.m. for the Midland Directors, the Duke of Devonshire, etc. According to the "Stockport Advertiser", congratulatory speeches were made, and it was especially remarked that the line was opened on the day originally fixed -a rare thing on railways! Not to be outdone, the S.D. & W.B. ran an official 'opening' train from Manchester and gave a luncheon at 3 p.m. in Buxton. But while the Midland line opened for traffic on 1st June 1863 the S.D. & W.B. extension to Buxton was not actually ready for public traffic until 15th June 1863. The two companies had separate stations at Buxton, glaring at each other across a common forecourt.

3. The Midland Enters Manchester and Marple. (1866-8)

Meanwhile work was proceeding apace on the extension to New Mills, despite problems encountered with the Peak under·ground rivers, problems so great that no contractor could be found to make Dove Holes Tunnel, and the Midland were forced to do it themselves. The line was ready by October 1866, and Midland goods trains were passing over it and through Marple to Manchester. However the autumn of 1866 was marked by torrential rains, and a remarkable landslip occurred on the Midland's new line at Bugsworth. All of a sudden 6 acres of land slipped off the hillside, and the railway viaduct, formerly curved, became straight as a result of the earth movements. Services were suspended, and the Midland immediately set about to restore the line; for 10 weeks 400 men worked day and night to construct a viaduct of timber, creating a deviation about half a mile long. The slip took place just east of Bugsworth station and the new alignment was carried North of the station, instead of to the South as previously, so that the station was turned back to front. Later on in 1885 a new embankment was constructed and the original masonry and the temporary timber viaducts were removed.

The line re - opened on 1st February 1867, this time for goods and passenger services. The Midland immediately started running a series of express trains from London King's Cross to Manchester London Road. The L.N.W. and G.N. were forced to countenance yet another competitor for London-Manchester traffic The Midland had at last reached Manchester despite all these companies had done to prevent it, and the Marple and New Mills line was the last but one link in this chain. Finally on 1st October 1868 the Midland opened their extension to London St. Pancras, which gave them an approach to the capital independent of the G.N. or L.N.W. The Midland commenced running two expresses each way between London St. Pancras and Manchester London Road, taking 5 hours only, which was then the timing of the G.N./M.S.L. and L.N.W. best expresses, despite having a much more difficult route through the Peak. A formidable new competitor had now arrived on the Manchester scene, and great must have been the excitement at stations such as Marple, as the Midland 5 hour trains swept through, drawn by a fine Kirtley 2-2-2 express engine, in the rich green livery then favoured by the Midland with a string of magnificent crimson lake coaches behind, so different from the dowdy M.S.L. stopping trains. At the same time the Midland began running local services from Manchester to Buxton and Derby, which supplemented the M.S.L. trains calling at Marple, and gave a direct outlet to the South. This however was merely the beginning of the Midland invasion of Lancashire and Cheshire!

4. The Sheffield and Midland Joint Committee (1868-72)

You will recall that the line from Hyde Junction to Hayfield had been built to take double track throughout but as each section had opened, it was with single track only. The arrival of the Midland made doubling of the line imperative, and the section from New Mills to Hyde Junction was doubled probably some time in 1866. Strines station probably opened as part of these works, and may have had two platforms from the outset. At the same time additional platforms were provided at all stations en route, though at first they would have had very little in the way of buildings. The wooden shelters which were probably erected at this time survived until quite recently at Hyde 'Junction' (now Hyde North), Woodley, Strines and New Mills and it is probable that at first Marple had such a building on the Up platform. The M.S.L. being an impecunious company decided that as the Midland were gaining such benefits from the New Mills - Hyde Junction line, the Midland might as well share the cost of maintenance and running. The Midland agreed, and an Act was passed on 24th June 1869 vesting the line from Hyde Junction to Hayfield in the 'Sheffield and Midland Joint Committee' (S. & M.) which had equal numbers of Board Members from the M.S.L. and Midland. This committee left numerous traces until quite recently. The monogram in the ironwork of Marple's roof were in fact the letters 'S.M.' entwined and until the 1970's there was a bench at Romiley with the words 'S. & M.J.C.' carved on the back. This is now in the National Railway Museum at York. There were as yet no goods or coal depots on the line from Hyde Junction to Hayfield, which is surprising as the early railways usually found goods traffic more profitable than passengers. Perhaps the M.S.L. was afraid to damage the goods traffic on their Peak Forest Canal, or perhaps they hoped the Midland would help pay for them when they started using the line. As might be expected the Midland soon requested that the S. & M. stations should have goods depots, and the M.S.L. agreed to their provision at Woodley, Romiley, Marple, Strines and Hayfield in 1870 and subsequently at Hyde and Birch Vale. Coal traffic was dealt with at these stations from 1870 and general merchandise followed in 1872. There was never a S. & M. goods depot at New Mills but the Midland built their own at New Mills East, and presumably the M.S.L. sent its traffic there.

5. Marple Station in 1872

By now Marple Station had grown considerably from the single platformed affair of 1865. By 1872 on the Down side a bay platform had been added, much in the same position as the later bay; the Down platform had been lengthened considerably to about 530 feet, not much shorter than its final length though it was very much narrower. The bay was used to stable trains terminating at Marple before they departed again for Manchester, or to shunt goods trains out of the way.

The Up platform was much shorter (c.350 feet) and extended from Brabyns Brow to the footbridge carrying Seven Stiles footpath over the line. On it there was a large set of waiting rooms, probably of wood, and a staircase at right angles to the line led up to Brabyns Brow. The Down platform buildings were unchanged from their original form of 1865. The goods yard was smaller than it later became, and contained two sidingsm - one against the retaining wall of St. Martin's Churchyard, for coal and one behind the Up platforms for merchandise and livestock. The Northern end of the station was not hemmed around with retaining walls as yet, but a sloping embankment divided the station from Brabyns Park and on this embankment was perched the station signalbox which controlled the primitive signalling of the day, and controlled the points, included those of the trailing crossover from Up to Down line in front of the signalbox.

The opening of a goods depot would have been a great boon to the district. The price of coal, a basic necessity of every home and industry, would have dropped several shillings a ton, as it could now be brought direct from the pits of the Midlands, Lancashire and Yorkshire without the need for road haulage from the nearest railhead or slow canal transport. The coal merchants therefore transferred their businesses to the railway goods yards. Local cotton mills found obtaining raw cotton and despatching finished products greatly speeded up by the railway, and found themselves better placed to compete with the mills of adjoining rail-served towns.

Agriculture was stimulated by the ease with which the new machinery of the 19th Century and all manner of general merchandise could reach the district. Livestock no longer had to be driven to market, losing weight and condition all the way, but could be conveyed in a few hours by train. Postal services were greatly speeded up, as mail could now reach Marple within a day or two from most parts of the Kingdom. The Railway also facilitated the conveyance of all kinds of merchandise to the district, which contributed to the rising standards of living of the 19th Century. To deliver these goods, the railway usually appointed existing carters as their agents, and so the whole transport system of the district came to revolve around the station. In Marple the canal continued to carry limited commercial traffic up until the 2nd World War, but it was gradually dwindling away.

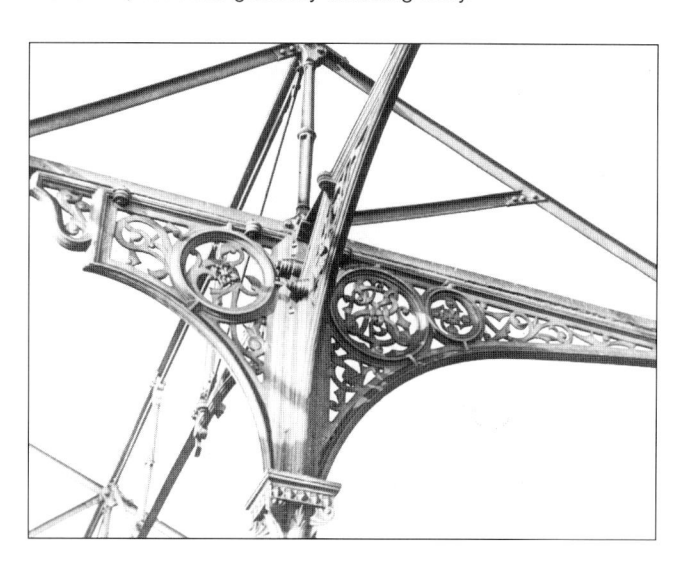

The 1875 ironwork of the canopies of Marple station shortly before demolition. Note that the large roundel in the canopy contains the intertwined letters "S & M" (here seen in reverse), standing for "Sheffield and Midland". (Rosemary Taylor)

IV. Marple's Expansion. 1872-1889

1. The Origin of the 'Cheshire Lines Committee' (1859-74)

To trace the steps by which Marple, now on the Midland through route to Manchester, became an important centre on that route we must retrace our steps to 1859. In that year two schemes were floated - the Stockport and Woodley Junction Railway, to run from the M.S.L. at Woodley to a low level station in Stockport, and the Cheshire Midland Railway, an extension of the M.S.J.A. from Altrincham to Northwich. Both were initially locally promoted, but Sir Edward Watkin, the forceful General Manager of the M.S.L., encouraged both these schemes seeing in them a means of occupying territory west of the M.S.L. main line. These lines were authorised in 1860, and in the same year Watkin engineered the "local" promotion of the Stockport, Timperley and Altrincham Junction Railway to link the two lines, and the West Cheshire Railway to extend the Cheshire Midland towards Chester and the Wirral. These two lines were authorised in 1861.

Later on the G.N. (which as you will recall had started running into Manchester in 1857) was also looking for further western outlets for its traffic and was induced to join the M.S.L. in financing, and when completed, working the four lines mentioned. A joint Board of Directors known as the Cheshire Lines Committee was set up in 1863 to do just this: at the time the name was appropriate as all the lines were in Cheshire, but became anomalous when the major sphere of activity became Lancashire!

The first line to be completed was the Stockport and Woodley which opened in 1863 to a temporary terminus in Stockport at Portwood; the Stockport-Altrincham line linked up with it in 1865 with a station nearer the centre of Stockport at Tiviot Dale. Portwood closed in 1875 but remained open for goods until 1972 and was open as a private siding until the mid 1980's. The lines on into Cheshire, and a Woodley-Godley Junction cut off, completed the original C.L.C. 'Main Line' from Godley Junction to Chester.

The M.S.L. had for many years been casting envious glances at the glittering prize of Liverpool. It had depended for access up till now on running powers over a variety of local railways, and over the L.N.W. into Liverpool proper. The M.S.L. and G.N. had however got hold of a local line, the Garston and Liverpool, opened in 1864, and made it part of the C.L.C. However the local line on which the M.S.L. depended for access to Liverpool had fallen into the L.N.W. net. Watkin therefore decided that an independent route to Liverpool was essential to their interests and would almost certainly attract the interest and financial support of the G.N. and Midland. The 1865 session of Parliament authorised the construction of such lines to run from Skelton Junction on the Stockport - Altrincham line, and from Manchester (Cornbrook) to Glazebrook and thence via Warrington to Garston. The final portion of the route into Liverpool Central station was already authorised. These lines received very widespread support in both cities, whose traders were very dissatisfied with the facilities provided by the L.N.W. and L. & Y.

The L.N.W. was furious and initiated instant reprisals and the M.S.L. was threatened with withdrawal of running rights between Ardwick and London Road. Watkin counter-attacked by proposing a railway across Manchester from Ancoats to the M.S.J.A. and C.L.C. lines at Cornbrook, with a large Central Station on Portland Street, and a wayside station at Piccadilly. Unfortunately this scheme met with opposition due to the interference it would cause to Manchester's streets. The L.N.W. then retaliated in another direction by promoting a 'Sheffield, Buxton and Liverpool Railway' to run from Sheffield to Chapel-en-le-Frith via Castleton. Sir Edward Watkin remarked that it was a "veritable High Peak line, evidently conceived in pique". The warring Companies however were eventually forced to compose their differences. The Midland was by now almost ready to enter Manchester but had no intention of resting on its laurels once it had got there. It would be content with nothing less than the subjugation of the whole North West! The Midland was therefore very interested in the C.L.C. and was admitted as third partner in 1866.

As Watkin had expected, the Midland and G.N. were prepared to put up capital for the Liverpool extensions, and construction pressed ahead. The lines had completely opened by 1874 though at Manchester the terminus was only a temporary one at Cornbrook. The new lines were a great success, not least between Liverpool and Manchester, where for so long the L.N.W. had used its monopoly as an excuse for high fares and slow services. The C.L.C. changed all this, and in 1877 reduced fares and started its famous hourly expresses, taking only 45 minutes. What is more the Midland from 1874 had access to Liverpool and immediately commenced a combined London St. Pancras to Liverpool and Manchester service. However the Liverpool portions had to be worked to Manchester London Road and back the way they had come to Woodley to gain access to the C. L.C., because Woodley was not a suitable place to divide or join trains. This was obviously a very time wasting procedure.

2. The 'Manchester and Stockport' Railway (1866-75)

When the Midland was still completing its line from Millers Dale to New Mills, the M.S.L. supported a nominally local scheme, the 'Manchester and Stockport Railway'. As originally promoted it was to have a main line from Ashburys to Brinnington Junction on the C.L.C. Main Line just east of Portwood. But the M.S.L. added a 'branch' from Reddish Junction to Romiley which would provide the Midland with better access to Manchester London Road than via Guide Bridge, knowing that the Midland would almost certainly help pay for this. The line was authorised in 1866, and while nominally independent, 4 of the 7 Directors were from the M.S.L.

The M.S.L. was correct in its assumption and when in 1869 the Sheffield and Midland Joint Committee (S. & M.) was formed to take over the Hyde Junction-Hayfield line, the Midland agreed to accept the unfinished Manchester and Stockport Railway as part of the joint line. At the same time it was agreed to jointly construct the so called 'Marple Curve' from Romiley Junction to Bredbury Junction (on the C.L.C. Woodley-Stockport line) to give direct access to Liverpool via the C.L.C.

Thus the Midland was to have a more direct route into Manchester than the circuitous and congested route via Guide Bridge, and a direct route from their main line via Marple to the C.L.C. permitting through running from the South to Stockport and Liverpool, without the need for a detour via Woodley. It was decided that Marple would be the most convenient point for the division and joining of the Manchester and Liverpool portions of St. Pancras expresses; hence the curve to the C.L.C. actually at Romiley, was known as the 'Marple Curve'. And so the stage was set for Marple, previously a wayside station, to assume great importance as a junction for Midland expresses, and interchange point between these expresses and other local services of Midland and M.S.L. It may be asked why Marple was chosen, and not Romiley, which was actually at the junction. Marple station was constricted but there was even less room at Romiley which was on an embankment in a built up area; and of the two Marple was the more important place.

The 'Marple Curve' opened early in 1875 for goods on 15th February and for passengers on 1st April. Immediately Liverpool portions detached from or attached to the main Manchester train at Marple began to use it. The sections from Ashburys to Romiley and Brinnington Junction were opened soon after on 17th May for goods and for passengers on 2nd August 1875. In September 1875 Belle Vue and Bredbury stations were opened and Reddish in December. The M.S.L. thereupon started a local service between London Road and Stockport Tiviot Dale, and diverted some of the Marple and Hayfield services via the shorter and quicker route via Bredbury. All Midland main line services were diverted onto the 'New Route' via Bredbury, though for some years Midland locals still ran from Marple via Guide Bridge.

The Midland was in many respects the most go-ahead railway company of its day, and in 1874 decided to introduce 1st class only Pullman Cars, then only known in America. These Pullman Cars, 60 feet long, were at their time the longest and largest vehicles running in the Country. They were so long and large in fact that in the course of tests, it was found that they would not pass through Marple South Tunnel, which had to be widened slightly and shortened by some 45 yards at its northern end to its present length of 225 feet, at a cost of £23,000. It is still possible to see traces of this work at the North portal, where a fragment of the old North portal and tunnel wall are still visible. The Midland wasted no time in introducing Pullman cars to their new territories in Lancashire, and Pullman Sleeping Cars for Liverpool began using the "Marple Curve" from the day it opened; Sleeping Cars soon also ran to Manchester, and day-time "Drawing Room" cars to both cities followed.

3. Marple Rebuilt (1875)

To cope with the greatness to be thrust upon it in becoming a main line calling point for Midland Express trains, Marple station had to be expanded. These alterations must have been decided on in the early 1870's when the Marple Curve and direct line via Bredbury were under construction, and were probably ready for the new Midland services of 1875. The pressing needs were for longer platforms to accommodate lengthy multi-portioned main line trains, broader platforms, more cover and waiting rooms for passengers changing trains, additional platforms to accommodate terminating and connecting services, and a turntable to turn engines. The great problem at Marple was lack of space, hemmed in as the station was by St. Martin's Churchyard on one side, and a steep hillside on the other. At the Northern end of the station the cutting was cut back to the west, and a retaining wall built at its foot, and on the east the cutting was replaced by the present sheer stone retaining wall. Any further expansion in this direction was prevented by St. Martin's Churchyard. On the Down side, the platform was slightly lengthened to 538 feet, exclusive of ramps, giving a bay platform about 300 feet long; at the same time it was broadened to about 25 feet throughout. A lofty glass and iron canopy, 350 feet long, was added to the existing canopy, with a glazed screen to fill the gap at the junction between the two different heights. Thus almost the entire Down side was under cover. On the Up side, the platform was lengthened to 550 feet, exclusive of ramps, and made 33 feet wide at its broadest point. A loop line was laid behind the Up platform, thus giving four platforms in all. Again a canopy was erected, slightly shorter than the Down, 315 feet long. A building comprising ladies and general waiting room, with lavatories was erected on the Up platform to cater for those changing trains. A footbridge, which was about the only item from the old station to survive until 2012 (except for the platforms themselves) linked Up and Down platforms. The addition of a loop line severed direct pedestrian access between Brabyns Brow and the Up platform, so an enormous footbridge 130 feet long was erected linking platform and road. It was originally open, but later roofed over.

The canopy on both platforms was very lofty, about 25 feet high from platform to apex and supported on a double row of cast iron columns, with curious capitals decorated with vaguely mediaeval foliage and 'dog tooth' ornament. The weight of the largely wrought iron roof girders was transferred by means of cast iron spandrels with elaborate scroll patterns and roundels. The outer spandrels contained a roundel about 17 inches across, with a monogram formed of the letters 'S.M.' (standing for 'Sheffield and Midland') entwined. The roundels were separately cast, and set in lead . One wonders if they were an afterthought. The roof girders had at their extremities notches which supported the timber rafter which carried the pitch pine glazing bars, which in turn supported the large 7 ½ x 2 foot sheets of clear glass which covered the whole. The roof must have looked magnificent when new, with clean glass and white paintwork.

Three Water Columns were provided on the station: two at the North and serving Down main and bay platform lines, while there was another at the south end of the Up main platform. These were to enable trains to take water en route, especially expresses on the last lap for Liverpool or Manchester, or about to tackle the gruelling climb through the Peak; it also enabled the numerous engines on terminating local trains or Liverpool portions to take water before the next trip. The water was stored in a large cast iron tank high on the cutting wall to the west of the station; the piers which supported it are still visible. The Water Columns were owned by the Midland, and water was supplied from the M.S.L. owned Peak Forest Canal - at Midland expense. To this day there survives at the North end of St. Martin's Road a small brick building which contained the valves of the pipe supplying the tank from the canal, and also a meter to enable the M.S.L. to charge the Midland for the water used. As the Midland paid for the water the drivers of M.S.L. engines were not meant to use the columns, but often did if they could get away with it!

Under the long footbridge from Brabyns Brow a turntable 45 feet in diameter was provided capable of taking the largest express engines of the day. This was used to turn locomotives arriving on trains from Liverpool, Manchester, or the South, to enable them to run back the right way round. Trains could depart in an Up or Down direction from the Up loop, and Down from the Down bay, but no train could run straight into either loop or bay, and all trains had to reverse to gain access to them. This was because of the railways' dislike of facing points on a passenger line, fearing that the points might move under the train and derail it. Facing points would have been necessary to allow trains to arrive at bay and loop, and so this was not possible; anyway if trains had been able to arrive at the Down bay, they would have had great difficulty in running round, as the locomotive would be trapped at the buffers. Up trains terminating would arrive at the Up Main platform, and shunt into the Up Loop. The engine would then detach and go on to the turntable, turn round, and run round the train and attach to the coaches standing in the Up Loop. It would either remain there ready for departure or propel into the Down bay, in either case then ready for a departure in a Down direction. Any Down trains terminating would follow a similar procedure, though few Down services ever terminated at Marple. Two crossovers, both trailing, were provided - one at the North, the other at the South end of the station (only the South crossover now remains). At the North end of the station were two sidings or headshunts useful for stabling locomotives and putting wagons out of the way when shunting. The goods yard, as before, consisted of a siding beside the retaining wall for coal, called the 'back road' and one parallel to the Up loop for general merchandise called the 'shed road'. On this siding a medium sized goods shed was erected to enable merchandise to be unloaded from wagons under cover and warehoused for delivery.

This was a massive timber structure 30 x 60 feet, with main beams of 9 x 10 inch timbers. At the Southern end was a small office where the documentation work was done. Locomotives were not allowed into the shed, because of the fire risk, nor were they allowed onto the 'back road' due to the sharp curvature of the siding; a 'barrier' of wagons had therefore to be used in shunting. The goods yard entrance was provided with a gate 15 feet wide and 8 feet high, prefabricated in sections and made up on the site - enough to deter most thieves! The whole layout was controlled by two main signalboxes - Marple North and Marple South. One was just North East of the Brabyns Park overbridge, and the other just South West of the Brabyns Brow overbridge. The sites of these boxes is still visible from their stone retaining walls in the embankment. There was a third subsidiary box controlling movement into the goods yard only, which was used when required . This was known as the 'knob-up' box and was housed under the footbridge steps on the Up platform. So many boxes were needed as there was a strict limit to the distance a box could be from the points it controlled, due to the heavy equipment used in the mid-Victorian era,

The first station master at Marple we have on record was a Mr. Rowbottom, who presided from the mid 1860s onward. By good fortune some of his correspondence survived in the attic of the station, and this casts an interesting light in these early days. One deserves quoting in full

Manchester, Sheffield and Lincolnshire Railway
Audit Office, Manchester. June 4th 1875
(To) Mr. Rowbottom, Marple.
Dear Sir,
I have not yet received your Goods Balance Sheets for the months of March and April though they are much overdue. The absence of these documents is causing us much inconvenience and you really must be good enough to see that they are compiled and forwarded here at once.
Yours truly,
Wm. Pollitt
(Chief Accountant, M.S.L.R.)

Mr. Rowbottom was in hot water no more than a fortnight later when he received another letter from Mr. Pollitt in which he had "to draw attention to the **loose manner** in which your clerk replies to the "Clearing House inaccuracies" and to "request you take up with him, and favour me with an explanation"! On a happier note we find Mr. Rowbottom in July 1875 sending a request to the office of the Superintendent of the line at Derby for more luggage barrows for the platforms. The need probably arose with the large number of people now using the station as a result of its new main line status. Incidentally the station master, being in charge of a joint station, was responsible to both companies but was always appointed by the Midland, in view of their more important interest in the station.

4. Train Services 1875

Let us now look at the train services which required such a complicated layout and commodious accommodation. In the October 1875 Bradshaw's Timetable, a total of 34 Up and 32 Down passenger trains are shown calling at Marple station, 66 in all. Of these 20 were M.S.L. trains, the remaining 46 Midland. So it can be seen that the Midland was now by far the dominant partner.

The basis of the M.S.L. service was 7 trains each way between Hayfield and London Road, usually via Guide Bridge and taking 35-45 minutes to Marple, depending on stops. This was supplemented by 3 trains each way between London Road and Marple only, 2 of which were routed via Bredbury. The best trains of the day were the business trains between London Road and Hayfield, which were routed via Bredbury and omitted calls at Ashburys and Reddish. These are the ancestors of the present morning and evening 'expresses'. In 1875 they took 25 minutes Down and 27 minutes Up - quite a creditable performance.

All M.S.L. trains were 1st, 2nd and 3rd class, but Midland trains were 1st and 3rd only. At that time it was general practice for 3rd class passengers to be only admitted to the painfully slow all stations 'Parliamentary' or 'Government' trains, so called because the railway companies were compelled to run them and charge a penny a mile fare, under the 1844 Railways Act. All the M.S.L. Marple trains in the October 1875 timetable are shown as 'Gov' (Government) trains, to indicate that they were of this type. All companies at that time only ran express trains for 1st and 2nd class passengers, and suitable 'express' fares were levied, However in 1872 the Midland dropped a bombshell by announcing that henceforth all trains, including the best expresses, would convey 3rd class passengers. Other companies were furious and Allport, the Midland General Manager, was accused of "communism" and "democracy" and of wishing to do away with all sorts of institutions. The Midland trains however merely grew at the expense of their competitors, who were soon forced to follow suit and admit the despised 3rd class to express trains, or see them all flocking to the Midland booking offices. Following this, in 1875 the Midland abolished 2nd class altogether, as it was found in practice that most people travelled 1st or 3rd class, and the trouble of providing 2nd class accommodation was not justified by the revenue. All 2nd class carriages were made 3rd class and it was announced that in future all 3rd class carriages would have upholstered seats. Other companies were even more horrified at this revolutionary step, and accused the Midland of "pampering the working classes".

The "working classes" however liked such "pampering" and the increase in Midland receipts was staggering. So by October 1875 all Midland trains were 1st and 3rd class only and you would get a good chance of reasonable comfort and upholstered seats, compared with the universal wooden seats of M.S.L. 3rd's. 2nd class lasted nearly 20 years more on the M.S.L. until 1892. What is more, 4 wheeled coaches all but disappeared from the Midland from 1874, the more comfortable 6-wheeler becoming the standard, while on Midland express trains bogie coaches were appearing giving an even better ride. 4 wheeled coaches however lasted on M.S.L. trains into the 20th Century. As has been said, 46 Midland trains called daily at Marple, 24 Up and 22 Down, Of these 7 Up and 6 Down were London expresses which called at Marple. All but one of these services attached or detached a Liverpool portion at Marple, the exception being the 7 a.m. from London Road to St. Pancras and Nottingham, which only had a connection from Stockport at Marple. Many Midland expresses were non-stop from Marple to Derby and none stopped between Marple and London Road. In fact with 11 Down and 12 Up, there were more Midland trains than M.S.L. between Marple and London Road; the fastest train took a mere 15 minutes, which has never been bettered.

A typical Midland express was the 4 p.m. from St. Pancras, which called at Kentish Town (for connections from the City and railways south of the Thames) Wellingborough, Leicester, Trent (where a Nottingham-Manchester Through Carriage was attached) Derby, and then non-stop to Marple, arriving at 8.28 p.m. The train then divided, the front, main portion leaving almost immediately for London Road, where it arrived 4 hours 45 minutes after leaving the capital. As soon as the Manchester portion was away, an engine waiting in the Down bay would then smartly back onto the waiting Liverpool coaches, left behind in the Down main platform and leave for Liverpool about 7 minutes after original arrival. The Liverpool portion conveyed a through Pullman "Drawing Room Car" from St. Pancras, and called at Stockport Tiviot Dale and Warrington Central only, arriving in Liverpool 65 minutes after leaving Marple. On the Up, a typical train, though not so fast, had a Liverpool portion which left at 12 noon, and called at Cressington, Sankey, Warrington, Cheadle and Stockport to arrive at Marple first at 1.10 p.m. After a brief call at the Up main platform. the train would draw forward and reverse into the Up loop; the engine would detach and run onto the turntable, to turn in readiness for its return trip to Liverpool. Meanwhile the main Manchester portion had left London Road at 1 p.m. ran non-stop "via the New Route" (via Bredbury) and arrived at 1.15 p.m. The express engine detached from its train, ran forward and then back onto the Liverpool portion in the Up loop, drew it forward, and then backed it onto the main Manchester train. The two portions were then coupled up, and left at 1.20 p.m. for St. Pancras calling at most principal and some not so principal stations en route, to arrive at St. Pancras at 6.40 p.m. A 'refreshment stop' of 7 minutes was allowed at Trent Junction. Most long distance express trains stopped at a refreshment station en route, for no train in 1875 had buffet or dining cars. Most trains stopped for 10 minutes at Derby, Trent or Leicester to change engines and this gave time to jump out and seize something from the station refreshment room. For the well off, it was possible to send a telegram requesting a luncheon basket (with or without wine) which could be supplied at principal stations for a few shillings. Stops were also necessary for as yet, except in Pullmans, there were no lavatories on trains.

In all 6 Pullman services called at Marple; the 10 a.m. ex St. Pancras conveyed a Pullman for Manchester, which returned on the 4.50 p.m. to St. Pancras. The 10.30 a.m. from Liverpool Central returning from St. Pancras to Liverpool at 4 p.m. conveyed 'Drawing Room Cars' while the 9.45 p.m. Liverpool-St. Pancras and 12 midnight St. Pancras-Liverpool had sleeping cars, which were in fact converted day coaches. There were as yet no Sleeping Cars to Manchester, but a footnote in the timetable reads "1st class passengers can avail themselves of Sleeping Berths upon payment of a small additional charge, changing into ordinary cars at Marple"- at 4.45 a.m. that is! A strange vision of Victorian businessmen, and perhaps theatre celebrities, stumbling out of Pullman luxury at Marple in the middle of the night to change into the Manchester coaches! These Pullman carriages must have seemed exotic in their rich greenish brown livery, decorated with gold arabesques, their luxurious fittings, and sonorous titles such as "Excelsior", "Britannia" and "Enterprise", though strange to English eyes with their end balconies and open interior saloons.

Many of the St. Pancras trains carried through Nottingham portions, usually attached or detached at Trent or Derby. There were 6 Up and 4 Down services between Manchester and Nottingham, all calling at Marple. On a more mundane level, the Midland also ran 4 stopping services each way between Manchester and Derby; one of the Down trains split at Marple, with one portion going to London Road via Bredbury, the other being sent round via Guide Bridge; another Derby train split for Liverpool and Manchester. In all 8 trains divided and 6 were marshalled up at Marple. To feed its express services, the Midland also ran two connecting trains between Marple and Guide Bridge each way; there were in addition a few trips between Marple and Stockport only. The services Marple enjoyed at this early date are best seen from the table below:-

	To	From
Manchester (M.S.L.)	7	7
London Road (Mid.)	11	12
Total	18	19
Stockport Tiviot Dale	9	10
Liverpool	7	7
Derby	11	10
Nottingham	6	4
London St. Pancras	7	6

On the other hand, though through services were in many ways lavish, the timetable was poor in others; there was for instance no M.S.L. service from Marple to Manchester between the 8.50 and 11.10 a.m. and the earliest Down train did not arrive at London Road until 8.10 a.m. The Midland express trains of 1875 were hauled by 2-4-0s built at Derby Works under Matthew Kirtley in the late 60's, with 6'2" driving wheels; or perhaps on the Liverpool and Derby trains older 'singles' with the 2-2-2 wheel arrangement. Both to our eyes would appear diminutive and picturesque with heavy frames, tall copper capped chimneys and elegant safety valve and dome, but little in the way of a cab to shelter the enginemen. The M.S.L. on its local services used even older and smaller engines, often tank engines without a tender.

However the passenger service was really only the icing on the cake as far as the Midland was concerned, and the most lucrative revenue lay in goods traffic. Vast tonnages of coal poured across the Peak to fuel the industries of Lancashire and the produce of Manchester and imports through the Port of Liverpool flowed the other way. Midland goods traffic had developed so rapidly that in the Spring of 1870 a vast new 70-acre goods depot was opened at Ancoats, costing half a million pounds, a fantastic sum then. Within a few months Midland goods trains were growing longer and heavier, hauled throughout by the ubiquitous Kirtley 0-6-0s. On one occasion, as one such locomotive pounded its way south up towards Peak Forest Summit, the blast from its exhaust blew the top of the chimney off! Marple station must have sounded day and night to the rumble of northbound coal and southbound merchandise trains; getting these through without delaying the prestigious passenger expresses must have been a headache to the signalmen, and the loop and bay at Marple must have many times held goods trains to let the St. Pancras expresses past. Such in fact was the flow of freight between Lancashire and the Midlands that severe congestion developed at Derby, which was only relieved when a series of avoiding lines linking Ambergate and Nottingham were created, thus incidentally creating the triangular station at Ambergate, and a new route to Nottingham which passenger trains from Manchester also soon began to use.

5. Manchester Central (1875-88)

However the growing traffic of the Midland, added to the equally growing traffic of the M.S.L., resulted in chronic congestion at London Road Station and its approaches, so that in 1875 the M.S.L. gave the Midland 3 years notice to quit. The Midland had therefore to find itself another terminus in Manchester. As the C.L.C. had the same year obtained powers to build a Manchester Central Station to replace its temporary Cornbrook terminus which eventually became the C.L.C. goods depot. As the Midland was a partner in the C.L.C. it was natural that it should try and gain access to the new station: the only problem was getting a route. In 1873 the Manchester South District Railway had been authorised to build a line from Manchester to Alderley, but had got nowhere until the Midland seized on the scheme. The line was tailored to suit its own needs, that is for a line from Heaton Mersey Junction, on the C.L.C. Godley-Liverpool line, west of Stockport, to a point on the C.L.C. Manchester-Liverpool line at Throstle Nest Junction.

Originally the line was to have been part of the C. L. C. but the G.N. was "going through one of its periods of wishing to wash its hands of the C.L.C." and refused. The M.S.L. was unsure whether to support the project, so the Midland with characteristic firmness, took it over on its own. The line opened on the 1st of January 1880.

Meanwhile the great new Manchester Central Station was rising, work starting in 1875. When finished the frontage was only intended to be temporary. It was hoped to build a C.L.C. hotel to form the station frontage, as at St. Pancras but this never materialised and the Midland built their own separate hotel in 1903, at a cost of £1 million. The roof of Manchester Central however was far from temporary as it was a clear span of 210 feet, and 90 feet above rail level, only 30 feet less than St. Pancras. In fact the station is all roof and little else - the side walls are merely to keep out the weather. The main weight, as in a mediaeval cathedral, is taken by the ribs of the roof vault, which continue downward into the earth to the foundations. The platforms are in fact built on the tie-beam of the arch, and the space underneath was used as warehousing. The station opened on 1st July 1880, and the Midland now had a first class Manchester terminal, and one that was in many respects the 'twin' of St. Pancras. As originally built Central had 7 platforms, but 2 more were later added on the South and were used for locals to Marple, Derby etc.

The Midland thereupon transferred all its principal services to Central, gaining access via Stockport Tiviot Dale and the South District Line. At first Liverpool portions were worked via Central, but it was soon found quicker to detach and attach at Marple once again or at Stockport in some cases. Marple therefore retained its main line services, though not all now called as they had before Central opened. This relieved pressure on London Road instantly, though for a time some Midland locals continued to run into London Road, and the M.S.L. ran some local services into Central. From 1884 however all Midland trains ran into Central, and M.S.L. trains were confined to London Road.

It is interesting to look at the train services given in Bradshaw August 1887 to see the pattern of service and how it had altered since 1875. The number of weekday trains calling was almost the same -67 (66 in 1875) with 34 Up and 33 Down. But the composition of the timetable was quite altered. With the Midland having given up running purely local services to London Road, the proportion of M.S.L. trains was much higher, and now M.S.L. trains marginally outnumbered Midland, with 19 in each direction. Of these 18 were to or from London Road, one each way terminating at Guide Bridge. Hayfield had a much more generous service than in 1875 of 10 trains each way, and a few trains now started at New Mills. In addition 7 trains turned round at Marple. Many more services were now routed via Bredbury. There were also more trains in the morning and evening, indicating the growing residential traffic, which was mirrored in the continued building in Marple in the 1870s and 80s, now spreading to Strines Road, Hawk Green and Ley Hey Park.

Fewer Midland trains called at Marple in 1887 than in 1875- 29 as opposed to 46, mainly because the Midland no longer ran its own locals over the S.& M. joint route to London Road, and also because some St. Pancras expresses no longer called at Marple. But in compensation for this, Marple now had services to a second Manchester terminus at Central, 12 trains Up and 8 Down. Some of these were provided by the new local service the Midland ran on the South District line, of which a few were extended beyond Stockport to Marple.

Now that Stockport was the effective junction for Liverpool, only one London express was marshalled up at Marple though three continued to divide. But the continued importance of Marple is shown in that many of the St. Pancras expresses still called to give connections to the M.S.L. services, 6 Up and 3 Down in fact; there were also still services to and from Nottingham, 3 each way calling at Marple. 4 services calling at Marple conveyed Pullman cars, including the Up overnight sleeper, which by now conveyed cars for Liverpool and Manchester so that passengers no longer had to stagger half awake in and out of sleeping cars at Marple. The best Midland express took 4 hours 40 minutes between Central and St. Pancras, giving a timing of about 4 hours 15 minutes from Marple to St. Pancras. Certain of the St. Pancras expresses ran non-stop between Marple and Central in as little as 22 minutes, Stockport being served by the Liverpool portion. There were four services to and from Liverpool, the fastest, the 3.40 p.m. ex St. Pancras, taking only 55 minutes from Marple to Liverpool with 4 stops. An added feature of the 1887 service was the provision of through services between Manchester and Bristol Temple Meads, via Birmingham and Gloucester, 3 of which stopped at Marple in the Down direction only, giving a variety of new destinations directly served from Marple.

6. The 'Midland Junction' Line (1889)

But the ever ambitious Midland was still not satisfied with its grip on Lancashire and Cheshire, though by now it had access to Manchester, Stockport, Warrington, Liverpool, Chester and Southport (the C.L.C. had opened a Southport extension in 1884), thus fulfilling the prophetic words of the 1861 agreement with the M.S.L. that the Midland should "run its own trains to Manchester, and every other place in Manchester, in Lancashire or Cheshire or beyond". In 1889 therefore a short but very important curve known as the 'Midland Junction' was opened linking Ashburys to the L. & Y. line at Ancoats Junction thus providing access to Victoria Station, the largest and busiest of the Manchester stations. Through coaches were introduced between St. Pancras and Manchester Victoria to draw passengers from the Lancashire towns onto the Midland route, and several of these coaches ran through to Bolton and Blackburn: mud in the eye of the L.N.W. which regarded East Lancashire as its own territory by virtue of its through services between Euston, Bolton, Blackburn and Colne. The Midland through coaches were detached from the main Liverpool and Manchester train at Marple, to proceed via Reddish, Ashburys and the Midland Junction and most of the St. Pancras expresses stopped once again at Marple for this purpose.

Certain connecting trains were also provided between Marple and Manchester Victoria, providing Marple with services in all to no less than 3 Manchester termini by 4 routes! The curve was also useful in permitting summer holiday expresses and excursions to pass direct from the Midland line to Blackpool, thus further extending the influence of the Midland. In 1862 the Midland had approached no nearer Manchester on its own metals than Ambergate; by 1866 it had arrived; by 1875 it had overrun most of Cheshire and Lancashire, and by 1880 it had a first class terminal at Manchester Central. The 'Midland Junction' Line was the latest move in its campaign to invade the whole North-West, but by no means the last!

The Cabstand on Brabyns Brow outside Marple Station. c.1900

V. The Macclesfield, Bollington and Marple Railway. 1863-1910

Seals of the M.B.M. and Macclesfield Committee (BR)

1. Origins (1849-64)

In order to present a continuous narrative of the Midland's drive for Manchester and its effect on Marple Station, no mention has yet been made of the Marple Wharf-Macclesfield line. It is now therefore time to turn to this, the lesser of the two lines serving Marple. It might be thought that such a line could not possibly equal the railway political significance of the line through Marple, passing through nowhere of any size but Bollington, and enjoying throughout its existence a purely local service. Far from it: the line had an origin as stormy as any, and can be added to the long list of 'might-have-beens' as regards Main Line significance. The ogre of the piece was, as usual, the L.N.W., ever jealous, ever obstructive. The origins of the line can be traced back to 1849 when the North Staffordshire Railway (N.S.), having reached Macclesfield, found the way to Manchester blocked by the L.N.W. The N.S. then proposed a branch to Whaley Bridge to join the proposed M.S.L. branch from Hyde Junction. Nothing came of this, but the N.S. continued to find the L.N.W. obstructive, and refusing to allow any traffic to Manchester to pass via Macclesfield, insisting it went via Crewe, thus ensuring a higher L.N.W. mileage. In 1863 Thomas Oliver, a Macclesfield businessman, promoted a scheme for a local line from Macclesfield to Marple via Bollington - the Macclesfield, Bollington and Marple Railway (M.B.M). It was particularly hoped to revive Bollington, then an important cotton town, but suffering from depression due to the American Civil War, and that Kerridge Stone from local quarries would be a valuable traffic. The collieries of the Poynton area were also expected to provide much revenue.

The N.S. seized on this scheme, seeing in it a route to Manchester independent of the LN.W., which was being particularly obstructive at that time. When the promoters approached the M.S.L. General Manager, Edward Watkin, he was enthusiastically in favour, seeing in the line another outlet for the M.S.L. to the south, and the start of a possible independent extension to London. In fact the Macclesfield Courier and Herald went so far as to proclaim Watkin the inspiring light of the scheme, second only to Thomas Oliver. With such support, the scheme prospered, though the L.N.W. only withheld opposition on the condition that the M.S.L. withdrew their support from various schemes west of Macclesfield. The line was therefore authorised on 14 July 1864, with the M.S.L. and N.S. empowered to subscribe £80,000 each for its construction, and work and maintain it when open. But almost immediately the original purpose of the line - to provide the N.S. with an independent route to Manchester- was lost, as the LN.W., in consternation at the success of the M.B.M., came to an amicable traffic agreement with the N.S.

2. Construction and Opening (1865-73)

The urgency had thus gone out of the scheme, and construction was very slow, despite there being no substantial engineering works, apart from a low 23 arch viaduct at Bollington, and deep cuttings approaching Marple Wharf Junction. The slowing down was also due to the general trade depression of the mid 1860's. In 1868 the N.S. board was considering means of disposing of the remaining £40,000 of unsold shares, and by June of the same year only £93,165 had been spent of the eventual cost of £187,079. However, the line eventually opened on 2nd August 1869 for passengers only. The line was single throughout, with the track on the Up side, though the formation was wide enough for double. Single platform stations were provided at Marple (Rose Hill), High Lane, 'Poynton' and Bollington. The initial train service consisted of 4 trains each way between Macclesfield and Romiley, where trains terminated for some while until the service was extended to London Road. There were two services each way on Sundays. Goods traffic began on 1 March 1870, and Goods Depots opened at Rose Hill and Bollington. In 1871 the line was doubled throughout at a cost of £16,000, and second platforms were provided at the stations. By 1872 a connection had been opened at Poynton to Lord Vernon's extensive colliery railway system. The line left the Main Line by a south facing connection

Middlewood Higher Down Platform, looking north from a train bound for Macclesfield Central, on 18th April 1954. Notice the tiny Booking and Waiting Hall, and the station sign advising passengers to "Change for Disley, Whaley Bridge and Buxton" (H.C. Casserley).

Middlewood Higher looking north in 1962, 2 years after closure.

just north of the station platform, and swept round in a wide circle, to enter the colliery to the west. Much traffic passed from this system on to the M.B.M. until the last colliery closed in 1935. The line in 1871 was vested in the N.S. and M.S.L., as the 'Macclesfield Committee Railway', with a board of 8, with 4 directors from each company. The M.S.L. ran the trains and provided staff, but the N.S. Civil Engineer was responsible for stations, engineering work and maintenance, though the M.S.L. agreed to provide a steam crane for bridge work.

The original terminus of the line was a temporary affair in Macclesfield, near the L.N.W. Hibel Road Station. For 2 years Watkin tried to persuade the L.N.W. to join the N.S. and M.S.L. in the construction of a tripartite joint station, but the L.N.W. refused to consider this, fearing lest a single passenger should escape their net and travel on the new line. So the N.S. and M.S.L. went ahead without the L.N.W., and built a link from the M.B.M. to join the N.S. main line about a quarter of a mile south of Hibel Road Station. A new joint M.S.L. - N.S. joint station was opened in 1873, and the original terminus turned over to goods; the new station was called 'Central', and was certainly more conveniently situated than Hibel Road, But the potential of the Central station was never realised, as the L.N.W. refused to permit any through N.S. - L.N.W. through trains to use the joint station, and so the best trains called at Hibel Road only, thus depriving Central Station and the M.B.M. of much of its connectional usefulness.

The line once more became a pawn in railway politics when

in 1876 the M.S.L. and N.S. came within an ace of amalgamating; had they done so the M.B.M. would have probably become a link in the M.S.L.'s route to London, of which Watkin dreamed. This all however came to nothing and the line settled down to a purely local existence.

3. The Middlewood Curve (1876-85)

In 1879 a station was opened at Middlewood, where the M.B.M. crossed the L.N.W. Stockport-Buxton line and almost directly above the L.N.W. Middlewood Station, for the purpose of interchange of passengers. To provide better facilities between Macclesfield and Buxton, a curve connecting the two lines at Middlewood was suggested in 1876, but did not materialise until 1885. The curve was laid out on generous lines with a flyover carrying the Down line from Macclesfield over the Buxton line to join the Up line to Buxton, thus avoiding conflicts with Down Buxton trains. Such an arrangement was very elaborate, and normally only found at the most important and busiest of junctions: it is in fact the only such 'flying' junction on the south side of Manchester. The promoters of the scheme must have had high hopes of its success.

The first trains, probably excursions ran on Whit Monday, 25th May 1885, and regular services between Macclesfield and Buxton began the next day. A through Stoke-on-Trent to Buxton service followed later that year. But the curve was not a great success, and soon services were confined to the summer months. Trains were always provided during July and August, and sometimes in May, June, or September, or any combination of these months, usually on Saturdays only, though some trains operated on Mondays, Tuesdays and Wednesdays as well.

Middlewood Low Level Station from the East c1910. Note the frock coated Station Master, the up buildings and the signals of the High Level Station visible on the left. (F. Hawley).

A scene of sylvan tranquillity broken by the arrival of the 9.35 Manchester-Whaley Bridge d.m.u. at Middlewood (Low Level) on 12th September 1978. The overbridge formerly carried the Marple Wharf Junction-Macclesfield line. (Author)

In the summer of 1896 for instance all the five Saturday, and three weekday trains started from Macclesfield only, but one or two conveyed through coaches to and from Stoke; all called at Bollington, and the odd one at Poynton as well. The N.S. tried to induce the L.N.W. to run a through London-Buxton service by this route to compete with the Midland, but the L.N.W. said that it was not practicable as "the through coaches had to be taken by a reverse journey between the two stations in that town (i.e. Macclesfield) - not a very satisfactory movement in any competitive through route". What the L.N.W. ignored was that if they had agreed to use Central as their Macclesfield Station, no such reverse move was necessary.

Through goods trains did however regularly use the curve, and three exchange sidings were laid, and later a siding to serve an adjacent clay pit was added. There was a daily early morning goods from Macclesfield to Buxton known as the "Knotty"; it was so named after the nickname of the N.S. which used the Staffordshire knot as its company badge. This ran until after World War 2, but when it ceased the curve was mainly used for storing old coaches.

4. Description of the line

The line diverges from the Manchester-Marple main line at Marple Wharf Junction, which was, as we have seen, a Junction for the Canal Wharf branch before the Macclesfield line was even conceived. The line, immediately on leaving the main line, begins rising, and curves round a full 90 degrees, necessitating a very low speed for trains negotiating the branch, which would have been a serious impediment to use of the line as an express route to London. Such a sharp curve is however necessary to make the M.B.M. line coming up from the south meet the main line, without the need for a separate viaduct over the Goyt on the one hand or on the other, a tunnel under the high ground on which Marple lies.

As it is, the M.B.M. only joins the main line on the brink of the viaduct, and the cutting leading up to the junction is deep enough as it is. In fact the cuttings between Marple Wharf and Rose Hill gave considerable trouble, and collapsed in one place in the vicinity of what is now Clifton Drive, due to one of the numerous pockets of sand in the geology. Accordingly the railway bought a strip of land all along the east side of the line to prevent anybody building on it, and claiming compensation if the bank collapsed - most of this land is now rented out, but still in railway hands. The railway skirts the hilly ground of Marple, until emerging into flatter terrain at Rose Hill, whence it skirts the base of the Pennine range all the way to Macclesfield.

At Rose Hill the main Stockport road was diverted over the line by a large hump back bridge, thus accounting for the kink in the road at this point, The original single line station buildings at Rose Hill were on the Up, or Macclesfield side, and were of the small unpretentious M.B.M. style found at all the other stations on the line: a small one storey brick building, with a low pitched slate roof, extended out on beams and bracket to form an elementary canopy. M.B.M. stations were built to N.S. designs and are similar to contemporary N.S. branch line designs. The accommodation consisted of four rooms all entered from the platform -a Porters Room, at the north, followed by the Station Office, with a booking window to the adjoining General Waiting Room-cum-Booking Office; a Ladies Room with lavatories completed the facilities, with a brick-built Gents adjoining. The only architectural feature was a small square bay, with clock, projecting from the Station Office, whence the Station Master could survey his domain. The Down platform probably originally had a rudimentary wooden shelter, similar to those which survived at other stations on the line. But the growing business at Rose Hill, particularly residential traffic to Manchester, called for greater facilities, which were probably provided in c.1880, in the form of a brick-built block on the Down side. This had a flat wooden canopy supported on cast iron brackets towards the Platform and comprised a Ladies Waiting Room, with a lavatory, and a General Waiting Room. Later on as the Manchester bound business grew, a second Booking Office was provided by tacking a lean-to wooden office onto the General Room, with a booking window into the latter. This second Booking Office was generally only open when a Down train was due, but survived in use until 1970. Incidentally the Down Ladies Room contained a Waiting Room bench with the initials "M.B.M." carved on the backrest. This was still in situ up to 1970, but was then purchased and is now in private hands.

The station would have probably been originally oil lit, but gas lighting had arrived by the turn of the century. Then, as now, there was no footbridge, access being by individual pathways from the main road, with a sleeper crossing for staff use. Originally the Signal Box was probably on the Up platform, in the recess with a stone retaining wall on three sides, still visible today, albeit filled up. However it was later found expedient to place the Signal Box nearer the points into the goods yard, just south of the Down platform. The goods yard initially consisted of a single siding running behind the present Down buildings, and terminating beside a loading bay. To the south three sidings served Tym's Rose Hill Brickworks, which remained open until the 1920's. The site later became the Marple Urban District Council Depot, and they too had a private siding and loading bay until the 1960's.

In c.1900 the goods yard was extended by the addition of a second siding to deal with the growing coal traffic, and a weigh bridge provided near the road entrance. At the same time the N.S. rebuilt the Signal Box on much the same site, and this box lasted until 1970; it was the most northerly N.S. style signal box. The mainstay of the goods traffic at Rose Hill was always coal, though there was some agricultural traffic. Both full wagon loads and 'sundries' were dealt with, the latter being the term used for general merchandise conveyed in less than wagon loads. Marple was however always the principal goods depot for such traffic with its superior facilities of goods shed and crane. To the south of the station, Park and Paterson in 1914 established a non-ferrous metal foundry on the site of another disused brickworks. The works was soon provided with a private siding, also closed after World War 2. When Rose Hill was built there was not a house in sight apart from the 'Gun Inn' which was on a slightly different site to the 'Railway Inn' which replaced it in 1879. The 'New Inn' had bedrooms and stabling to deal with railway clientele. Its is now just the plain 'Railway' and is flourishing. However the Inn sign currently shows a L.N.E.R. express loco which would have rarely if ever appeared on the line. The station was named after the nearby Rose Hill House, which stood where The Drive now runs. Development around the station itself came after the 1st World War, but after the opening of Rose Hill, houses began to be built more on the Rose Hill side of Marple and building began to creep down Stockport Road towards the station and on to the fields on Cross Lane and Bowden Lane.

A pair of houses were even built next to the station. But a passenger before the 1st World War, arriving at Rose Hill, thinking from the timetable that it was in Marple, would have been somewhat surprised to find it set amid fields and quite some way from the village: a surprise no doubt matched by the stranger who arrived at Marple station, and was confronted unawares by Brabyns Brow. From Rose Hill the line ran southward through undulating countryside, with alternate low embankment and shallow cutting, with stone road overbridges, some underbridges and one unmanned level crossing just south of Rose Hill.

High Lane station was as equally in the middle of nowhere as Rose Hill, except that it was on the Stockport-Buxton turnpike road; it took its name from the small settlement about half a mile away. Unlike Rose Hill it was never surrounded by much building, and remains largely encircled by fields to this day. The original buildings here, as at Rose Hill, were on the Up side, and had identical accommodation, except that the rooms were in reverse order, with the addition of a brick outhouse for the storage of coal at the north. The Down platform had a small wooden building, with a glass fronted waiting room, heated by a coke stove in the centre. To the south of this was a tiny second booking office, as at Rose Hill. to supplement that on the Up. Also as at Rose Hill, inclined paths connected platforms to road, and there was no footbridge, only a sleeper crossing at the south end. There was a signal box at the north end of the Up platform controlling a crossover and Up and Down line signals; it is not known when this closed, but it was probably as early as the 1930's.

Such modernities as gas lighting never reached High Lane, which remained oil lit until it closed in 1970. High Lane, like 'Poynton', never had a goods depot, but dealt with parcels by passenger train, and such general merchandise 'sundries' as could be manhandled out of wagons onto the platform. The 1956 Railway Clearing House Handbook of Stations indicates that packages of up to 1 cwt. could be dealt with, but this facility probably ceased soon after. There would almost certainly be an arrangement with a local haulier to deliver such traffic as and when required. Station staff would consist of Station Master, 2 Signalmen, 2 Booking Clerks and 2 or 3 Porters.

Just over half a mile to the south lie the two Middlewood stations. Here no houses, and very little at all, in fact, could be seen from the station, which as its name suggests lies deep in the middle of a wood. The station had no road access, but was served by 3 footpaths which disappeared from a variety of wicket gates on the platforms into the depths of the encompassing wood. The stranger might be surprised at the rural nature of the surroundings on arriving at Rose Hill or High Lane but at Middlewood he had every right to wonder where on earth he had got to, especially if it was a dark windy night. There was little local traffic, but the stations were quite busy with passengers changing from one line to another, for which purpose staircases connected the L.N.W. Low Level and Macclesfield Committee High Level station platforms; one staircase connected up High Level and down Low Level platforms while a footbridge crossed from High Level down platform to link up with a ramp to the up Low Level platform. The Low Level station also had the refinement of a footbridge - one feels that the link up could have been much simpler. The stations were designed to provide interchange for passengers between e.g. Macclesfield and Buxton, but to the chagrin of the M.S.L. and N.S. many of the passengers using the station were transferring from their trains from Bollington and Poynton to use the quicker L.N.W. route to Stockport and Manchester!

The Low Level station had standard L.N.W. type buildings of the mid 1870's, entirely wooden, with horizontal timbering and a low pitched slate roof. On the Up platform, were a Ladies Waiting Room and W.C., General Waiting Room and Ticket Office, plus a Gentleman's Lavatory. The same facilities were provided on the Down, minus the Ticket Office. Gas lighting never came to Middlewood, and the Low Level station remained oil lit as late as 1972, when electricity arrived. A signal box with the title 'Middlewood Low Level Junction' stood at the divergence of the curve, some yards to the east. The High Level station was set high on an embankment, and was entirely constructed of wood, set on stilts in the bank, with the result that it shook alarmingly in the wind. The buildings were rudimentary, the waiting shelter on the Down was open to the elements and due to the exposed situation of the station it used to drift up with snow so that it was impossible to get into the little office adjoining. This Booking Office was so tiny that it proved a furnace to work in when the coke stove was lit, and once in, to get any working surface it was necessary to lower a folding table flap, which blocked the door! The Up platform had a larger building containing a Waiting Room adjoining the Ticket Office, Ladies Room, Porters Room, and Ladies and Gentlemens toilets, which were of the chemical variety. Middlewood being without sanitation, the embankment was liberally manured with the contents of these. The Macclesfield Committee accommodated their Station Master in a house beside the station, and this is still standing. In the early days at least there were 2 signal boxes, one at High Level Junction where the curve diverged, and another

High Lane, 1st March 1951. Ex Great Central C.14 4-4-2T No 674477 on the 1035 London Rd Maccesfield (R. Gee).

Rose Hill Station c.1914, looking South. Note the chimney of the rail served Tym's brickworks.

MIDDLEWOOD c.1910

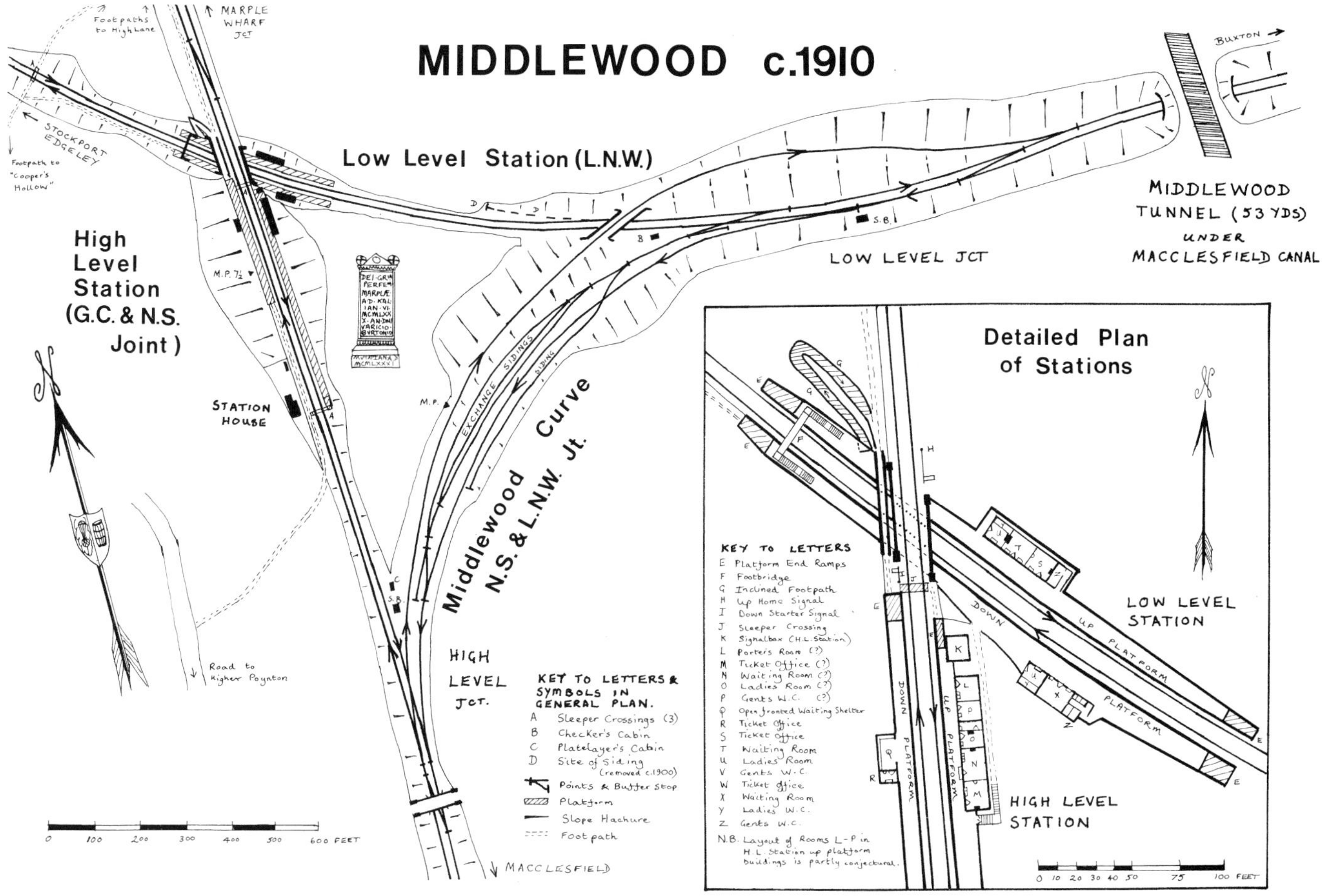

ROSE HILL STATION c.1900

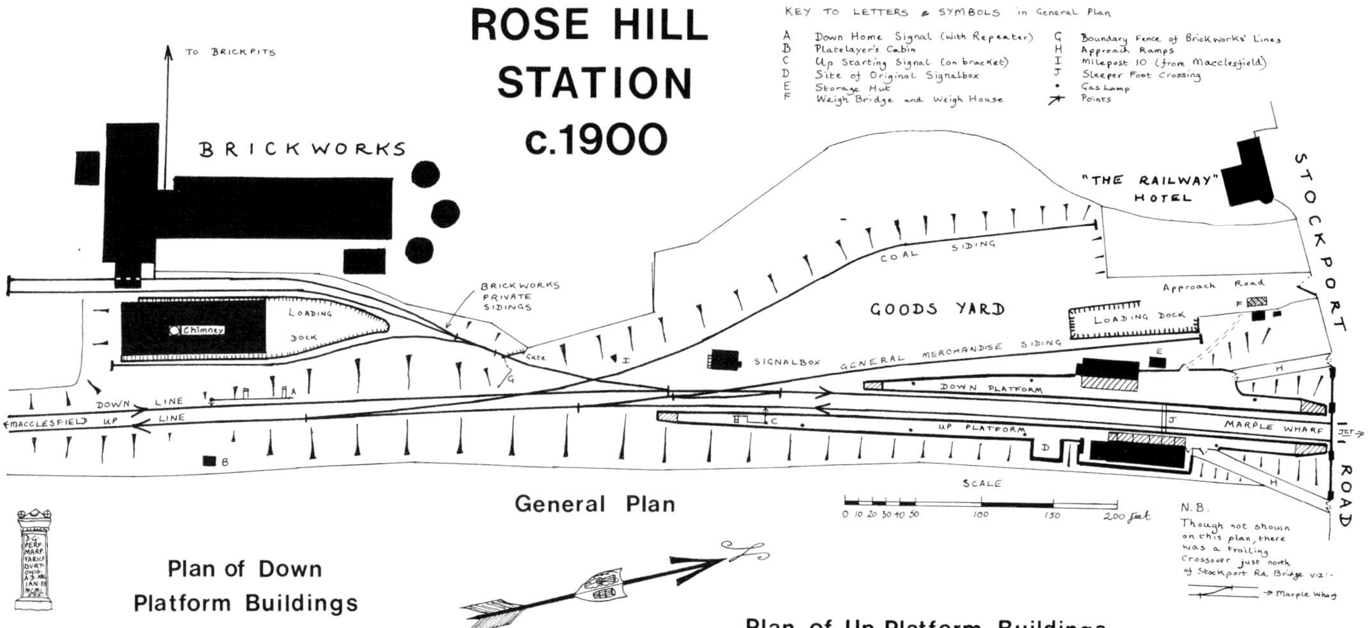

General Plan

Plan of Down Platform Buildings

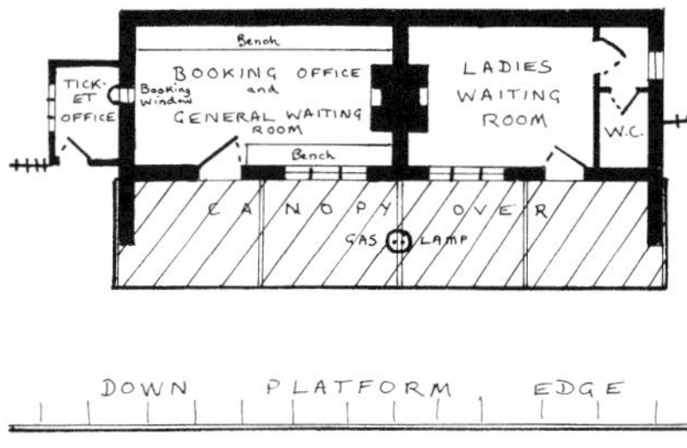

Plan of Up Platform Buildings

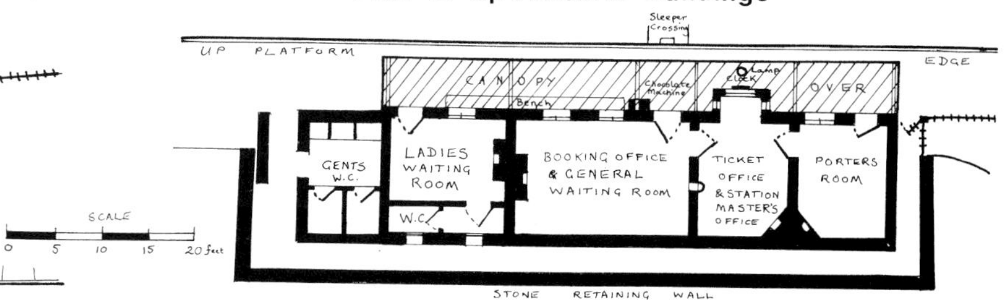

Rose Hill - train arriving from Manchester 1951 (R.Gee)

Rose Hill from the north in 1962 (Mowat Collection)

Rosehill Station C1910 looking North

controlling a crossover north of the station, though the latter closed at an unknown date, probably early in the 20th C. At High Level Junction, a small brickworks developed around the same time, where the clay pit had previously been. It possessed quite a set of sidings, but these closed in the 1950's. And so the line continued its uneventful way on to Higher Poynton, Bollington and Macclesfield - but outside our chosen area.

5. Train Services

The initial train service of four each way and two on Sundays was soon found inadequate, and in Bradshaw for October 1875 this had risen to six each way (seven on Saturdays) and four on Sundays. All the Sunday services ran through to or from London Road, though of the weekday trains one Down terminated at Romiley, and one service ran to Hyde, returning from Woodley. Of the 6 London Road trains each way, half were routed via Guide Bridge and half via Bredbury. The latter had some pretensions to the title of express, as they omitted most of the intermediate stops: the 9.10 a.m. from Macclesfield ran non-stop from Romiley reaching Manchester at 9.55 a.m., and the 4.20 p.m. from Manchester, non-stop from Ardwick, reached Rose Hill in 18 minutes, and Macclesfield in 45 minutes - which is much faster than anything on offer to Rose Hill now. The 5.30 and 6.30 p.m. trains from Manchester were almost equally fast. It would appear that the M.S.L., who ran the passenger service (the N.S. ran the goods) was out to try and capture some of the Manchester-Macclesfield traffic from the L.N.W. In these early days, 4 wheeled coaches and tank engines would have maintained the service, all provided from the M.S.L. carriage sidings and loco shed at Gorton. By August 1887, Bradshaw shows a service substantially unaltered, with 7 trains to London Road on the Down, and on the Up 6 trains from London Road, and one starting from Woodley. In addition on Saturdays a late evening train ran each way between Macclesfield and Woodley, with connections at the latter to and from Manchester. Also on Saturdays, a train ran at 1.30 p.m. from London Road, to cater for workers, who in those days worked half day on Saturdays, returning home, and for half day trippers from Manchester seeking the countryside. Between Rose Hill and Macclesfield most trains called at all stations, though one or two did not call at Middlewood, and others only called by request. There was also now a shuttle service of 3 trains each way between Bollington and Macclesfield. Eleven years later in August 1898, the service was little altered, though all trains now called at Middlewood; most services were now routed via Bredbury, but called at most or all stations. Most 'express' running had thus been given up by the M.S.L., and services wisely concentrated on intermediate traffic, with the result that timings were slower, and most trains took about an hour to reach Macclesfield; on the Manchester-Rose Hill run the fastest Up timing was 24 minutes, 23 minutes on the Down - still comparing favourably with today. The Macclesfield - Bollington shuttle had meanwhile risen to 5 trains each way, with 8 on Saturdays. An interesting feature of this high summer timetable were 2 early afternoon Saturday only trains from London Road, and another from Guide Bridge, with corresponding evening return trains, to cater for day trippers on their Saturday half day. Such was the number of these trippers that 2 of the trains were 3rd Class only, and were really excursion trains. By then Macclesfield trains would almost certainly consist of mainly 6 wheeled coaches, though 4 wheelers were still in evidence. Compartment stock without corridors was the order of the day, and lavatories unheard of, except in the 1st Class coaches- hence the generous provisions of lavatories at stations. Superannuated ex-Main Line M.S.L. 2-4-0 tender engines were much in evidence, as well as some of the 2-4-2 tanks built specifically for local work. Goods train would almost certainly be worked by antique standard goods 0-6-0's, which would operate on the 'Knotty' Macclesfield-Buxton trip, and on the daily all stations pick-up, the 'Woodley Goods', which ran from Macclesfield to Woodley and probably Guide Bridge. The line was also used by through M.S.L. and N.S. goods trains to the Potteries. By Bradshaw April 1910, the passenger service had grown to 9 each way on weekdays and 10 on Saturdays, though 2 trains each way used Hyde or Woodley as their terminus. A significant feature is however, the appearance of the first morning 'commuter' train, leaving Macclesfield at 7.40 a.m., Rose Hill at 8.4 a.m., to arrive at London Road at 8.53 a.m. in time for a 9 a.m. start in the office. This indicates that residential traffic was just beginning to build up, but at this point, well into the 20th C., and well out of chronological sequence, we must leave the backwater of the M.B.M. and return to Marple on the Main Line, about to witness its palmiest days.

VI. Fin de Siècle - Marple's Heyday. 1890-1898

1. The Dore and Chinley Line (1888-94)

You will recall that Chapter IV ended with the opening of the 'Midland Junction' Curve, giving the Midland access to the L. & Y. system. The ever ambitious Midland was not however satisfied with its grip on the North-West. A need was felt for a better link between the new empires in Manchester and Liverpool and the older territories centred on Sheffield and the West Riding. When therefore a local Dore and Chinley line was promoted in the 1880's, the scheme was eagerly snapped up by the Midland, and, with its support, authorised in 1888. Work began immediately, but was slow; for out of the 20½ miles of line, over one quarter - 5¾ miles were in tunnel. Totley Tunnel (6,226 yards) is the second longest tunnel in Britain. Cowburn Tunnel (3,727 yards) by contrast is one of the deepest below ground level. Great problems were encountered with underground water in these tunnels. The Manchester Guardian remarked at the time that "every man seemed to possess the miraculous power of Moses, for whenever he struck rock, water gushed forth!" At one point in fact a natural underground reservoir was tapped, and the resulting flow was estimated at 5,000 gallons a minute. The route, usually now known as the Hope Valley Line eventually opened on 13 May 1894. With a route between Manchester and Sheffield only 5 miles longer than the M.S.L., the Midland tried to capture some of the express traffic between the two cities. Fast trains were run from Manchester Central calling at Stockport, Marple and a few selected Hope Valley stations - the services at Marple were thus further diversified and increased. Local services on the line at first usually ran to and from Buxton, but were soon diverted via Marple to Manchester. The express service never really challenged the M.S.L. route, and dwindled away in the early years of the 20th C, but the route prospered for goods traffic, and carried great tonnages between Lancashire and South Yorkshire. It was also found to be a useful alternative to the heavily graded, and by then very busy route through the Peak, and for some years the occasional St. Pancras or Nottingham and Manchester service ran this way via the South Curve at Dore. Meanwhile goods traffic was causing such congestion on the approach to Manchester that the Main Line was being quadrupled south of New Mills.

2. The Marple Landslip of 1893

An important piece of Marple Rail history not included in the original book is the landslip which occurred on the night of 23rd December 1893 between Marple Goyt Viaduct and Marple South Tunnel, just north of 'Arkwright's Footbridge'. The slip carried away the Up line and led to Single Line working by Pilotman (a human single line token) between Strines and Marple South signal boxes using the Down Line. Marple Goyt Signalbox was taken out of use temporarily. A notice to this effect was issued on 25th December - Christmas Day - 1893! By 29th December a temporary 'Marple Cutting' signal box, open continuously, was provided at the site of the slip controlling temporary crossovers and signals to keep the single line section as short as possible. The signal box was on the Strines Road side of the railway and cut into the embankment. The debris from the slip was removed and repairs effected by two large shear leg like cranes. The work was rapidly completed and double line working restored after a few weeks of disruption on 7th January 1894. The dislocation and delay to Midland Main Line and freight and M.S.L. locals must have been dramatic. But the repairs were apparently nowhere near completed. On 10 June 1894 the Engineer was still engaged in sluing the lines to their permanent positions between Strines and Marple, and on 24 June 1894 he was to slue the Up main line into its final position after treatment of the slip. The slip was repaired by the construction of blue engineering brick arches in the form of a dummy viaduct to stabilize the steep hillside; this is still there to this day. The slip caused a great deal of loose earth to pour down the hillside towards the River Goyt and up against the walls of Marple Lodge, which stood by the bridge across the Goyt to Oldknow's Mellor Lodge and the site of Mellor Mill. The Lenthall family living in Marple Lodge had to flee and stay with friends in Marple and Mellor, They eventually moved back into Mellor Lodge. But the slip was the end of Marple Lodge and looking at the site today it is difficult to imagine there was ever a house on the site. The footpath from Strines Road via 'Arkwright's Bridge' was also blocked but soon reinstated.

3. Marple Train Services: August 1898

Thus with lines radiating to Manchester Victoria, Central and London Road, Liverpool, Stockport, Sheffield and Derby, Marple had by the late 1890's reached the zenith of its main line importance as a Midland main line calling and connectional point. Meanwhile the M.S.L. had opened an independent extension to the Capital in 1899, terminating at Marylebone, changing its name in anticipation to 'Great Central Railway' (G.C.) in 1897. Now yet a fourth route was added to the competitive lines between London and Manchester. The Midland was particularly affected, as the G.C. line passed through Leicester, Nottingham and Sheffield en route, hitherto mainly served by the Midland. Cut-throat competition ensued, so that by the turn of the century the best St. Pancras-Manchester trains had been accelerated to 4½ hours. This was only achieved on a few trains, omitting most stops, but even so most services continued to stop at Marple, the best of which only took 4 hours 20 minutes between St. Pancras and Manchester. Let us therefore look at the August 1898 train service for Marple, culled from Bradshaw. In all a staggering 109 trains used the station daily, 60 Up and 49 Down. Of these only 37 were G.C. trains, the remaining 72 being Midland, over double the number of Midland trains calling in 1887, such had been the growth in traffic. On Saturdays the total was even higher at 122, with 5 additional Midland and 8 G.C. trains. To these must be added almost as many goods trains, mainly Midland, as well as special trains, excursions to Blackpool, Southport or the Peak District, and the 8 daily express passenger trains which did not stop at Marple. All told then about 250 trains passed through Marple in 24 hours - an average of 10 an hour, or one every six minutes, day and night! One wonders if the occupants of the station house got any sleep at

The Marple landslip on the 28th December 1893 looking south - note the temporary signal box (Science & Society Photographic Library/ NRM)

all with the almost continual rumble of overnight goods trains.

The busiest period was the 2 hours following 8.15 a.m., when no less than 23 trains were booked to call, terminate or start at Marple, in addition to those passing through without stopping. In fact analysis of the timetable shows a continuous stream from the 7.35 a.m. to St. Pancras until the 6.35 p.m. from St. Pancras arrived at 10.40 p.m., with trains on average every ten or so minutes, with only four half hour breaks in this cascade of trains. At times this flow reached a torrent with so many trains that one wonders how on earth they all got through. For instance, in those two hours from 8.15 a.m., this was what happened. The first of the torrent was a Midland Up local from Stockport, which terminated at the Up platform, and quickly shunted into the Down bay. This was followed at 8.27 by a Down G.C. New Mills-London Road train, the morning business express. At the same moment an Up Midland local for Millers Dale was calling at the opposite platform. 7 minutes later the same Up platform received the 8.35 arrival from Manchester Victoria, which terminated and shunted into the Up loop, before the train with which it connected, the Midland West of England Express from Central, drew in at 8.48, and soon departed again for Bristol. Meanwhile at the other platform, a Down G.C. Hayfield-London Road local departed at 8.47, followed 3 minutes later from the Down bay by a local for Stockport and Altrincham, formed by the loco and coaches of the 8.15 arrival from Stockport. 7 minutes later another Up local from Stockport arrived and shunted out of the way. After a break of 10 minutes, an Up Midland semi-fast for Matlock Bath drew in at 9.07. Behind it at 9.15 arrived another Up train, a Midland non-stop service from Victoria, to connect with the following St. Pancras express. The Victoria train had however to quickly shunt out of the way into the Up loop, as 4 minutes later at 9.19 an Up G.C. local for New Mills was due, while at the same time in the Down platform a Midland semi-fast from Rotherham and Sheffield halted for 3 minutes. It left for Manchester Central at 9.20, closely followed 3 minutes later by the return to Manchester Victoria of the train which had arrived at 8.35 - this would leave from the Down bay, if there had been time to get the stock across between trains, or if not, from the Up loop. Traffic was now reaching a crescendo, and at 9.25 an express from Liverpool Central arrived, terminated in the Up platform, and was quickly propelled into the Up loop, and the engine turned on the turntable. Within a few minutes the Manchester-St. Pancras Dining Car express drew in at 9.31, with through coaches for Nottingham and Sheffield also attached. Promptly the shunter detached the rear 3 or 4 coaches destined for Sheffield, and the main express departed at 9.36. The Sheffield coaches were quickly provided with an engine (probably off the 8.57 local arrival from Stockport) and left 4 minutes later. At the same moment as this caravan like train was being dealt with at the Up main platform, a Derby-Manchester express was being divided at the Down main platform. Arriving at 9.30, the rear 2 or 3 coaches were shed for Manchester Victoria, and left in the Down platform; once the main train had left for Central at 9.35, the loco and coaches which had been waiting in the Down bay since arrival from Victoria at 9.15, drew out, backed onto the Derby coaches and left for Victoria at 9.38. Hard on its heels, the connecting 9.44 for Liverpool left from the Up loop, with the train that had arrived at 9.25. It can thus be seen that at approximately 9.35, all four platforms were occupied with 7 trains or portions standing in them simultaneously destined for Liverpool, Manchester Victoria, Manchester Central, Sheffield, St. Pancras and Nottingham, and one from Stockport; two trains were dividing simultaneously, there were 4 departures within 5 minutes and three light engines shunting from line to line. No sooner had all these trains left however than an Up Midland Derby Slow called at 9.45, at 9.52 an Up G.C. Hayfield. At 10.01 a Midland Down Millers Dale - Manchester Central Slow halted for 4 minutes for water, followed at 10.08 by a G.C. Hayfield-London Road. There then mercifully followed a rare 30 minutes break until the next train was due, a gap which was no doubt filled with a steady stream of goods and special trains. This pattern of intensive usage was repeated several times during the day, though not quite to such a fever pitch. As has been said, the Midland stopped 42 Up and 29 Down trains at Marple, of which about three quarters were express as opposed to local services. 6 trains from and 7 to St. Pancras called, and of these 5 each way stopped to detach or attach through coaches to or from Manchester Victoria, Bolton and Blackburn. These portions to and from the L. & Y. system were very popular in their day, as Midland coaches were so comfortable by comparison with those of other companies. The coaches used on these trains were 12 wheeled bogie 1st and 3rd composite non-corridor stock, hauled throughout by Midland locos. They usually called at Darwen, Bolton, Salford and Manchester Victoria, though one or two called at Bromley Cross and Turton stations- what on earth such trains were calling at such remote places high on the Lancashire moorland can only be surmised- perhaps some important personage lived nearby. Trains conveying 1st class sleeping cars between Manchester and St. Pancras also stopped at Marple; Liverpool portions were usually attached or detached at Stockport, though a few expresses had Liverpool connections at Marple. But the Up overnight train was marshalled up at Marple with portions from Liverpool, Blackburn and Manchester Central, which must have been quite a task.

Some of these St. Pancras trains were very fast indeed: the 12 noon from Central ran non-stop to Marple, where it picked up a Blackburn portion. From Marple it ran non-stop to Leicester (avoiding Derby via the Chaddesden Loop) in 98 minutes for the 87 miles, an average of nearly 54 m.p.h. - not bad for 1898! The train reached St. Pancras without any other stop at 4.20 p.m., 3 hours 55 minutes from Marple. It is difficult now to imagine a St. Pancras express calling at Marple and Leicester only after leaving Central! There was another non-stop Marple to Leicester run on the 4.10 p.m. from Manchester, and another on the 12 noon St. Pancras-Central; such was the competition for London-Manchester traffic that on occasions even Derby was avoided. Cross Country services to Bristol and between Liverpool, Manchester and Nottingham called, and there was also the Midland's Sheffield-Manchester service, some of which ran to and from Rotherham Westgate. While some of these trains were entitled 'Sheffield Expresses', others called at nearly all the stations on the Hope Valley line, and even the best usually stopped at Heeley, Dore and Hope or Edale, or some other station, even if only to take up or set down. There were in addition some even more exotic through coach workings, such as one from Southport Chapel Street to St. Pancras, via the C.L.C., Manchester Central and Marple. In the summer there were several Blackpool services calling at Marple. For instance the 4.50 p.m. Blackpool (Talbot Road) -Sheffield train was first stop Marple, though the through train to Leicester and Nottingham on the Up stopped at Salford and Manchester Victoria, and the equivalent Down train at Miles Platting (change for Victoria) and Poulton. The basis of the local services was the slow stopping trains between Manchester and Derby, which took over 3 hours for the 60 miles, and other locals which had their terminus at Millers Dale, Matlock or even Ambergate. There were also semi-fast trains which called at principal stations such as Chapel-en-le-Frith and Rowsley to Matlock, Derby or Nottingham. The number of services Marple enjoyed to various principal points in August 1898 are best summarised in table form:-

	To Marple	From Marple
St. Pancras	6	7
Leicester	8	7
Nottingham	-	6
Derby	12	15
Birmingham	-	3
Bristol	-	3
Sheffield	5	6
Rotherham	1	3
Liverpool	7	8
Blackpool	2	1
Southport	1	-
Blackburn	5	5
Manchester Victoria	12	8
Manchester Central	17	20
Manchester London Road	20	17
Stockport Tiviot Dale	16	22

The coaching stock employed on Midland trains had an enviable reputation for comfort, especially for 3rd class passengers, and for internal and external cleanliness. All were painted in a rich shade of red known as 'crimson lake', lined out black and gold, and embellished with the Company's coat of arms. By now the Pullman cars, which had been running since the 1870's were becoming rather antiquated, and were replaced on night trains by specially built 1st class sleepers. There was also a growing demand for dining cars, and refreshment stops were going out of favour as causing delay. In 1897 the Midland introduced magnificent 1st and 3rd class dining cars on the Manchester run. These were 60ft. long, with 6 wheeled bogies and had handsome clerestory roofs.

At the same time new coaches were being provided with lavatories reached by short internal corridors - as yet the public were not ready for full corridor trains as they were regarded as invasions of privacy. Another feature of Midland coaches was steam heating, as on most British trains people had to rely on footwarmers for warmth. These were giant 'hot water bottles' of brass, filled with hot water or heat giving chemicals. A Marple gentleman still living until the 1970's remembered using these on trains from the station, his father tipping the fireman for a fill of hot water, and he and his brothers and sisters squabbling about who should have their foot on it. Not for nothing did railway guides enjoin wrapping up well against the cold when making a train journey. Trains were also still gas lit, as electric lighting was still in its infancy. The engines hauling these magnificent coaches would seem very small to our eyes, but were supremely elegant, and beautifully finished since c.1883 in the same crimson lake as the carriages, with black and gold lining out, and the Company's armorial embellishment. They were always in immaculate condition, even underneath. They could also run remarkably fast on occasions, despite their small size. The most famous class of engine in use on Midland expresses at this time were the Johnson 'Spinners', so called because of their 7'9" single driving wheels, which had a tendency to slip and spin when starting, but were exceptionally fast and free runners. Other 4-2-2's and also 4-4-0's, with almost equally large driving wheels were also common on the express services calling at Marple. Less up to date engines would have been seen on local and stopping services, though the Dore & Chinley Line had fifteen 4-4-0's built specially for it in 1893. Goods trains were still worked by the ubiquitous 0-6-0's, some of great antiquity - as Midland engines were so well maintained, they tended to last a long time! Coaches on local and semi-fast trains were composed of 6 wheeled coaches, and some 8 wheelers. The G.C. share of activity at Marple was far less intense than that of the Midland, and hardly changed from 1887 - seventeen Up and twenty Down trains were run of which a few started or terminated at Marple. One G.C. train was even marshalled up at Marple: separate trains left London Road at 5.10 p.m. calling at all stations via Guide Bridge and at 5.37 p.m. calling at Ashburys to take up, and Romiley, reaching Marple in 23 minutes, where the two trains combined to go forward to Hayfield. Of the G.C. trains 11 each way ran to and from Hayfield, and 2 used New Mills as a terminus. Trains were almost equally divided between the Bredbury and Guide Bridge routes, if anything favouring the latter. The G.C. trains ran at irregular intervals, with gaps in departures of well over an hour throughout most of the day. On Saturdays 2 extra trains were run to and from Hayfield, and another as far as New Mills only, for the benefit of trippers from Manchester, Ashton, Hyde etc. enjoying a half day trip into the countryside. Some of them started from Guide Bridge or even Gorton, and were 3rd class only. G.C. services were generally worked by green-liveried tank engines from Gorton or Hayfield Shed (whereas Midland engines came from depots as far afield as Liverpool, Leicester, Derby and Sheffield, or nearer home - Heaton Mersey, Trafford Park, Belle Vue, or Rowsley), such as the class Three 2-4-2 tanks. The coaching stock livery was changed in 1896 from varnished teak to a very smart style of buff lower panels and French grey upper, lined out gold. But the new livery did not wear well or stay clean in the industrial north, and in 1908 coaches reverted to varnished teak. In all 45 trains each day left Marple for Manchester, and 49 arrived from that city, linking Marple to the 3 most important Manchester termini by a variety of 4 routes. All told the 109 daily trains terminated at 22 different places, linking Marple directly to well over a 100 different stations in 13 counties. Incidentally, in 1904 as a result of the change of name of the M.S.L. to G.C. and the joint acquisition of a colliery branch from Shireoaks to Haughton in South Yorkshire, the Sheffield and Midland Committee was renamed the G.C. and Midland Joint Committee, which thus controlled two distinct and remote lines. Similarly in 1907 the old Macclesfield Committee became the G. C. & N.S. Joint Committee.

4. Improvements to Marple Station

The station as completed in 1875 and described in Chapter IV.3, remained much as built until demolition in 1970. The Midland must have often wished for additional platforms and facilities, with the vast and growing number of trains calling and passing through. But there was no room to expand without formidable engineering works on one side, or sweeping away St. Martin's church on the other. Various small scale improvements were however made. On the Down side the original 1865 waiting room was proving inadequate, and a large bay fronted wooden waiting room was provided between the station house and bay platform - it is not known when, but was probably about 1885. The old waiting room became a 1st class waiting room. Behind the new waiting room was erected another wooden building to house the platform foreman; this building had originally been the checkers office in the goods yard, but was moved and re-erected. An improvement to the goods yard in the last years of the 19th C. was the addition of an additional siding between 'shed road' and 'back road' to deal with additional coal traffic, which became known as 'middle road' - between it and 'back road' a cobbled cart road was laid and beside its buffer stop a weigh bridge was installed. This was later moved to beside the gateway onto Brabyns Brow.

As we have seen a number of trains terminated, divided or were marshalled up at Marple - in fact the August 1898 timetable would have required about 25 engines to use the turntable in one day. The turntable installed in 1875 was 45 feet long, and was becoming rather short for the increasing size of engines of the late 19th C. We find a reference in the minutes of the Midland Board's Loco Committee in 1896 as follows; "it was suggested that the 45' turntable at Marple be replaced by one of 50'. This was sanctioned by the General Purposes Committee", and in 1897 "it was reported that the S. & M. Joint Committee agreed to a 50 foot engine turntable being put in at Marple, the Midland Co. to bear the whole cost of the work, and to pay £10 rent for the site of the turntable" (i.e. to the M.S.L., per annum). The turntable was installed, probably in 1898, in a hollow carved out of the embankment, just S.E. of Brabyns Brow; this great excavation is still visible today, though the actual table pit is filled in. The reason that a completely new turntable was required was because there just was not room for a larger table under the footbridge between main line, 'shed road' and retaining wall. For a time the old turntable remained in use alongside the new one (it is still shown on the 1909 O.S. 25" map), but was eventually removed and a siding laid over its site; this was still however known as 'table road'! There are no records

Marple Station from the south C1890. Note the 'knob-up' signal box under the footbridge on the Up side.

The Harwich 'Boat Train' from Manchester Piccadilly heads south, 12th Sept 1978. (Author)

of when the second 50' turntable was removed, but it would have declined in usage with the great alterations to Midland services in the early 20th C. It was probably removed sometime after the 1st World War, and it is known that the new turntable was taken away for re-use at Buxton Midland Loco Shed. The Midland Railway was responsible for the maintenance of half of the Works and Ways on the S. & M. Joint Line, which came under Derby North Maintenance District. The Midland share extended from Hayfield, through Marple, to Woodley Junction on the Hyde line, to Bredbury Junction on the C.L.C. and Reddish Junction on the Bredbury Route. The Midland were responsible for all track, signalling, signal boxes, bridges, viaducts, gradient posts, mile posts, telegraph wires, stations and lighting. Station maintenance and painting was let out on contract, but the rest was performed by the Midland. The track was maintained by gangs of platelayers stationed all along the route, each of whom had his 'length' to patrol each day; for bigger jobs they would form a larger gang to tackle it. All other general maintenance work was done by staff based at Romiley, and included carpenters, painters and a blacksmith. The Midland erected its mile posts along its portion of the S. & M.; accordingly a Midland style mile post reading 176 ¾ (from St. Pancras via Derby) was placed at Marple Station affixed to the retaining wall of St. Martin's Churchyard, near the site of the 1905 signal box.

5. Operating at Marple

To deal with these 109 trains a day, a very large staff was required. Presiding over the hierarchy was the Station Master. After Mr Rowbottom, whom we have already met in the1870's, came Mr. Hawkins who left in the 1890's, and was the last to live in the Station House for many years. He was followed by Mr. Keighley, who was only a small man, but he ruled with a rod of iron, and his staff were always careful to call him 'Sir'. He supplemented his railway income by giving shorthand lessons at a 1d. each Below the 'boss', in the Booking Office was the 'Chief Clerk', and several 'Second Clerks' on various turns, plus a Junior Clerk to assist in the busiest part of the day. These Clerks would book tickets, give information, and deal with all the station accounts, and also the documentation for parcels by passenger train. The Junior Clerk was no doubt often sent to the Parcels Office to do this. Also under the boss, were two Platform Foremen on each shift, one for the Up and one for the Down. Under them they had two Porters each, and an additional Porter to assist as required. The Porters also had to help load and unload parcels traffic. There were normally also two Ticket Collectors on duty, one from each company, the G.C. and Midland. Tickets were collected from each of their own company's trains, to be bagged up and sent to Manchester or Derby - no doubt however they helped each other out on occasions! They had a little office beneath the footbridge on the Down platform. There was also one shunter on duty on each shift to couple and uncouple coaches and locomotives on all trains dividing, joining and terminating.

On the goods side there was a Chief Goods Clerk, and a Junior Clerk, who did all the goods documentation in the little office attached to the goods shed. There was also a Checker, who checked all the wagons sent out of the yard were correctly labelled, took details off wagons coming into the yard, kept a watch on road vehicles entering the yard, and operated the weighing machine. There were also day and night goods porters who loaded and unloaded all goods traffic from wagons. Originally, when there were three signal boxes, north and south required two full time signalmen, plus a porter-signalman for 4 hours of the night (men worked 10 hour shifts then), and the centre 'knob-up' signal box had a porter-signalman on early and late turns. However when one box replaced three, only two full time signalmen and one porter-signalman were required. Finally a Lampman was employed to keep all the signal lamps filled with oil, and generally clean and in order. He was housed originally under the signal box, but later a corrugated iron hut was provided between the two short sidings at the north end of the station. In all therefore the Station Master presided over about 40 staff, of whom 15 or so would be on duty at any one time; labour was cheap and plentiful in those days.

But a station with such a heavy train service required a large staff. Passengers changing trains often carried heavy luggage, especially businessmen with their heavy 'skips' of samples, which the platform porters had to deal with. In many cases the gentleman would require a cab to take him to his destination - there were always a rank of horse drawn cabs or carriages awaiting on Brabyns Brow, and sometimes the queue extended back to St. Martin's Lych Gate. The unfortunate porter would have to heave the luggage up the stairs to the cab. Porters also had to attend to trains, load and unload parcels and passengers' luggage, help passengers out, close doors, collect tickets if there were more passengers than the ticket collectors could deal with, and keep the station clean and tidy between trains. The porters also had to handle mail bags, which G.P.O. staff used to drop down the stairwell from Brabyns Brow - one hopes railway staff were more careful with their parcels! The goods yard was also a hive of activity. There were four basic types of traffic dealt with at Marple: coal, livestock, general merchandise in full wagon loads, and general merchandise in less than wagon loads ('sundries'). General merchandise could be delivered or collected by the Railway, usually through a local carrier, except at the larger goods depots, or carted by the customer. Coal was entirely in the hands of the various merchants who came to collect their coal from wagons in the yard. It was difficult to deal with livestock at Marple, as the lack of space precluded permanent pens. On Monday, which was cattle market day, temporary pens were erected by inserting wooden posts in permanent sockets in the yard, and roping up between them. To get cattle, and other livestock, out of vans or wagons, which were usually placed in 'shed road' on the south side of the shed, a portable wheeled ramp was used. Livestock traffic grew so much that early in the 20th C. a cattle market was erected opposite side of Brabyns Brow, and at one time the provision of a permanent siding beside the second turntable was considered to avoid driving the cattle across the road. Sheep, cattle and pigs also arrived by train on Tuesday night for slaughter in Marple's butcher's premises. There was also quite a lot of milk traffic, with churns being despatched daily by passenger train each morning for dairies in Manchester and Didsbury.

General merchandise was dealt with out of doors if it was not likely to take harm e.g. agricultural machinery, or minerals, but the rest which needed to be protected from the weather passed through the goods shed. The purpose of the shed was to allow goods to be loaded and unloaded under cover, and to warehouse traffic for collection or delivery. To facilitate this the interior was provided with a raised platform, occupying the entire floor space, except for the railway line on one side and two loading bays on the other, which permitted a road vehicle to back into the shed and load under cover. Both bays were provided with cranes of 1½ tons capacity. Through this shed would pass such merchandise as sacks of corn to be ground into flour at Flowerdew's Corn Mill at Marple Bridge, chemicals for the Mellor Bleach Works at Hollywood, farming produce, raw cotton and coal for the mills of the district and returning consignments of finished cotton or calico from Compstall. The entire requirements and produce of the district passed through this shed or the yard, unless it went by railway owned canal. G.C. Goods Services were provided by a daily pick-up from Guide Bridge and Woodley to Marple and Hayfield, and by Midland Goods trains to and from Ancoats, Sheffield, Rowsley and Buxton. One train, nicknamed the 'Bull', perhaps because it carried livestock, was due from Ancoats every morning at 1 a.m., but was frequently late, with a result that the unfortunate goods porter who had to deal with it often had to wait about for it all night until it came. There was also a night fish train from Fleetwood to Derby, which called to set down some of the catch for Marple fishmongers. The Railway Companies usually employed local agents to perform cartage except at the larger depots. In Marple at the turn of the Century this was a Mr. Yarwood, more commonly known as 'Old Yarwood'. The Midland also had a local parcels receiving agent in Marple, Mr W.. Bradley of Church Lane.

In the early 1900's as a result of the burning down of Oldknow's Mill in 1892, the great mill ponds were turned into boating lakes; the boats for these arrived by train, and were carted down to 'the Lakes' on Bowden's horse drawn coal lorry. These 'Roman Lakes', as they were called, proved a great attraction for trippers from all the Manchester district. Marple, and also Strines, New Mills and Hayfield, were already very popular destinations for excursionists, and Saturday half day trippers, as we have already seen from the extra trains run on Saturday afternoons to cater for them. For instance a handbill for the Easter Bank Holidays of

1898 advertises morning and afternoon excursions from Oldham and Ashton to Marple and Hayfield at 1/- (5p) return. A particular attraction advertised at Marple, before the Roman Lakes were established, were a set of pleasure gardens half way down the west side of Compstall Road formerly known as the 'Spring Gardens'. But the Roman Lakes brought a vast influx of visitors, for whom Marple was the nearest place offering beautiful countryside and amusements within reach of the city. On occasions the queues of excursionists waiting to return home of an evening stretched several hundred yards up Brabyns Brow as far as the canal bridge. According to a G.C. handbook of 1900, a third class season ticket between Marple and Manchester London Road via Hyde or Reddish cost £7 per annum! For an extra 10/- (50p) p.a. it could be made available to Manchester Central or Victoria, and for £8 all told it was available to all three termini by the four routes. Rose Hill was a little dearer at £7 12s. 0d. (£7.60p) p.a., via Hyde or Reddish, but they were also available to Marple.

For Middlewood very complicated arrangements were in force. For £12 2s. 0d. (£12.10p) p.a. your season could be made available from Middlewood or Disley to London Road via Hyde, Reddish or Longsight which gave 6 possible permutations of route in all. A Marple - St. Pancras return ticket cost £1 9s. 3d. (£1.46p) 3rd class, £2 7s.2d. (£2.36p) 1st, though it must be remembered that the 3rd class fare was about equal to a skilled artisan's weekly wage, the equivalent of perhaps £200 in today's values. If you took your dog with you it cost an extra 4/- (20p). Through bookings were available from Marple to almost any station in Great Britain and Ireland. The Midland was particularly generous in the issue of 'Tourist' tickets at reduced rates. For instance a return 'Tourist' to Lowestoft cost 29/- (£1.45p) or to Southport 6/6d (32½ p). If you fancied a trip to Bideford for Westward Ho! in Devon, this would cost you 37/- (£1.85p), while if you choose to go a little further afield, the Great Central would be delighted to oblige with a through booking to Hamburg via Grimsby at £1 11s. 6d. (£1.57p) 3rd class 'Steerage' or £2 18s. 10d. (£2.94p) 1st class 'Saloon'. Some of the regulations of the Midland Railway make interesting reading, and give some indication of the type of passenger and traffic to be expected at a busy station. Commercial Travellers, for instance, were not allowed to take with them free In their luggage such things as "children's mail carts, patent corking machines, small gas engines, patent scrubbing machines, polyphons, chair legs, orchestraphone cases, and automatic penny-in-the-slot pianos", but had to pay full parcels rates on these. Special reduced rates were however available for the excess luggage of "Strolling Players, Burlesque and Musical Companies, Equestrian Parties, Emigrants", and for the "demonstration plant of Lecturers employed by the Church of England Incorporated Society for providing Homes for Waifs and Strays, and that of Lady Lecturers employed by cooking stove manufacturers, lecturing apparatus of the National Refuge for Destitute Children (when accompanied by the Secretary) and 'Dissolving View' and other apparatus accompanying Band of Hope Lecturers". Quite a mixed company! You name it, the railway had rates for it, from black puddings and samples of temperance beer (whatever that was) to mistletoe and patent clips for horseshoes. The Railway Companies were obliged by law to carry everything (the so-called 'common carrier obligation'). Hence we find that "small wild animals such as pumas, jackals, tiger cats are charged at 6d (2½p) per truck per mile" while "elephants carried in covered carriage trucks are charged at 1/- (5p) per mile per truck - whether the truck is specially strengthened or not". Potential consignors of wild animals in the early 20th C. would have been relieved to know however that "camels and zebras are charged at the horse rate, according to the number of stalls occupied", and could even be conveyed by passenger train in horse boxes.

In 1900 the railways had an almost complete monopoly over all inland movements over a few miles for both goods and passengers, and accordingly even a smallish goods yard like Marple was very busy. It is however too easy to look back to this as a 'golden age'. It must be remembered that the steam engine was dirty, that manual work in the age of coal and iron was hard without modern aids, that clerical work involved much drudgery over ledgers of hand written figures by gaslight, and that men at Marple Station worked 10 or 12 hours a day for little over a £1 a week. But it is fair to say that the railways were at the height of their power, pride and prosperity, and on a well run line like the Midland things were spick and span and beautifully maintained, and that men had a real pride in their work and loyalty to their Company, and railway employment was very secure.

6. Strines

Strines Station first appears in Bradshaw on 1st August 1866. The original buildings on the Down were of stone and consisted of a low, one storey waiting room, with a veranda type shelter in front, adjoining the waiting room, and under the same roof was a tiny booking office about 6' wide. Behind this was the Station Master's house, with living room and kitchen on the ground floor, and 3 tiny bedrooms above. Next to this were the Gents. A Ladies Room was later added behind the main waiting room. The buildings on the Up consisted merely of a wooden open fronted shelter, probably dating from when the line was doubled. A footbridge linked the platforms, and the station was gas lit, at least by 1900. Adjoining was a goods yard, with one siding to the West for coal, and another to the East, serving quite a sizeable goods shed, where traffic to and from the large Strines Calico Print Works provided the bulk of the business, with a little agricultural merchandise. There was a small outdoor crane of 2 ton capacity, and another in the shed.

Strines, like Middlewood, had almost no houses nearby. Passenger traffic was never heavy, but in the days before the bus and car, it was the only public transport in the area and with the passage of years, houses were built in Strines village, and some residential traffic built up. Few houses were however built near the station due to the presence of Strines Mill and the unsuitability of land in the wet valley bottom or on the steep hillside. The goods yard was however busy enough. Staff would probably consist of Station Master, Signalman, a Clerk (one on each shift) for goods and passenger work, and a couple of Porters, again for goods and passengers. In all perhaps 10 staff were employed at the station, and in the busiest part of the day 5 might be present at once. The mainstay of Strines' service were the M.S.L and later G.C. Hayfield-London Road trains, though the Midland stopped some of its local trains between Manchester Central and Derby or Sheffield as well. In 1875, 7 M.S.L. trains called in each direction, and 2 Down and 3 Up Midland 'Derby Slow' trains, a total of 19 trains in all. By 1898 still only 5 Midland trains called en route to or from Millers Dale or Derby, but the G .C. total had nearly doubled, with 13 each way and 18 on Saturdays, for the benefit of half day trippers, some of whom came to Strines. By 1910 the number of G.C. trains had increased to 18 Up and 17 Down. Midland services were down to 2 each way, though they were a fair assortment -on the Up, one to Chinley and another to Matlock, and on the Down one from Millers Dale, and one from Buxton! Strines was in the early 20thC. a good example of a small but thriving country station, as Marple was of an important medium-sized station.

Strines in its heyday C1910, looking south.

Strines looking north on September 12th 1978. (Author)

THE RAILWAYS AROUND MARPLE 1910

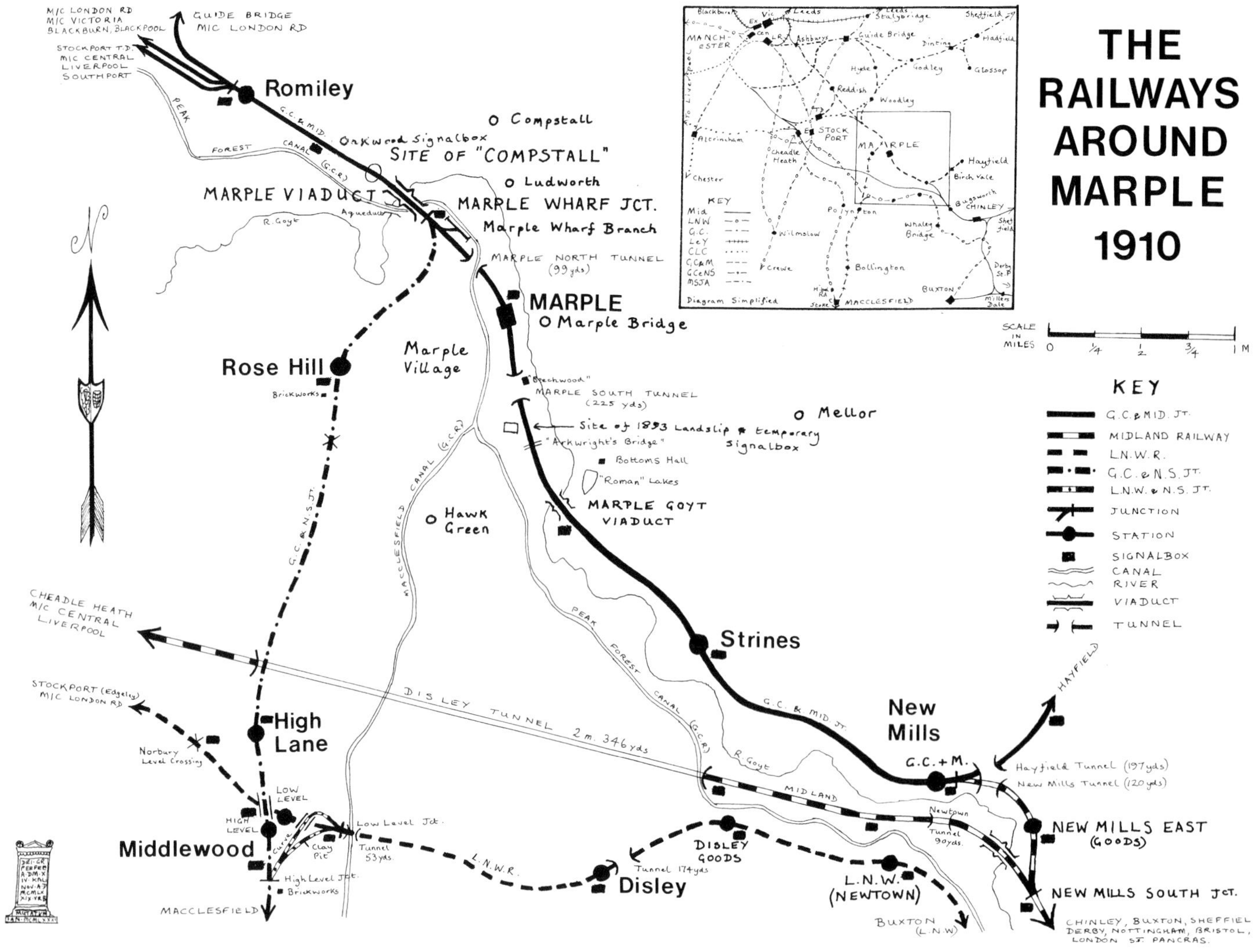

STRINES STATION c.1900

General Plan

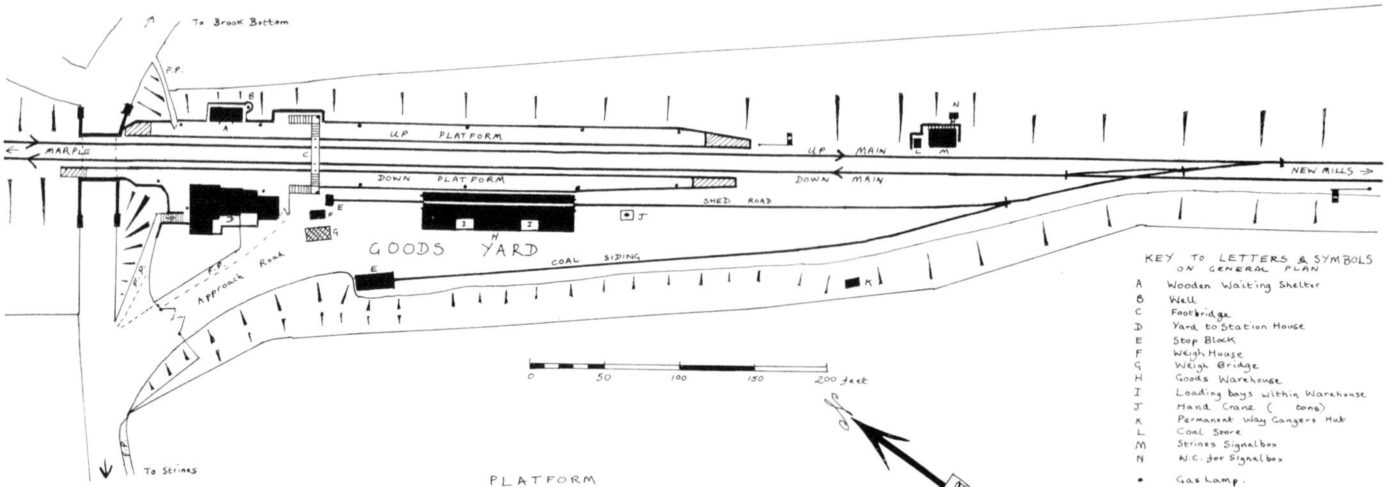

Plan of Down Platform Buildings

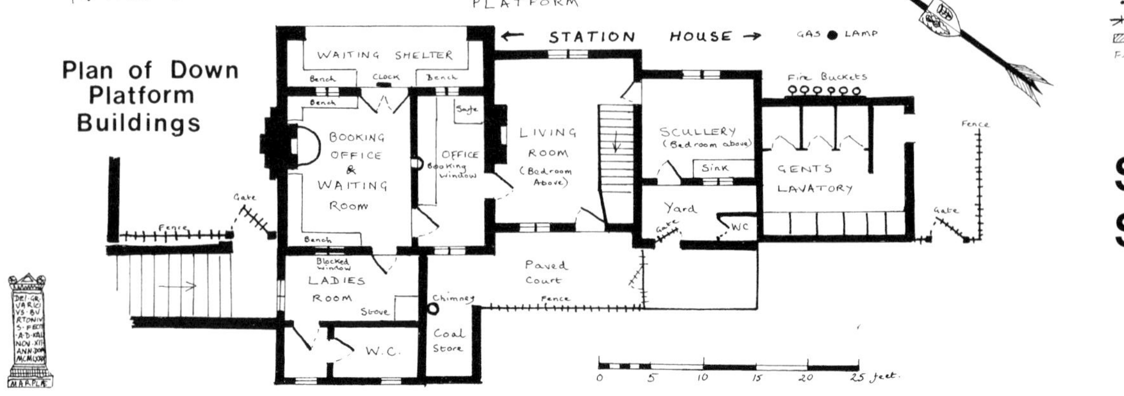

VII. Marple By-passed. 1898-1911.

An Up Great Central train of fourteen 6-wheeled carriages headed by a tank engine crosses Marple Viaduct. As some of the carriages are in the new G. C. livery of French grey and brown, and some are still in MSL livery, approx c.1900. On the extreme right note the old tall brick Marple Wharf Junction Signalbox replaced in 1927 by the box which remained in use until July 1980. Compare with inset taken by Author on 12th August 1979.

1. The Need for the 'New Line'

The last decade of the 19th C. had seen a vast increase in the volume of passenger and goods traffic on all the railways of Great Britain, not least on the Midland, and especially on the Main Line via Marple to Manchester and Liverpool. The Midland had arrived late, but had extended its hold by leaps and bounds. Midland passenger and goods trains in the late 90's were much longer, heavier and more frequent than even 10 years before. As a result lines laid down even in the 1860's and 70's were proving inadequate to handle traffic. For instance the section of the Midland Main line from Chinley, where the Hope Valley and Peak lines converged, to Heaton Mersey, where there was the split for Liverpool and Manchester, was becoming increasingly congested. This was particularly serious between New Mills and Stockport, where Midland expresses had to jostle for line space first with G.C. locals as far as Romiley. and then, once on the C.L.C., with another intensive service of passenger and goods trains. Some measure of the growth in traffic can be judged from the fact that in 1887 67 Up and Down trains of both companies had called at Marple; 11 years later in 1898 this had risen to 109 in all on weekdays, and more on Saturdays. In Chapter VI we have seen something of this incredible activity at Marple, such as in the two hours from 8.15 a.m., when 23 Up and Down trains called, with over a dozen shunting moves arising out of trains dividing, terminating or being marshalled up, to say nothing of the goods and non-stop passenger trains which had to find a path through all this. The station, and whole line was working at full pitch, and at Stockport Tiviot Dale congestion was equally bad as at Marple. What is more, the Midland route into Manchester from New Mills onward showed its mixed origins (it was in fact built in 8 quite distinct stages by 7 different companies) in numerous sharp connecting curves, switchback gradients and conflicting junctions. This physical unsuitability of the Marple route for express traffic, compounded by congestion, made it increasingly difficult for the Midland to reduce timings to Liverpool and Manchester and so keep up with its competitors, the most recent of which was its erstwhile ally, the G.C. By the late 1890's it was obvious that something had to be done to facilitate the passage of the ever increasing Midland traffic in and out of the North-West. It is said locally that the Midland toyed with the idea of greatly expanding Marple Station to handle their growing passenger traffic, but that this was prevented by the violent opposition of the Hudson Family of Brabyns Hall. This is probably folk myth, but it is certain that, had the Midland so wished, such objections could have been overridden by compulsory purchase and Act of Parliament. In any case the expansion of Marple would only relieve congestion at the station itself, and could not have given any extra line capacity or provided the desired fast route to Manchester. The Midland therefore decided to build a new 'cut off' line from just south of New Mills to Heaton Mersey, to be laid out on the most generous lines for high speed running, and to avoid the congestion and junctions of New Mills, Marple, Romiley and Stockport. This route, known as the 'New Line' was authorised by Act of Parliament in 1898. In addition a large, new junction station was to be built on a relatively level site at Chinley to replace Marple as the connectional and marshalling point for trains to and from Liverpool and Manchester in one direction, and Derby, Sheffield and Buxton in the other. Four tracks were to be extended southward from Gowholes to be continuous from the junction of the Sheffield and Derby routes at Chinley North Junction, to the divergence of the 'New' and 'Marple' routes at New Mills South Junction, thus providing much needed capacity in what was becoming a bottleneck. At the same time, a large yard was to be built to ease the flow of goods traffic, by providing a convenient marshalling point for traffic from Manchester, Liverpool and the North-West generally for either the Hope Valley route of the Main Line to Derby. This was to be sited at Gowholes, just south of New Mills. All this work was authorised in 1900. Thus the writing was on the wall for Marple as a Main Line station on the Midland's Manchester Main Line, though it is interesting that in the same year as the 'New Line' was authorised, the Midland decided to install a larger turntable at Marple, as we have seen, so obviously Marple was to have a continuing if reduced role as a Midland traffic centre.

2. Construction and Opening

Construction of the 'New line' began straight away, and the works were on a generous scale, with most cuttings, bridges etc. made wide enough to take four tracks. Meanwhile work also began on quadrupling from New Mills South to Chinley, which necessitated the opening out of Bugsworth Tunnel, and the construction of Chinley Station, which was to have five through platforms, and a bay for Hope Valley locals. The largest work however, was the construction of the 2 mile 346 yards long Disley tunnel, which preserves the fine alignments and consistent gradients of the 'New Line', by going under the Pennine outliers which the Marple route is forced to skirt. Despite its name, over half of the Disley Tunnel is under Marple, running underground about quarter of a mile north of the A6 in High Lane. The tunnel emerges at its western portal almost underneath the Macclesfield line just north of High Lane Station.

The construction of the tunnel brought the last great influx of navvies into the district. They were accommodated in temporary villages at New Mills and Wybersley. There was even a tin church erected at Wybersley, where the Midland had an office, later converted into a house. Some idea of the level of activity can be gained from the fact that 300 navvies' children attended local schools. The method of construction was to drive the tunnel bore from both ends, and from 11 shafts sunk along the line of the tunnel. The miners worked outwards both ways from each shaft, thus giving 24 working faces in all. All but one of these shafts were later used for ventilation, and these are still in use and visible as large blue brick towers dotted along the line of the tunnel. The Midland bought the land above the tunnel and though most has been restored to agricultural use, much remains in railway ownership, and to this day boundary markers made of old rails, with the initials 'M.R.', can be found along the line of tunnel, especially in Disley Golf Course. To facilitate construction a standard gauge contractors line was built, using steam locos and a 'steam navvy'. This ran from exchange sidings just north of High Lane Station to the vicinity of the Andrew Lane Shaft, crossing Windlehurst Road on the level, and the Macclesfield canal by a temporary bridge. The line roughly followed the subterranean course of the tunnel. No traces however are visible as the line was extremely lightly laid and quite ephemeral. On the eastern side of the tunnel however narrow gauge tramways running from the shafts to wharves on the Peak Forest Canal were built, though these too were largely ephemeral. A substantial embankment in Stanley Hall Wood near Disley is said to be the remains of one of these tramways.

The line opened in two sections: first in 1901 the initial section from Heaton Mersey to Cheadle Heath where a large station was erected to serve Stockport, which like Marple, was by-passed by the 'New Line'. The section from Cheadle Heath to New Mills South Junction finally opened to passenger traffic on July 1st 1902. Apart from Cheadle Heath, there was only one intermediate passenger station at Hazel Grove (South). This never prospered - very few trains stopped - as it was an inconvenience on an express route, and closed in 1917. The prime function of the line was not local traffic, but a fast cut-off line for express trains.

3. Train Services in the Early 20th C.

Immediately the Midland St. Pancras expresses began to use the 'New line', and the best Manchester - London timing was reduced to 3 hours 50 minutes, and again in 1904 to 3 hours 35 minutes. Chinley was now the hub of the Midland system in the North - West, a function previously performed by Marple. But Chinley with its greater platform capacity and quadruple track approaches was much better suited for the role. From Chinley lines radiated to Sheffield via the Hope Valley, to Derby and Buxton, to Liverpool via the C.L.C., Manchester Central via the 'New line', or via Marple to Stockport, and Manchester Victoria and the L. & Y. Thus connections were available in many directions, and many a local journey involved "change at Chinley". Expresses were also marshalled up and divided at Chinley, for which it was much better suited than Marple. But Marple continued to be served by through portions to and from Manchester Victoria and Blackburn, attached to or detached from the main train at Chinley. Some expresses were also routed via Marple to serve Stockport en route, while most local services continued using the Marple route. Marple was thus no longer on the main line, but still enjoyed quite lavish services to main line destinations by virtue of through coaches.

By 1910 fewer trains in all called at Marple than there had been in the Main Line days of 1898-87 on weekdays in 1910 as opposed to 109 in 1898. But the local services provided by the G.C. had increased from a total of 37 in 1898 to 47 in 1910, an increase of about one-third in only 12 years. Whereas in 1898 the Midland trains calling at Marple outnumbered the G.C. almost 2 to 1, by 1910 the G.C. had a sizeable edge on the Midland. The shift of emphasis from a main line to a suburban station had begun, until today only local services remain. But the growth in local services reflects the growing size of Marple, and especially the increase in residential traffic to Manchester. Building of new houses continued unabated in the district, and now spread e.g. further along Longhurst Lane in Mellor, up Church lane and Hibbert Lane in Marple, while Ley Hey Park near the station was developed with fine residences for well-off Manchester businessmen. One reason the Midland continued to stop main line services at Marple was probably to provide such people with services to London and other cities for business purposes, and prevent them making their way to the rival L.N.W. or G.C. routes. The Midland with its longer route to Manchester Central could not hope to compete for local traffic, but they evidently made an attempt to provide a service for the wealthy businessman who started at 10 a.m., with a service arriving at Victoria and another at Central at about that hour, the latter provided by stopping a fast business service from Sheffield and Buxton at Marple and Stockport only. In all there were 40 weekday services from, and 39 to Manchester, over half running in and out of London Road, the rest, the Midland services, being roughly equally divided between Central and Victoria. The fastest services were often the Victoria trains, which were usually non-stop and taking just over 20 minutes, though one each way called at Bredbury. The fastest G.C. services were the morning and evening 'expresses', stopping e.g. at Romiley, Bredbury and Ashburys only, taking 22 minutes. The normal timing was slower - 28 minutes, or thereabouts, via Bredbury, and around 40 minutes via Guide Bridge. Trains to and from Central took anything from 25 to 45 minutes depending on the number of stops. As has been said, Marple did however continue to be served by Midland main line trains. The overnight St. Pancras sleeping car trains continued to call at Marple, and while the Down train merely called to set down, dividing at Stockport for Liverpool, Manchester and Blackburn, the Up train attached the Blackburn coaches at Marple. Two day-time St. Pancras services each way also conveyed through coaches for Blackburn, which called at Marple, and the 4.2 p.m. ex Victoria was also a through coach for London calling at Marple. In the opposite, Down, direction a Leicester - Victoria through service called at Marple. One interesting service was the 7.45 a.m. ex Liverpool Central which, calling at Garston, West Timperley and Baguley to take up, and Stockport Tiviot Dale, left Marple at 8.47 a.m., ran to Chinley and divided into a fast portion for Sheffield, while the main express ran on via Butterley, Nottingham and Melton Mowbray to St. Pancras, arriving at 1.15 p.m. The 8.45 a.m. through service from Blackburn, called at Marple at 10.6 a.m., was attached to the main train at Chinley, and then ran non-stop to St. Pancras. which was reached at 1.50 p.m., - 3 hours 51 minutes from Marple. In all there were 5 services to and 3 from St. Pancras. Certain cross-country trains were also routed via Marple, the most remarkable of which was the 11.30 a.m. from Liverpool Central, which called at Warrington, reversed in Manchester Central, then calling at Didsbury (to take up only) and Stockport, left Marple at 12.52 p.m., before running to Derby, one portion being attached to the Newcastle-Bristol Restaurant Car Express, calling only at Birmingham New Street and Gloucester; the other coaches ran forward via Nottingham and Melton Mowbray on to the single track Midland and Great Northern Joint line via South Lynn and Melton Constable, calling at such unlikely places as North Walsham (Town) deep in the Broads, and coming into the line's terminus at Yarmouth Beach, where the coaches were now shunted onto the rear of a stopping train to Lowestoft, which was reached at 8.03 p.m. Surely the most exotic through coach service ever calling at Marple, taking, incidentally, over 8½ hours to get from West Coast at Liverpool to East Coast at Lowestoft! Up to 1907 the Midland had run a Southport Chapel Street (C.L.C.) - St. Pancras through coach via Marple, and in the summer there were even more such through coaches and trains to holiday resorts, notably from the Midlands and Sheffield to Southport and Blackpool, and from the North West to Cromer, Yarmouth, Lowestoft and even to Dover, Folkestone & Deal. Many Midland local services between Buxton, Millers Dale, Derby or Sheffield and Manchester Central continued to run Via Marple, though quite a few went via Cheadle Heath. Some locals calling at Marple started or terminated at Chinley, as did those trains to and from Victoria which were not through coaches, to give connections with the main line. In all 21 Up and 17 Down Midland trains called at Marple on a weekday, several of which were shuttle journeys between Marple and Stockport.

As yet on Midland services calling at Marple gas lighting and compartment coaches were the rule, for electric lighting and corridor coaches were found only on the latest main line trains, though lavatories and steam heating were becoming commoner even on local trains. In contrast G.C. stock was still very archaic with 4 and 6 wheelers, where the Midland had 6 wheelers and bogie carriages. On its best Main line trains the Midland was beginning to use its famous 4-4-0 'Compound' Locomotives; these were larger than anything hitherto seen on the Midland, which always had a 'small engine' policy. These 'Compounds' must have occasionally been seen at Marple, especially on Sunday Main line diversions, but the bulk of Midland trains would have been hauled by older ex-express engines, such as the 'Spinners'; in some cases the engines were antiques of 30, 40 even 50 years

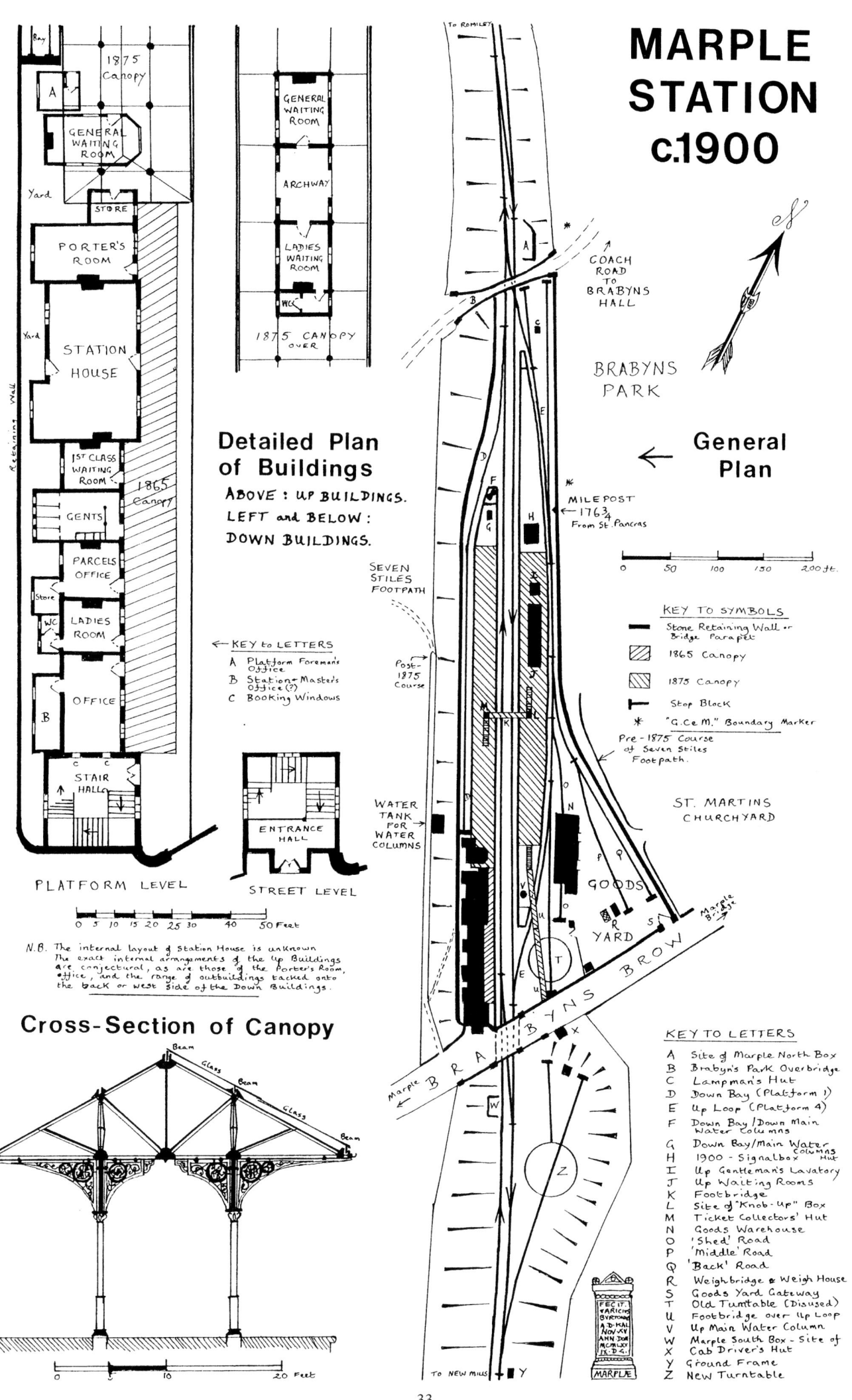

MARPLE STATION c.1900

Detailed Plan of Buildings

ABOVE: UP BUILDINGS.
LEFT and BELOW: DOWN BUILDINGS.

Down Buildings (Platform Level):
- Bay
- 1875 Canopy
- A
- General Waiting Room
- Yard
- Store
- Porter's Room
- Yard
- Station House
- Retaining Wall
- 1st Class Waiting Room
- 1865 Canopy
- Gents
- Parcels Office
- Store
- WC
- Ladies Room
- Office
- B
- Stair Hall
- C

Up Buildings:
- General Waiting Room
- Archway
- Ladies Waiting Room
- WC
- 1875 Canopy over

Street Level:
- Entrance Hall
- Y

KEY to LETTERS
- A Platform Foreman's Office
- B Station-Master's Office (?)
- C Booking Windows

0 5 10 15 20 25 30 40 50 Feet

N.B. The internal layout of Station House is unknown. The exact internal arrangements of the Up Buildings are conjectural, as are those of the Porter's Room, office, and the range of outbuildings tacked onto the back or west side of the Down Buildings.

Cross-Section of Canopy

Beam — Glass — Beam — Glass — Beam

0 10 20 Feet

General Plan

- To Romiley
- Coach Road to Brabyns Hall
- Brabyns Park
- Milepost 176¾ from St. Pancras
- Seven Stiles Footpath
- Post-1875 Course
- Pre-1875 Course of Seven Stiles Footpath
- St. Martins Churchyard
- Water Tank for Water Columns
- Goods Yard
- Marple Bridge
- Brabyns Brow
- To New Mills
- MARPLE

0 50 100 150 200 ft.

KEY TO SYMBOLS
- ▬ Stone Retaining Wall or Bridge Parapet
- ▨ 1865 Canopy
- ▩ 1875 Canopy
- ⊢ Stop Block
- ✱ "G.C.&M." Boundary Marker

KEY TO LETTERS
- A Site of Marple North Box
- B Brabyn's Park Overbridge
- C Lampman's Hut
- D Down Bay (Platform 1)
- E Up Loop (Platform 4)
- F Down Bay/Down Main Water Columns
- G Down Bay/Main Water Columns
- H 1900 - Signalbox Hut
- I Up Gentleman's Lavatory
- J Up Waiting Rooms
- K Footbridge
- L Site of "Knob-Up" Box
- M Ticket Collectors' Hut
- N Goods Warehouse
- O 'Shed' Road
- P 'Middle' Road
- Q 'Back' Road
- R Weighbridge & Weigh House
- S Goods Yard Gateway
- T Old Turntable (Disused)
- U Footbridge over Up Loop
- V Up Main Water Column
- W Marple South Box - Site of
- X Cab Driver's Hut
- Y Ground Frame
- Z New Turntable

old, but lovingly maintained and polished. The opening of the 'New Line' via Cheadle Heath, and the accompanying expansion of passenger and goods facilities at Chinley and Gowholes respectively allowed the Midland to compete much more effectively for traffic in the North West, particularly Manchester, so that by 1910 the Midland's hold had greatly increased on what it had been only 10 years before. Marple might be by-passed by the Main Line, but it retained quite a lavish provision of through services, and had access to all the rest of the Midland's express trains via connections at Chinley. And the Marple route was still an important freight link to the principal Midland goods depot in Manchester at Ancoats, and also the L. & Y. system. In fact in the early years of the 20thC. traffic on the Marple route continued to increase to such an extent that congestion got worse rather than better. It was a requirement then (as it still is) of the 'Absolute Block' System of Signalling operating on the route that only one train must be in a block section at once (a block section being the length of line between two signalboxes). It follows therefore that the more signalboxes there are, the more trains that can use a line at once. By now the 1860's and 70's signalling was badly out of date.

In the early years of the 20thC. therefore the Midland resignalled the Marple area. First Romiley signalbox was rebuilt in 1899. Then, to shorten sections, new signalboxes were provided at 'Marple Goyt Viaduct' between Marple and Strines in 1904, just south of the viaduct, but replacing an earlier signal box there, and at 'Oakwood' between Romiley and Marple Wharf in 1907. At Marple a new signalbox, in use until July 1980, was erected in 1905 at the north end of the Up platform. This replaced Marple Station North, South and Goods Yard Boxes, greatly facilitating station working, as all was under the control of one man, instead of two or three as previously. As however the points for the 1898 turntable were now too far from the new Marple Box to be operated by the signalman, a ground frame was provided at these points and were operated when required with permission from the Signalman. To compensate for the reduction in the number of sections and thereby capacity at Marple, 'outer home' signals were provided, which allowed the signalman to accept another train into his section while there was already a train in the station.

Another device was to install 'inner' and 'outer' distant signals, which allowed the signalman two chances of giving a train a clear run: that is if a train passed Marple's outer distant at caution, due to the presence of another train ahead it would commence braking. If however the train ahead then moved on, the signalman could clear the inner distant, to indicate to the driver that he could proceed at full speed. This was an invaluable aid to the flow of traffic in an area like Marple where sections were short. The Midland also provided 'splitting distants', e.g. North of Marple Wharf Junction, to indicate whether the train was to take the faster route to Marple or the slower one to Rose Hill. These signalling devices were characteristic of the Midland and remained in use until 1980. At the same time the Midland erected new lower quadrant signals (i.e, ones which show 'proceed' when lowered at an angle of 45 degrees) all along the route. They were mounted on elegant wooden posts with 'gothic' finials, some of which survived until resignalling in 1980. The electrical block bells and indicators of solid brass and polished mahogany installed in the 1900's lasted until a few years ago in most boxes in the area. Marple Wharf Box was not however rebuilt until 1927 by the L.M.S., but following Midland designs.

In many ways the year 1910 marked the high water mark of railways of Great Britain, not least for both Midland and Great Central. Marple's Main line heyday of the 1890's may have passed, but such had been the growth of traffic, especially suburban passenger and goods in the early years of the 20th C. that in 1910 Marple by-passed was probably not a great deal less busy than it had been in its Main Line days, and as more and more people came to live in Marple, continued growth seemed assured. Coaching stock might seem archaic to our eyes, but it was well cleaned and maintained, at least on the Midland, and, like the locomotives, decked in colourful liveries. Stations were still beautifully kept, and staff to help passengers and manhandle merchandise were plentiful, and while wages were low and hours long, the real purchasing power of the working man had risen over the previous 30 or 40 years. Heyday it might have been, but in truth it was an Indian Summer; the end of the confident Victorian era , the beginning of the end of the age of steam, gas, iron and coal. The 'New Line' of 1902 was almost the last piece of railway expansion in the district, and the non-stop, hectic construction of the previous 70 years slowly came to a halt. For in 1910 the storm clouds were just appearing for England and for the old Europe, as well as for the Railways.

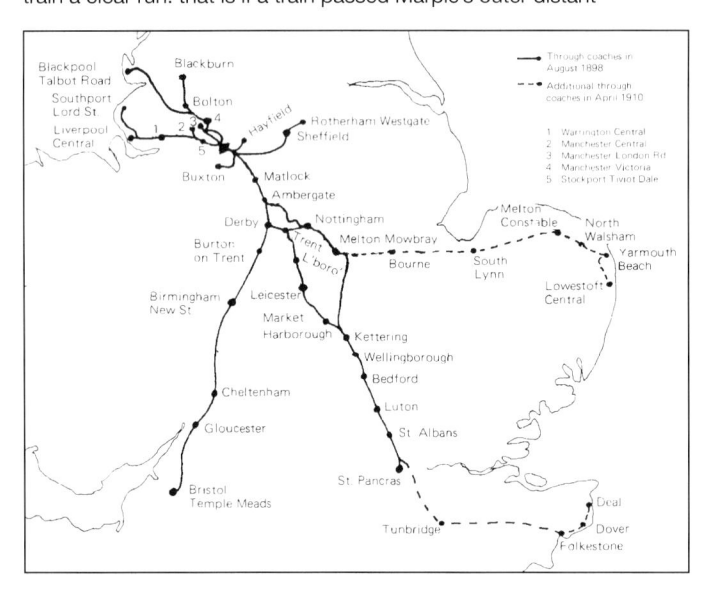

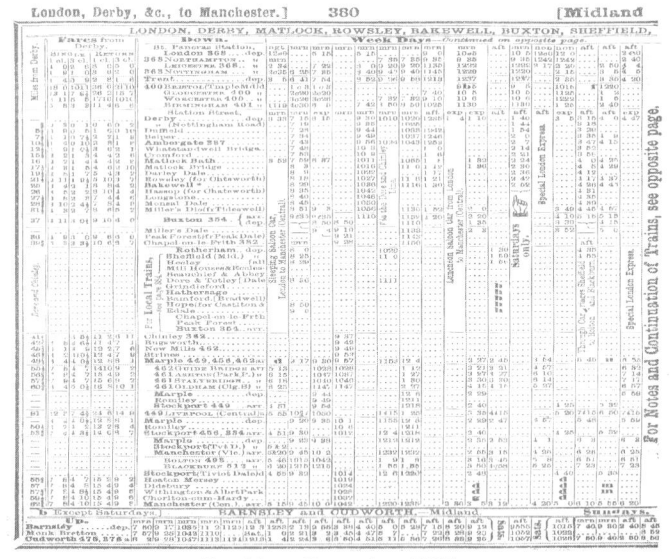

Bradshaw December 1895

VIII. A Changing World. 1911-1939

1. World War I

The first signs of a changing world came in 1911 in a great national railway strike which began in the North West of England. This not only showed that railwaymen were tired of long hours and low pay, but were now sufficiently organised to demand better conditions on a national level - and get them. This was followed in 1912 by a coal strike, which had a very serious effect on the railways. Outside the station horse drawn cabs and carriages might still wait to meet passengers, but the early years of the 20th C. saw the start of privately owned petrol driven omnibuses. At first in Marple, as elsewhere, they connected with trains and ran from Marple Station to Mellor, Compstall, and Hawk Green. But soon the operators realised that where the railway service was poor, infrequent or indirect, they could draw passengers from the railway - and so the 1900's saw the start of a bus service between Marple and Stockport, where the bus could provide a service much more convenient and not much slower.

As yet buses were unreliable and uncomfortable, but it was

an augury for the future. The storm clouds burst in August 1914, when World War I broke out, and immediately the Railways were taken under Government control. As the war progressed, the Railways increasingly felt the pinch. More and more of the staff left for the ranks, voluntarily at first, then under conscription, so that the Midland for instance lost nearly 30% of its total staff to the armed forces, and of these one-third were killed. Railway Works became munitions factories, and locos, wagons and carriages were sent all over Europe for military traffic. Despite losses of men, equipment and repair facilities, the railways were called upon to handle an unprecedented amount of military traffic, for which they got little reward. In this situation, something had to give: maintenance and repairs to track, stations, engines and rolling stock fell into arrears, so that by 1918 one-fifth of all the engines in Great Britain were awaiting repair. The strain soon began to take its toll, and by the end of 1916 the Midland had withdrawn some of its best Manchester-St. Pancras trains, and most of the more exotic through coaches. In January 1917 further savage cuts were ordered by the Government, leaving the Midland with a basic service of local and semi-fast long distance trains, while fares rose 50%. Overcrowding was severe. and timings slow, but the railways had little alternative. The G.C. suffered equally badly. but its services to Marple, Hayfield and Macclesfield were local and non-competitive, so that even by 1918 the service was only a couple of trains down on 1914. However the N.S. service over the Middlewood Curve ceased at the outbreak of war.

But by 1918 Midland services at Marple were just under half what they had been in 1914. Almost all the lavish pre-war through coaches had disappeared. The only Main line train to call was in fact an overnight through coach from Manchester Victoria to St. Pancras - in fact this was the only service linking Marple and Victoria. For the rest Marple was served by locals between Central or Stockport and Chinley, Sheffield, Buxton or Derby. In such a crisis there was no place for through workings to Liverpool, Blackburn or Bristol, or holiday trains to Blackpool, Southport, Yarmouth or Lowestoft. Instead troop and munitions trains ran day and night.

2. The Aftermath of War and the Grouping (1918-30)

Terrorist attacks are nothing new-on 25th June 1921, at ten past midnight, the Signalman at Marple Wharf Junction, John Axon of Romiley, was shot in the groin and threats were made to burn the signal box down. The aim was perhaps to derail the midnight mail train and may have been the work of Irish Nationalists. The culprits were never identified and the Signalman mercifully recovered from his injuries! The war ended in 1918, but the Railways remained in Government control until 1921. Some lines, such as the L.N.W. and Midland, were in relatively good shape, and some of the Midland's pre-war through coaches and trains calling at Marple were restored such as those to Victoria. But others such as the Blackburn services were never restored. Other lines however were in very poor shape, having been worked to death and starved of essential maintenance. It was obvious they could not survive unless supported by stronger companies such as the Midland. War-time control had also removed the worst of pre-war competition which had led to a proliferation of duplicating and triplicating services and routes, and shown the advantages of some form of unified working. It was therefore felt desirable to amalgamate the 150 or more railway companies into regional groups. This process was known as the 'Grouping'. It was originally intended to form separate Midland and L.N.W. based groups; but eventually the Midland joined its old rival, along with smaller companies such as the L.&Y. and N.S. to form the London Midland and Scottish Railway (L.M.S.). Despite the large number of lines owned in the North West, the G.C. was obviously part of the Eastern group, which also included its old ally the G.N.- this was the London and North Eastern Railway (L.N.E.R.).
Coming into existence on 1st January, 1923, these new companies took some time to knit together, particularly the L.M.S., where the rivalries of Midland and LN.W., such antagonists in the past, and differing in practice on nearly every point, did not really die down for over a decade. The old G.C. and Midland Joint Line was now L.M.S. and L.N.E.R. Joint, as was the former G.C, and N.S. Macclesfield line; the C.L.C. was also joint between these two great companies. The L.M.S. adopted Midland Red for its locomotive and carriage livery, which infuriated L.N.W. men. The L.N.E.R. however adopted a pleasing shade of apple green for its engines, and continued the old G.C. (and G.N.) coaching livery of varnished teak. While the elaborate lining-out and armorial embellishments of the Company days soon disappeared, the liveries were thus very similar to what had gone before. With this and the gradual re-instatement of many of the old Midland through services, which continued into L.M.S. days, it might seem at Marple that only the names of the Companies had changed, and railwaymen looked forward to a return of the palmy pre-war days. But those days had gone for good, though it took railwaymen a long time to realise it. The Railways never received proper compensation for war damage; a return to financial stability was sought in an all round increase in rates in 1919, with passenger fares rising to 75% above pre-war level, goods rates being doubled, except for coal, and small merchandise rates up 150%. This however was a very unfortunate move, as it made the Railways look even more expensive compared with the growing number of private hauliers taking to the roads.

Before the war there had been about 82,000 petrol driven goods vehicles, mostly employed in connection with the railways; by 1922 alone there were twice as many, and as often as not competing with the railway. In a railway strike of 1919, traffic was lost in bulk to the private hauliers, and the increase in rates referred to above merely made the matter worse. What is more the Railways by law had a 'Common Carrier' obligation; that is they had to quote public and fixed rates for all goods carried, and they were obliged to accept anything. The road hauliers, by contrast, could pick and choose what they liked, and could easily undercut by charging slightly less than the Railways' published rates. The road hauliers paid little tax, and nothing for the maintenance of the roads they used. As if this was not enough, in 1920 the Government flooded the market with 20,000 army surplus motor vehicles at knock down prices. Many ex-servicemen snapped these bargains up, and set up as road hauliers. Two such ex-soldiers from Cheshire bought a Ford 'Tin-Lizzy' van on their service gratuity. One day when carrying a load from Liverpool, they came racing down Brabyns Brow. They lost control, and crashed into a horse-drawn lorry going down the hill, knocking the lorry into the sunken front yards of the houses at the foot of the Brow, killing both Driver and his horses. The driver was 'Old Yarwood', who delivered the parcels and sundries from Marple Station for the Railways, and he was just going home for his dinner. This tragedy, of runaway road vehicle crushing the slow, and somewhat old fashioned, railway carrier is strangely symbolic of the changes taking place in the years following the First World War.

Goods traffic at all the stations in the district began to decline, except coal, which continued to increase as more and more houses were built. What is more Marple was becoming primarily a residential district for Manchester and Stockport, a process begun by the Railways in the 1860's, and less of a manufacturing community. The cotton spinning mills and other textile works began to decline, especially in the depression of the 30's, under the pressure of foreign competition. Further troubles, notably the General Strike of 1926, did little to help the Railways out of their plight. Meanwhile the Railways were losing passengers as well to the roads. In Marple the bus operators soon captured much of the Stockport traffic, as Marple Station could hardly be called conveniently situated, and the trains infrequent, while Rose Hill had no direct services to Stockport, and Tiviot Dale Station was not convenient for much of the town. Some attempt was made to combat competition by introducing more trains worked by a 'Sentinel' Steam Railcar of C.L.C. origin. This looked like a conventional coach from the outside, though a miniature steam locomotive was concealed in the bodywork at one end. This had some success, but many were won to the bus, which could often set you down almost on your doorstep. Buses never drew much Manchester traffic from the Railway, as the train service was good, and the road indirect. But the growth in private car ownership in the immediate post-war years was phenomenal, and many took the roads for all journeys. Marple was however growing all the time as new houses were built in Mellor, Ludworth, Hawk Green etc., and so the numbers of passengers using the stations, particularly Rose Hill, actually increased, though there were fewer main line passengers at Marple. It was not really until about 1930 that the Railways woke up to the grim reality of road competition, having been used to nearly a century's monopoly. The Government was slow to respond, and it was not until the 30's that Road Traffic Acts were passed to license and regulate road passenger and goods transport. By then it was too late, and the railways were in a slow general decline, though there were many specific improvements. In such an economic climate, with accompanying rising wages and the reduced working day, it was impossible to keep up appearances as the Midland or G.C. had done, and by the mid 30's L.M.S. engines in particular had become generally shabby and dirty, except on express trains, under the rigid economy drive of Lord Stamp, President of the L.M.S. It is probably as well that from the 30's all but express passenger engines on the L.M.S. were painted black! Nor were things any better on the L.N.E.R. services. But as yet Marple station still had a large staff, though the lampmen and shunters were cut out as an economy measure in World War I.

Stations in the district were still well maintained - even too well maintained, if this story is anything to go by. One year, in the late 20's, in order to paint it, the boarding was being removed from the interior of the long footbridge over the loop linking up platform and Brabyns Brow. The Station Master, Mr. Walsh, took umbrage at this, saying there was no need to take the boarding out, and that he would stop this nonsense, and write letters of complaint to both companies. This he did, and accordingly a Works Inspector arrived one afternoon on the 1.30 p.m. train from London Road. He asked the paint foreman what all this 'to-do' was, and was told that they were only taking down the boarding to paint it. The Inspector was a sensible fellow and replied "Oh well, we can't stop that then, can we? Now what time do the pubs shut?" On being informed that the 'Midland' was open by special licence until 4.30 p.m. that afternoon (it being market day) there he went, and stayed until closing time!

3. Train Services between the Wars

With the grouping, the point of much of the pre-war competition and duplication of services became irrelevant, as the two great rivals, Midland and L.N.W. were now in the same camp. One benefit was the renaming of many stations with similar names belonging to different companies to avoid confusion. In our district on the Macclesfield line for instance, 'Poynton' station actually about 1½ miles from the place, better served by the ex L.N.W. station, was renamed 'Higher Poynton'. But it is surprising how long some of the competitive services lasted, and of course L.M.S. and L.N.E.R. continued to compete. Midland services to Liverpool gradually faded away, and those that remained were for the benefit of cross-country passengers from intermediate stations rather than London. But the L.M.S. if anything promoted the Midland Manchester route, though this was via the 'new line' and not Marple, while Blackburn and East Lancashire were considered the province of Euston. In the changing economic conditions of the 20's there was no room for much of the lavish pre-war provision of through coaches, especially as many of them had lost their point, that is competition.

By March 1927 four years after the grouping, the war time total of 18 Midland line services at Marple had risen to 32, which was however less than the 1910 total of 38. Of these the majority were stopping trains between Manchester Central and Derby, Sheffield or Buxton. There were also one or two peculiar workings such as an Altrincham - Marple working, and a Chinley - Liverpool semi-fast train which called at Marple. A couple of day time trains ran to and from Manchester Victoria, calling at Marple, of which one each way was a St. Pancras through coach. For some reason the Up overnight Manchester Central-St. Pancras continued to call at Marple, to take up the Manchester Victoria coach. There was also a through train from Victoria to Nottingham which called each afternoon at Marple, and ran fast to Ambergate, but then turned into a semi-local service calling at such unlikely places in Nottinghamshire as Langley Mill and Ilkeston Junction.

Gone however were the regular exotic through workings to Bristol, or Lowestoft, and an increasing number of trains calling at Marple had Chinley as their terminus, where connections were made with all manner of services. But the L.M.S. provided a somewhat better local service than before and at last there was a reasonable business service to and from Central, arriving at 9 a.m. and leaving at 5.8 p.m. in the evening, though the journey took over 50 minutes. The L.N.E.R. local service continued to grow, so that by July 1938 the timetable shows 31 trains to and 32 from London Road. Of these about half used Marple as a terminus which would have kept the loop and bay well occupied. The total of 63 L.N.E.R. trains was over 25% higher than the G.C. service of 1910. With the 32 L.M.S. trains the 1938 total of all trains, Up and Down, both Companies, was slightly higher than the pre-war figure of 87, though well below the staggering 1898 total of 109. If the 1938 service lacked the main line aura of pre-war days, it was more frequent and convenient. There were more peak hour trains, though there were still long mid-morning and afternoon gaps. If you were unfortunate to miss the 2.23 p.m. from London Road, it was a long wait until 4.10 p.m. for the next train home to Marple.

By 1938 the main line service still lingered on, but was increasingly patchy. There were two services to, but none from St. Pancras - one was a daytime Manchester Victoria through coach and the other was the overnight train from Central and Victoria which marshalled up at Marple. The late afternoon Manchester-Nottingham semi-fast train continued to call at Marple, but now ran from Central, with a connection from Victoria (also calling at Marple) at Chinley. As before, however, the bulk of the service was made up by locals between Manchester and Chinley, Sheffield, Buxton or Derby. The L.M.S. ran quite a few shuttle services between Marple and Stockport Tiviot Dale only, rising to 6 or 7 each way on Saturdays, giving quite a reasonable service combined with the Central service of 14 each way on weekdays and 17 on Saturdays. But due to the disadvantages already mentioned, the buses seized the lion's share of the business, though the shuttle was busy on Saturdays. The July 1938 timetable shows some interesting summer trains calling at Marple. One, recalling the most exotic pre-war trains, was a Saturdays Only train from Yarmouth Beach to Manchester Victoria via South Lynn, Melton Mowbray, Nottingham and Marple, while in the other direction a Blackpool to Sheffield Saturdays Only train called as well. A fast, summer holiday train ran daily from Nottingham and Derby to Southport Chapel Street via Marple and the C.L.C.

The engines and coaches of the 1920's differed little from before the war. The L.N.E.R. continued to use 6 wheel coaches of great antiquity, which were extremely rough to ride in. Some regulars said they had triangular wheels while others maintained they were square, but It was generally agreed they could not possibly be circular. Nobody had a good word for L.N.E.R. coaches, and in a council minute of 1926 we read that the Mellor Parish Council had approached Marple Council enquiring whether they were "favourable to the formation of a joint committee of representatives of the Marple, Ludworth, Compstall and Mellor Councils with a view to approaching the L.N.E.R. for improved conditions as regards cleanliness and lighting of railway coaches running between Marple and Manchester". Whether they ever formed such a joint committee is not known, but there was certainly no improvement for some years yet. L.N.E.R. trains were generally composed of eight coaches, all compartment non-corridor stock, with one 1st and five 3rd class carriages, and two brake thirds (half guard's van, half compartments). The morning and evening peak trains were strengthened to eleven coaches by the addition of one more 1st and two 3rd class coaches. Most coaches were steam heated and gas lit. A few of the newer ones had a primitive form of electric light, while as yet lavatories were rare.

L.M.S. trains were rather better, largely because of the coaches inherited from the Midland, which had a head start ever since the abolition of the second class in the 1870's. By the 20's, almost all L.M.S. trains serving Marple were composed of 8 wheeled compartment coaches, with upholstery much superior to those of the L.N.E.R. On suburban trains to Central 9-coach sets were used, with three 1st class coaches - a very high proportion. The Derby slow trains were often composed of 4-coach sets, with a Brake 3rd composite 1st and 3rd coach, 3rd class coach and brake 3rd, giving the equivalent of one complete coach for parcels, and only three for passengers; on busy trains two four coach sets were amalgamated, giving four separate vans, a rather excessive provision! In the 1930's the L.M.S. was replacing these old 8 wheelers by modern steel panelled, electrically lit corridor or compartment bogie carriages, just as the L.N.E.R. was introducing 8 wheelers, These were made up into sets consisting of only 5 coaches, as they were longer than the 6 wheelers they replaced. As the coaches often came from other lines no two within a set were ever the same!

A feature of Marple station at this time was the large number of children from Marple Bridge, Ludworth and Mellor (then all in Derbyshire) travelling daily to New Mills Grammar School, outward at about 9 a.m., returning by the 4.18 p.m. train. The Headmaster used to complain that his school hours were fixed by the railway timetable. Consequently, station platforms were crowded with school children, and, as you can imagine, they were not always as well behaved as they might be. An ex scholar recalled one day at New Mills when some second formers were trying to take by storm a compartment held by first formers, who tried to keep the door shut by holding on to the window strap. Unfortunately their forces were equally matched, and in the strain something had to give - and it was the window, which shattered. Next morning the Station Master stopped everybody on the platform at New Mills until the culprits owned up. Another ex-scholar recalled that an old Midland Dining Car used to run on the 4.18pm from New Mills, and they used to play shov'ha'penny on the tables, and that the goals were "permanently and indelibly marked" thereon! In 1936 however Mellor became part of Cheshire and the scholars went to Hyde Grammar School instead, and presumably the outrages between New Mills and Marple ceased. For some years a railcar ran between Hyde and Marple for the school childrens' benefit.

On the locomotive side, L.N.E.R. trains were generally hauled by 2-4-2 tank engines of M.S.L. vintage, but later on these were ousted by more powerful engines such as 4-4-2 G.C. tanks. L.M.S. locals continued to be hauled largely by superannuated Midland express engines, at least into the mid-30's, and such things as the 4-2-2 Johnson 'Spinners', often over 40 years old, were often still seen on easy turns like the Manchester Victoria through coaches. But following the introduction of the 'Class 5' 4-6-0 mixed traffic engines ('Black Fives') and the 'Jubilees' (both designed by Sir William Stanier the L.M.S. Chief Mechanical Engineer) on the main line between Derby and Manchester in the years just before the war, the 4-4-0 Midland 'Compounds'. which since 1909 had worked the best trains out of Central, began to appear regularly at Marple on L.M.S. local and semi-fast trains. Goods still remained in the hands of pre-grouping 0-6-0's, some of them dating from the 1870's and 80's, though by the late 30's more powerful 0-8-0's and 4-6-0's were also seen on through goods trains.

On the whole, the physical appearance of the railway changed little in this period, except that as old Midland type lower quadrant signals became due for renewal, they were replaced by more up to date upper quadrants (that is signals which show 'proceed' when raised 45 degrees instead of lowered) on tubular steel posts of standard L.M.S. design, though some ex Midland signals lasted into the late 1960's. In the drive for economy, Oakwood and Marple Goyt Viaduct Signalboxes were closed in 1930. These boxes had only served to shorten the sections between Romiley and Marple Wharf Junction, and Marple and Strines respectively. With the development of 'Track-circuits' in the early 20th C., it was now possible for a signalman to know the position of a train he could not see, perhaps many miles away. This opened the way for the use of 'Intermediate Block Signals', set in mid section to divide it into two, and with the track circuit indicating exactly where a train was. Accordingly in the Marple area, Intermediate Block Home Signals were provided where Oakwood and Marple Goyt Viaduct Signalboxes had been, permitting a reduction in staff, but without any loss in line capacity. One piece of work done at this time was the renewal of parts of Marple Viaduct. The spaces in the spandrels of the stone arches had originally been filled with clay, but over a period of years in the 30's this was dug out and replaced with concrete, which was more stable, but with less 'give' in it than clay.

4. The Macclesfield Line.

There was a considerable growth of housing, particularly the ubiquitous 'semi', in Marple, Mellor, Ludworth and Hawk Green, resulting in a 20% increase in the number of L.N.E.R. locals at Marple comparing 1938 with 1918 or 1910. There was less growth around Strines, due to the remote site of the station and the lack of suitable building land. But at Rose Hill the growth was positively phenomenal. In 1920 only a handful of houses were visible from Rose Hill station, and only perhaps 30 were within a quarter of a mile, but by 1938 the station was engulfed in a sea of red brick. Semis, and high class detached houses spread the entire length of Stockport Road to the top of Dan Bank, and down all the side roads, such as Cross Lane, Dale Road and Bowden Lane, former fields were developed to form new estates such as Claremont Avenue. In the ten years around 1930 the aspect of the Rose Hill area had completely changed from rural to suburban. The growth was no doubt stimulated by the existence of the station, and in turn the new housing stimulated a great increase in the number of trains. In 1910 there had been 9 weekday services each way on the tine; by 1938 there were 11 trains to and 13 from Macclesfield, and 5 services each way to and from Manchester, introduced in about 1935 or thereabouts, terminating at Rose Hill, in recognition of its new importance as a suburban station. All told then, there were 16 Up and 18 Down services at Rose Hill by 1938, nearly double what it had been twenty years before.

These 'turn back' services ran round at Rose Hill and the loco usually ran tender first to Manchester. Most trains ran to or from London Road, but one train started from Guide Bridge and another from Ashburys. To cater for residential traffic, trains left Macclesfield at 7.20 a.m., and Rose Hill at 7.44 a.m., running non-stop from Hyde to reach London Road at 8.14 a.m., followed by the 8.13 a.m., from Macclesfield (depart Rose Hill at 8.38) which was non-stop from Romiley, reaching Manchester at 8.56 - 18 minutes from Rose Hill. In the homeward direction the 5.6 and 5.33 p.m., were first stop Romiley, reaching Rose Hill in 22 and 19 minutes respectively. The L.N.E.R. was obviously making a conscious attempt to stimulate residential traffic. The Macclesfield to Bollington shuttle was also intensified, to combat bus competition, and by 1921 had reached 15 journeys each way, though this was down to 12 by 1938. There were in addition odd Saturdays Only shuttle workings to and from Higher Poynton and even Middlewood High Level. The shuttle was for some time after the war worked by an experimental Westinghouse petrol-electric railcar introduced by the G.C. in 1912 on the basis of the success of similar railcars in Hungary. It had cost £2,500, ran at a maximum speed of 40 m.p.h., and had seats for 50 passengers on tramcar-style reversible seats, with hanging straps, hopefully for standing passengers. It was not really a success, and was sent to end its days on the Bollington shuttle, where it earned the name of the 'Bollington Bug' because of its buzzing noise.

It was 3rd class only, and was regularly seen at Rose Hill, as it provided the Saturdays Only late night service each way between Romiley and Macclesfield. It was eventually withdrawn in 1934, and replaced by a steam railcar. The Macclesfield - Buxton summer service via the Middlewood Curve was restored in 1922 and ran erratically until 1927, when passenger services ceased to use the curve for good. There was some housing development at High Lane, and to a small extent around Middlewood in the 1920's and 30's, but not anywhere near the stations, which retained a quite rural aspect. Middlewood in particular remained a peculiar back water - as it still is. An old railwayman who was the Porter-Clerk at the High Level station there for many years from 1933 onward, recalled that the early morning workmens' train to Manchester had only two regulars - and one of those lived in the Station House. There were some regulars - cotton-workers in the mills of Bollington - who changed at Middlewood to and from New Mills Newtown, and on Tuesdays and Thursdays the Muffin Man used to come from the bakery at Bollington and take his wares to stations down the Buxton line. Middlewood was also apparently a favourite place for pigeons to be released, due no doubt to the great tranquillity of the surroundings!

Surprisingly, however, between the Wars, Middlewood was a hive of activity on summer Saturdays, with day-trippers from Manchester, Gorton, Hyde, Ashton etc. There is a pleasant hollow near Middlewood station, and here a Mr. Cooper erected two large Tea Rooms. 'Cooper's Hollow' was particularly popular with Sunday School parties, with plenty of space for games. Special excursions were run on summer Saturdays, which having disgorged trippers at Middlewood, ran to Macclesfield to stand to return later in the evening to pick up the excursionists. The Porter recalls taking over 300 tickets on some Saturdays, and seeing the platform jam-packed with returning excursionists. It is difficult today to imagine Middlewood as a mecca for excursionists. It was however also apparently a mecca for burglars, who found its isolated location ideal for their activities, but in fact never got any money, as the 30/- (£1.50p) float was kept well hidden in the bottom of the ticket stamping machine. After one break-in the detectives came and found the footprints of a rather distinctive size 8 workman's shoe on the chair, which was therefore wrapped up, and taken away to trace the owner of the footprint. All sorts of people were questioned - campers in 'Cooper's Hollow', passengers at the station and so on - but none had shoes to match the footprint. The mystery of the footprint was however solved when the other porter clerk at the station, who was a short man, arrived for duty, and asked what all the fuss was about. When told about the footprint, he replied "oh they're mine - I stood on the chair to turn t'light out!" The culprit of the crime was however never caught.

As on the Marple services the locomotives provided by Gorton shed were ex G.C. Robinson 4-4-2 tanks, or occasionally older M.S.L. engines. The coaches were the same as on the Marple and Hayfield services, though the Rose Hill 'turn backs' were formed up of half of the old 8 coach sets of 6 wheelers. One half-set was thus without 1st class accommodation, so some ancient 1st and 3rd lavatory composites were dug up and attached to the half set lacking 1st class. But despite these improvements, on both Marple and Rose Hill lines, the railways were losing ground to the roads on a national as well as local scale. The buses and now the private car were creaming off many passengers, while those left expected higher standards of comfort than before. Wages and costs rose, business dropped off in the wake of a world wide depression, while the invisibly subsidised roads continued to despoil the railways who were still labouring under legislation designed to protect the public and traders from a railway monopoly which no longer existed.

IX. World War II and Nationalisation. 1939-1961

1. World War II (1939-45)

Once again at the start of hostilities the railways came under Government control. At first there was something of a panic - the "phoney war"- and savage cuts were made in services. From the 1st November 1939 the L.N.E.R. reduced its services from London Road to Marple from 32 to 20, and on the Macclesfield line from 13 to 8, while all but one of the Rose Hill turn-backs were withdrawn. These cuts were later seen to be somewhat excessive, and even by the end of the war more services were running than in late 1939. The L.M.S. at the outbreak of war swept away the last remnants of the Midland line through coaches serving Marple, most of them never to re-appear, leaving a basic minimum service of 9 Up and 8 Down trains by 1944, all of them locals between Central and Chinley, Sheffield, Buxton or Derby.

The Marple-Stockport shuttle, as well as the L.N.E.R. Macclesfield-Bollington shuttle also disappeared forever. The L.M.S. total of 35 trains in 1938 was down to only 17 by 1944. All told only 61 L.N.E.R. and L.M.S. trains called at Marple in 1944 compared with 94 in 1938. Trains that did run were overcrowded, dirty and often hopelessly late; posters everywhere invited you "to give up your seat to a shell", and demanded "Is Your Journey Really Necessary?" The war also brought the blackout; as the railways were particularly vulnerable to attack but at the same time vital, great precautions were taken. For instance the glass of the roof canopies at Marple, along with many others in the area, such as Belle Vue, were covered with tarred hessian to prevent any light from being seen from enemy aircraft. This filthy black stuff remained on some of the glass panels until the roof was removed. Marple Viaduct was repaired during the Second World War but due to wartime restrictions the repairs were in blue engineering brick rather than stone.

The blitz, as far as I know, had little effect on Marple itself, but Manchester was badly bombed. On a more amusing note, a barrage balloon straying somewhat from its proper position, dislocated working at London Road for twelve hours with its trailing cables!

The locomotives and rolling stock were once again requisitioned, repair works turned over to munitions, staff conscripted, and the railways called upon to carry unprecedented amounts of traffic. When peace came after six years of war, the railways were in a sorry state, far worse than 1918, with stations and bridges bombed, repairs to locos, wagons, carriages and track in hopeless arrears due to shortage of men and lack of materials. Nor were the railways rewarded any better for their efforts than they had been in 1918. If anything worse, as the Labour Government of 1945 was determined to stifle any charges of 'profiteering' and would only sanction essential safety based repairs, rather than tackling the arrears of maintenance.

2. Nationalisation (1945-8)

With a Labour Government returned to power in 1945, large scale Nationalisation was embarked upon. Despite very vigorous campaigns by the "Big Four" Railway Companies against nationalisation, the 1947 Transport Act authorised the state take-over of all heavy land transport, under the "British Transport

Ex-G.C. CT3, 44-2 Tank Engine No. 67425 brings a Manchester-Macclesfield round the sharp curve from Marple Wharf Junction in 1956. (E. Oldham)

Marple station from south c.1910 (Ann Hearle).

Marple station exterior c.1910 (M.L.H.S.).

FOMS — Friends of Marple Station

Interested in finding out more about FOMS?

Want to get involved in projects that benefit the station?

Could you lend some free time?

Have you a hobby that could be used at the station?

Friends of Marple Station are having their first meeting at

The Navigation PH, Stockport Road, Marple

Wednesday 30th April 2014, 7pm

'The Marple Tiger' by Dan Lightman, 2015 version.

Dan Lightman fixing 'The Marple Tiger'.

Removing 'The Marple Tiger'.

Rear of 'The Marple Tiger' painting,

Marple Station footbridge demolition, rebuilding and opening (Arthur Procter).

Foundations Down platform, 13th March 2012.

Lift shaft Down platform, 4th April 2012.

Lifting new footbridge span, 15th April 2012.

New footbridge span almost in place, 15th April 2012.

Two footbridges in place simultaneously. Above: 28th April 2012, right: 1st may 2012.

Old staircases demolished, 11th June 2012.

Removing old span, 18th June 2012

Removing old span, 18th June 2012

Loading onto lorry, 18th June 2012

Ready for off to Peak Rail, 18th June 2012

Formal opening of the new lift, 24th August 2012. Paul Rice is the first to use the new lift.

Marple from the south. Both footbridges in place, new one nearing completion. 21st May 2012 (Arthur Procter).

Strines from the south, 10th October 2014 (Arthur Procter).

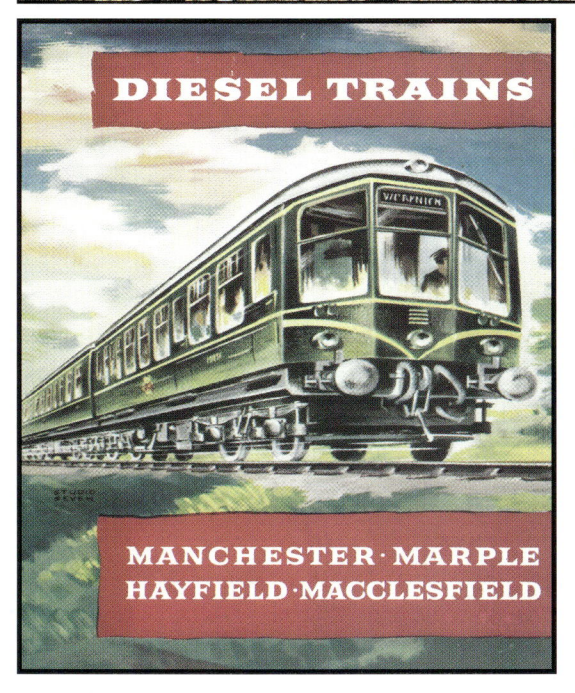

Left: Dieselisation leaflet, 1957.

Right: Sue Day of the Horse Boating Society with 'Bilbo Baggins' proving that a horse can pass through the horse tunnel under Possett Bridge, 21st April 2014, (Arthur Procter).

DIESEL TRAINS

MANCHESTER · MARPLE HAYFIELD · MACCLESFIELD

Rose Hill from the north, 10th April 2013. (Arthur Procter).

Rose Hill, loading bike on to train, 2008 (Stockport Lib Dems). *Rose Hill mural by local schoolchildren (Friends of Rose Hill Station).*

Rose Hill, Santa Special, 1st Dec 2012, (Friends of Rose Hill Station).

1947 winter, train snowed up near Torkington Lane south of Rose Hill

Commission", with a "Railway Executive" to manage the Railways. The Canals and heavy road haulage also passed into state ownership. On 1st January 1948 the L.M.S. and L.N.E.R. along with the Southern and Great Western Railways ceased to exist, and the newly unified, state controlled system was titled "British Railways" (B .R.). The network was divided into six Regions; most of the L.M.S. outside Scotland became The London Midland Region (L.M.R.), while the L.N.E.R. South of the Humber became the Eastern Region.

It was not however until the end of 1948 that the C.L.C. was finally dissolved, after 83 years of existence. At first Regional boundaries followed the old L.M.S./L.N.E.R. divisions and were correspondingly chaotic, as the two railways had overlapped a good deal, especially with the G.C. in the North West. Former joint lines such as the Marple and Macclesfield lines were even more of an anomaly, but were soon assigned to one Region or other. The lines in our district became part of the London Midland Region, along with the L.M.S. ex-L.N.W. and Midland lines. Soon locomotives began appearing in the district bearing the legend 'British Railways', and in the newly adopted standard livery of black, lined out red and cream, which was adopted for all but express passenger locomotives. Various trial liveries for the latter were tried, with the ex-G.W.R. Brunswick green being the eventual choice, but such engines were a rare sight on our lines. In about 1950 a new livery for coaching stock was introduced consisting of red lower and cream upper panels ('blood and custard'), but this did not last long. It was replaced in the mid-50's by a version of the old 'Midland Red' for all coaching stock (except diesel and electric multiple units), though the quality of the paint, like the cleanliness of the coaches, had deteriorated a lot since Midland days.

The L.M.R. also adopted a sort of maroon as the Regional colour for use on station signs, publications etc. In the early to mid-50's this maroon was used on enamel station name boards which were designed with distinctive 'double sausage' shape (officially known as 'Totems') and the 'Gill Sans' style of lettering favoured by the former L.N.E.R. These were put up at all stations in the district, and replaced the signs put up by the L.M.S., which were of cast iron, and of the 'bar and circle' shape. These had originally been painted with a sort of yellow reflecting paste, which, with the name and border picked out in black, were meant to make the signs visible at night. These L.M.S. signs erected in the 30's had in turn replaced the old Midland type station name boards, with cast iron letters screwed onto wooden boards, which were mounted at platform ends in pairs, each at an angle, so as to be visible from the side as well as face on. The Midland and L.M.S. had only placed station name boards at the ends of platforms, but B.R. placed the new 'Totems' on lamp-posts and roof pillars the whole length of the platform, as well as providing a large sign at the end, giving a much better level of signage. At the same time matching maroon enamel 'Way Out', 'Waiting Room' etc. signs were put up to replace the old Midland wooden signs.

Soon after the formation of B.R. the process began at the grouping of adding suffixes to distinguish separate stations serving the same place was continued. The two Middlewood stations became officially Middlewood Higher and Lower while the G.C. and Midland stations at New Mills and Reddish were titled 'Central' and 'North' to distinguish them from the L.N.W. 'Newtown' and 'South' stations in the same place.

3. The Post War Period (1948-55)

But for many years after the war, 'Austerity' was the watchword, and with coal and especially steel in short supply for some years to come, it was not until the early 50's that B.R. could even think of restoring something of the level of pre-war services. By which time, as in the 20's, it was too late and much traffic, both goods and passenger, was irrevocably lost to the roads. The number of road goods vehicles reached one million in 1952, the cheap motor cars became more common, and foreign oil poured into the country. Meanwhile, the war-battered railways, laboured on with old equipment, increasing costs and wages, and receipts that did not keep pace. B.R. made their first deficit of £1.8m in 1955, and attempts began in earnest to reduce costs by closing less used stations and lines. Around Marple for instance, Bugsworth closed in 1958 and Middlewood Higher in 1960. Middlewood's interchange function was much less than formerly, and Cooper's Hollow out of favour as an Excursionists' resort. What is more, the Down platform of the Higher station had been swept away by the collapse of the embankment in the early 50's, and had been replaced by a short 3-coach length wooden platform. The lower station however continued in business, though only for the very meagre local traffic. The Middlewood Curve finally closed to goods trains in 1955, and a further foretaste of things to come was given when Reddish North closed to goods in 1957 - road competition was now really beginning to bite. Station staff were also reduced for economy, and at Marple some of the ticket collectors and porters were withdrawn. Later on the clerical staff in the Goods Office were cut out, this work being transferred to the Booking Office. Smaller stations such as High Lane lost their Station Masters, and one man now supervised several stations - in this case the Station Master at Rose Hill took over High Lane.

To show how slow recovery was after the war, one has only to look at the 1952 timetable. There were only a couple more services between London Road, Marple, Hayfield and Macclesfield than in 1944, after five years of war. In 1952 only 18 Midland Main Line services called at Marple compared with 17 in 1944 - or 38 in 1938. Surprisingly one Midland Main Line train was still routed via Marple, the 3.22 p.m. Liverpool Central Buffet Car Train to Nottingham via Manchester Central, Marple and Derby. But for the rest, the trains were all locals between Central and Chinley, Sheffield, Buxton or Derby, and the service to and from Central and Stockport Tiviot Dale was very poor. There had been a slight improvement on the Macclesfield line with an extra Manchester to Macclesfield train and 2 more Rose Hill turn-backs each way compared with 1944. But in 1952 the level of service on all fronts was below that of 1938 and little better than 1918. In the motor car era it was impossible to attract enough passengers to such infrequent and inconvenient services, and patronage declined.

In this period many of the carriages on our lines were pre 2nd or even 1st World War vintage and in many cases just not up to modern standards. Eventually newer, steel bodied coaches with efficient heating and lighting, bogies for better suspension, and in some cases corridors and lavatories, which had begun to appear in the 30's on L.M.S. trains, became the norm - but none too soon. Suburban services from London Road in the early 50's were usually hauled by a variety of tank engines of G.C. origin, such as the Class C13 and C14 4-4-2T's and the A5 4-6-2T's, now forty or more years old. On the Midland line services the old Main Line 'Compounds' or the 2P class 4-4-0's of Midland build were the staple of motive power, though the new B.R. standard class 5MT 4-6-0 steam locos were occasionally seen at Marple on running-in turns after being built at Derby works. On goods trains Stanier L.M.S. standard 2-8-0's were common, though older Midland 0-6-0's were still much in evidence. But it was now proving difficult to get staff to maintain and clean locos, and obtain coal suitable for raising steam, with the result that steam engines were usually very dirty. Travel by train was increasingly seen as dirty and old fashioned by comparison with the roads and airways.

On some lines such as the Manchester South District which had once been very busy, the service had become so poor that patronage declined to the point of no return, and in desperation in 1961 B.R. closed stations at Heaton Mersey and Withington which only made matters worse. It was already apparent in the mid-50's that unless something was done, the whole system was in danger.

4. The Modernisation Plan (1955-61)

There had already been some modernisation in the district. In the late 1930's the L.N.E.R. had intended to electrify the Woodhead route to Sheffield and there had been talk of extending the wires to Marple and Hayfield; but the war put a stop to these plans. B.R. revived the Woodhead scheme, and in 1954 the line was opened to electric traction throughout, with a new Woodhead Tunnel, the first electrified Passenger and Freight Main Line in Britain. Glossop and Hadfield also got a frequent electric suburban service.

With the quite obvious decline in the railways in the 50's the Government decided in 1956 to implement a Modernisation Plan. The aim was to re-equip the railways to enable them to compete more effectively and work more efficiently. The plan included large scale replacement of steam locomotives by diesel railcars for local work, and diesel locomotives for freight and main line work, with the eventual aim of electrification.

A start was to be made with the electrification of the ex-L.N.W. main line from London Euston to Manchester and Liverpool via Birmingham, Crewe and Stoke. While this work was under way, virtually all the Manchester-London traffic was diverted via the Midland route, including the 'Midland Pullman', taking 3'10" from Central to St Pancras. But in April 1966 the full electrified service was introduced between Euston and Manchester, which sounded the death-knell for the Midland route. The Central - St. Pancras service immediately dropped from 8 trains each way to 4, and was henceforth mainly for the benefit of intermediate stations. In conjunction with the Euston electrification, Manchester London Road Station was reconstructed, and not before time, as it was chaotically laid out; both G.C. and L.N.W. had each had a virtually separate station, with a great iron railing between the two where platform 5 now is: L.M.S. and L.N.E.R. had perpetuated this dichotomy. Added to this were the quite separate M.S.J.A. through platforms, and beyond them the annex of Mayfield, built in 1910 as a relief to the L.N.W. side of London Road. With Nationalisation the station came under one management, but remained a shambles. In the reconstruction, only the roof of the old station was left, the platforms completely re-arranged and the frontage rebuilt. Main line services were diverted to Central, Exchange and Victoria, while local trains were in chaos, departing from any platform but their normal one. During this, a porter when asked what platform the such-and-such train for Hayfield went from, replied "Don't know: that's the L.N.E.R. line- don't even know the stations on it" - old loyalties died hard! Eventually the work was completed, and there were now 12 terminal platforms (compared with 9 before) and 2 through platforms for the M.S.J.A. service. The Marple, Hayfield and Macclesfield services however continued to leave from the old G.C. side, under the northern-most span of the roof, now platforms 1 to 4. The station was renamed 'Piccadilly' in 1960, though this was well before reconstruction was finally completed in 1966, giving a much improved terminus for long distance passengers as well as for local passengers from the Marple lines.

At the same time it was decided to concentrate passenger traffic in Macclesfield on one station - at last. Central Station was re-built in 1960 for the electrification and thereupon became Macclesfield's only station, with the closure of Hibel Road. Thus at last Main Line connections were available at Macclesfield for the line to Rose Hill, and a special platform was provided for the M.B.M. line trains. Excellent connections with the electrified service gave a best ever timing of well under three hours from London Euston to Marple (Rose Hill) and other places on the line, but this facility was never publicised at all. If only this were available today! Meanwhile, our lines too were benefiting from modernisation. On 17th June 1957 the first diesel passenger trains appeared on the Hayfield and Macclesfield services in the form of 'diesel multiple units' (d.m.u.'s). The sets originally used were the 'Derby Lightweights', which as the name implies were built at Derby, and were of light construction. After about a year, these were transferred to the Eastern Region, and former North Wales sets used on the line; which is why for many years trains used to arrive at Marple with a destination blind occasionally showing such bizarre destinations as 'Afonwen' or 'Bangor', when the driver had forgotten to set the blind correctly!

The sets consisted of two cars, with a driving cab at one end of each car, ideal for suburban work with no need for the train's engine to run round at the terminus. At one end was a first class compartment with twelve seats, and there was a sizeable guards van in the middle with ample room for parcels, prams and bicycles. The rest of the train was given over to 2nd class accommodation in open saloons, with a central gangway between bus-type seats

Ex GC C13 Tank No. 67401 brings a Macclesfield - Manchester train towards Marple Wharf Junction, 1956 (E. Oldham).

all facing the same way. Capacity was much greater than in conventional stock, yet without a reduction in comfort. (3rd class had been replaced by 2nd class in 1956).

Originally d.m.u.s were painted green, but from 1967 appeared in the new B.R. standard turquoise blue, at the same time as the Main Line coaches were changed from maroon to a blue and grey livery. It is difficult to imagine the impact of the d.m.u.'s in 1957 and they were originally very popular, and considered airy, spacious and comfortable. Especially popular was the fine view through the many windows particularly forward through the driving cab. The d.m.u.s displaced the ex-G.C.C.13 and C.14 4-4-2 and A.5 4-6-2 Tank engines from the bulk of the workings on the line, and at the same time Gorton Shed received an allocation of L1 2-6-4 Tanks of more recent L.N.E.R. build from the King's Cross suburban lines in London to work the remaining steam-hauled services, which were mainly in the rush hour, when the d.m.u. fleet could not cope. In 1960 Gorton went 'Midland', and the Stanier Class 4 Mixed Traffic 2-6-4 Tank engines, displaced by diesels from other work, were allocated to the remaining steam services. The last regular steam-hauled service was the 08.10 express from Marple to Manchester, and 17.20 return service, which was usually 8 coaches. Attempts were made to dieselise it on several occasions but it was too long and heavy a train. However by 1966 the number of passengers had declined- the private car being largely responsible - and it was possible to use an 8-car d.m.u. on the train.

Dieselisation was accompanied by a great increase in the number of trains run, as more efficient use of the coaches could be made due to the ease of reversal, and this stimulated usage. In 1955 the services on our lines were little better than they had been in the war, with only 35 departures daily from London Road for the Marple, Hayfield and Macclesfield lines, compared with 48 in 1938. After dieselisation this figure had risen to 57 by 1958. The basic pattern of services, was one train an hour via Bredbury to Hayfield, and one an hour terminating at Marple, giving Marple a half-hourly service; there were of course additional trains in the peak. In the 1961 winter timetable, there were 42 weekday trains from Marple to Manchester and 41 in the other direction. Of these about half ran to and from Hayfield, one or two terminated at New Mills, and the rest turned back at Marple. This was undoubtedly the best Manchester service Marple had ever had to date, having the additional advantage of being on a regular basis instead of irregular as before. The basic Midland line local service continued at 9 trains each way, making a weekday grand total of 102 trains calling at Marple, which almost equalled the all time high of 109 in 1898.

In the late 1950's, as they were displaced from Midland Main line turns, the Stanier Mixed Traffic Class 5's ('Black-Fives') and 'Jubilee' express engines appeared on Midland line local turns displacing older engines such as the Compounds. Additional interest was provided for many years on Sundays when all Main line trains were diverted via Marple to permit repairs to Disley Tunnel, bringing premier Main line classes of locomotives such as 'Royal Scots' and 'Britannias' through the station. However diesels appeared in increasing numbers from the mid-50's onward, and the line was used to run in the new Main Line Class 44 and 45 'Peak' class locomotives from Derby Works, and as a test ground for the ill-fated 'Fell' experimental diesel. After that the 'Type 2' Metro-Vic diesels, followed by the Class 24s settled down to form the mainstay of the local Midland line services, except for a few which remained steam-hauled.

Unfortunately, despite dieselisation, the Rose Hill and Macclesfield service remained irregular. With 15 trains each way, and several more terminating at Rose Hill, there was at last some improvement on the wartime level, but the improvement was not as dramatic as the Marple line, especially as most trains were via the slower Guide Bridge route. As a result usage did not grow as it should have done, and especially south of Rose Hill dwindled. While the usage of Marple and Rose Hill Stations on the whole remained steady, and even rose, that of Strines, Middlewood and High Lane declined, due to their unfortunate siting. The 50's saw a vast increase in private car ownership, and the buses were still taking passengers from the railways due to their lower fares, so the general state of the railways continued its slow decline. Goods traffic, particularly general merchandise, was also dwindling in the 50's, leaving coal as the staple of most of the goods yards in the area. However coal too began to decline, as gas and electric fires, and even oil central heating in later years, replaced coal, and 'smokeless zones' extended. Even so at Marple there was enough livestock traffic in the early 1950's to make B.R. consider installing a proper siding for livestock with pens on the site of the second turntable, to serve the cattle market.

Marple 29th Sept 1958. Steam age rush-hour. L1 2-6-4 T 67751 on the 17.29 Manchester - Hayfield. 17.00 ex M/C in Up loop (R. Keeley)

X. The Beeching Era. 1962-1970

1. The Beeching Report

Despite the effects of the Modernisation Plan, and the piecemeal closures of grossly uneconomic lines in the 50's, B.R.'s losses continued to mount, so that by 1962 the annual deficit had reached £104m - a fantastic sum then. The Government therefore appointed as Chairman of the newly formed British Railways Board (which replaced the old British Transport Commission and Railway Executive), a certain Dr. Beeching, to review the state of B.R. In 1963 appeared the results of his review in a Government document entitled 'The Reshaping of British Railways', usually known as the 'Beeching Report'.

Much of what was contained in the report was very true: that many of the lesser used lines and stations, passenger and freight, ran at such a loss as to completely submerge the profitability of the busier lines; that the railways had for too long in the face of road competition concentrated on small freight consignments instead of the large, heavy flows to which they were well suited; and that many suburban lines were an expensive luxury, as they were only busy for two or three hours of the day. His remedy was therefore simple- close all the unprofitable stations and routes, concentrate on heavy Inter-City passenger and bulk freight movements, and make the commuter pay the real costs of their peak hour services.

In our area the Beeching Report advocated the closure of the Hayfield and Macclesfield branches, the Hyde loop, the Midland route from Central to Chinley via Cheadle Heath, the Buxton L.N.W. line, the Midland Buxton branch, the Hope Valley, and all stopping services between Manchester and Derby. The idea seems to have been that a Manchester-Derby semi-fast service should continue to serve Belle Vue, Reddish, Bredbury, Romiley, Marple, New Mills, Chinley and Matlock but all other stations in the area were to close. The Hope Valley Line was to close, while the Woodhead route was earmarked 'for development'! In the event the Woodhead route closed and the Hope Valley line is now running at almost full capacity Later proposals went even further, and the only line not threatened with total closure was the electrified Main line from Piccadilly to Euston via Crewe and Macclesfield.

As may be expected, this Report produced a terrific outcry of protest, and Beeching was dubbed the 'Axe-Man'. There was a great deal of truth in what Dr. Beeching said but the remedies he suggested were too severe. There was much talk of 'pruning', but the danger was that the indiscriminate lopping of branches might lead to the death of the trunk, or in another metaphor, that if too many tributaries were stopped, the river might dry up. Dr. Beeching and the whole British Railways Board dismissed too much traffic and too many lines as hopeless cases: the Axe was excessively draconian. What the report also ignored was that there was a growing feeling throughout the country that the running of rail services in many rural and suburban areas should be regarded as a 'social service' like as a hospital. and not expected to run at a profit; the Government should subsidise lines and not shut them down. This was not however officially recognised until the 1968 Transport Act, which set up the system of Government grant aid for socially necessary loss-making lines.

Before however any line could be closed, the Transport Users' Consultative Committee (T.U.C.C.) set up under Nationalisation in 1947 as an early consumers' protection body, had to hold a public hearing to assess the hardship that would be caused by the closure of a line, and report to the Minister of Transport; he would then decide whether the line should close or not. When therefore notices were posted late in 1963 that all services were to be withdrawn from Buxton - from both Millers Dale and Stockport, the T.U.C.C. was deluged with protests. Buxton was an unfortunate choice for a test case, as the objectors had a very good case. The roads to Buxton were often cut off by snow in winter, while it was plain that the A6 road was already overcrowded. After a long and bitter campaign, in the end even the anti-rail Minister of Transport, Mr. Marples, was forced to refuse his consent to closure. Several subsequent attempts were made to close the line, including a crackpot scheme put forward in 1973 to convert the track-bed beyond Hazel Grove into a bus-way. But all have been defeated, and now the line's future seems assured. It must be remembered that Dr. Beeching closed nothing. He merely recommended and it was up to the respective Ministers of Transport, Labour and Conservative, to approve or refuse permission to close a line to passengers. In retrospect, with growing road congestion, it is reckoned that about one third of 'Beeching' closures were a mistake and some have re-opened, the most spectacular being the Waverley route from Edinburgh to Tweedbank, which is due to re-open soon with Scottish Government money. In our area there is no doubt that the Hayfield, Macclesfield, Chinley-Matlock and Romiley-Stockport Tiviot Dale 'South District' lines should not have closed and if they had been spared a few more years would have survived and prospered. There were virtually no closures after 1975.

The Twilight of Steam. 'Black Five' 45073 pounds through Marple Wharf Junction on an evening Sheffield Midland-Manchester Central local in March 1966. (J.R. Hillier)

2. The End of the Midland Main Line

Throughout the 60's private car ownership rocketed and usage of lines dropped, under the impression that "they'll all close soon anyway". In 1966, accompanying another attempt to close the Buxton L.N.W. line, B.R. put up for closure the Millers Dale to Buxton Branch, along with all stopping services between Manchester and Derby via Marple, Chinley and Matlock. Again a great fight was put up, and while the Buxton L.N.W. line was saved, the Minister of Transport, Barbara Castle, approved the rest for closure. Closure took place in two stages; 2nd January 1967 saw the official closure of Cheadle Heath Station, Chorlton-cum-Hardy, Didsbury and Stockport Tiviot Dale Stations, along with the 'Marple Curve' near Romiley, thus finally depriving Marple of links with Stockport and Manchester Central via the South District Line. These trains were the last regular steam-hauled passenger trains to call at Marple, though steam-hauled goods trains continued to pass through almost up to the very end of steam in August 1968.

Two months later in March 1967, stopping services between Chinley and Matlock were withdrawn, along with the Millers Dale-Buxton Branch service. Main Line services however continued to run from Central to Nottingham and St. Pancras via the South District Line, and Disley Tunnel.

At the same time a new service was put on from Sheffield Midland to Piccadilly to replace the old Central service; there were 5 Up and 4 Down trains each day, formed by d.m.u.s. They called at all stations from Sheffield to Chinley via the Hope Valley, then New Mills, Marple and Romiley only to Piccadilly. There were also a few of trains each way between Piccadilly and Chinley only via Marple, giving Marple 7 Up and 5 Down Midland line services. All connected at Chinley with Main line trains, and gave Marple a better Sheffield service than since the opening of the 'New Line' and extra fast services to and from Piccadilly.

But the Midland Main line into Manchester was fast disappearing, as it had lost its purpose when the L.N.W. route was electrified. From 1st January 1968 most of the remaining Midland line services were transferred from Central to Piccadilly, thus reversing the Midland's move from London Road to Central of 1880. The remaining trains continued to call at Chinley to connect with the Piccadilly-Marple-Sheffield services. A few peculiar late night and seasonal trains continued to run via the 'New Line' in and out of Central, and one very peculiar Sunday train ran each way between Liverpool Lime Street and Sheffield via Manchester Central, the G.C. suburban line via Fallowfied and Guide Bridge, and so to Marple, where the train called, and Sheffield. This was in fact the last service between Marple and Central, though it only ran once a week! The service, which began in the mid 60s, also strangely revived a Marple-Liverpool service, last seen in 1939.

In July 1968 the Chinley-Matlock link closed completely; the Matlock-Derby portion remained open as a branch line, while the Chinley-Peak Forest-Buxton section remained open to freight traffic. But the great Midland Main line through the Peak, which had arisen out of such intrigue, and taken so many years, and so much capital and labour to construct, was closed for the most part in a day. The Midland line services shifted route once again to run from Piccadilly via Marple to Chinley and now via the Hope Valley and the Dore South Curve to Chesterfield and Derby, a route much better graded, and not much longer than via Matlock, and which had been used by occasional St. Pancras-Manchester services in Midland days. Chinley was also now no longer a junction though it remained a Main line calling point for another four years yet. May 1969 saw the demise of Manchester Central, 90 years after first opening; its remaining services were transferred to Oxford Road and Piccadilly, including the peculiar Sheffield-Liverpool Sunday service, which continued to call at Marple.

The South District line was quickly lifted, and remains a disused, rubbish strewn strip of land for much of its length to this day. The 'New Line' however remained open, as it was and is, a valuable freight link between the limestone quarries of the Peak and the industries of Cheshire and Mersyside. And so the wheel came full circle, when once again all Midland trains ran into Manchester London Road (renamed Piccadilly) via the Marple and Reddish route, as they had done prior to the opening of Central in 1880 - except that they no longer deigned to call at Marple. Central has been left to brood over its past glories, like some prone giant.

No new purpose was initially found for its train shed, unless you count its use as a car park, most unsuited to its status as a listed structure of exceptional importance. However from 1982 it was refurbished by Greater Manchester Council as an exhibition centre, which opened in 1986 as the 'Greater Manchester Exhibition and Conference Centre' or G-Mex. It was subsequently renamed 'Manchester Central Convention Centre'. In these Beeching days no line seemed safe from closure: in January 1970 the old Great Central Main Line from Manchester to Sheffield Victoria, only electrified 16 years before, lost its passenger service, though local services continued to run to Glossop and Hadfield. Thereupon a fast service was put on between Piccadilly and Sheffield, via Reddish, Marple and the Hope Valley, all of them non-stop. All were formed of d.m.u.s except the 'Harwich Boat Train' which ran daily each way between Manchester Piccadilly and Harwich Parkeston Quay, via Sheffield, Nottingham and Peterborough to connect with Continental boat sailings. This train was diesel-hauled, usually a Class 45 or 46, with a long rake of

Mark 1 Main Line coaches, and usually a pre-War Gresley buffet car, at least until 1976, but did not stop at Marple. Thus between 1968 and 1970 the Hope Valley Line, built so late, and for so many years a purely local line, had greatness thrust upon it as it replaced the older pioneering lines to North Manchester and the Peak District quarries across the Southern Pennines to Sheffield or the Midlands.

With the closure of the Woodhead route to all traffic in 1981, the Hope Valley has ended up as he only link across the southern Pennines. As a result of these changes, the Manchester-Marple-Sheffield semi-fast trains were cut-back to ply between Sheffield and New Mills, where they could connect with the local services via Marple to Manchester. The remaining Midland Main Line services to Nottingham and St. Pancras continued to make a ritual stop at Chinley, out of habit rather than anything else, as they rarely connected with anything - all the lines which had made Chinley so important a junction had closed, and only the couple of Hope Valley locals terminating at Chinley connected with anything Main Line. Chinley's end was nigh, and came in May 1972, when the remaining Midland Line services were further cut down to only two trains each way daily between Manchester and St. Pancras, now virtually a stopping service, taking about 4½ hours - compared with 3 hours 35 minutes in 1904. In addition, they ceased to call at Chinley, which was thus left almost entirely without Main line trains - the few trains now remaining called at New Mills. At the same time alternate Manchester-Sheffield expresses began stopping at New Mills to connect with the Hope Valley locals. Some of the Sheffield expresses were also extended East of Sheffield to destinations such as Doncaster. Hull and Cleethorpes.

And thus in 1972 New Mills finally supplanted Chinley as the connectional king-pin of the remaining Midland line services in the North West, as Chinley had once supplanted Marple. Chinley Station, now largely flattened, and reduced from 6 to 2 platforms, thus reverted to its pre-1902 status as a wayside halt. New Mills by contrast was a relative hive of activity, mainly due to the constricted layout, which made it necessary to shunt terminating locals from Manchester or Sheffield into a siding or the Hayfield line tunnel to make way for through trains. But it was hardly as busy as Marple or Chinley in their respective heydays.

The remaining St. Pancras services gradually disappeared as they were poorly patronised, and very poorly publicised. In May 1976, they were down to one each way daily, and in May 1977 the last Up and Down trains were withdrawn altogether -except on Sundays, when for some reason two services continued to operate each way, reversing at Sheffield. And so in just over 10 years the Midland line services into Manchester have been reduced almost to nothing and the great Midland terminus of Central closed, while the Hope Valley and Marple route remains the sole link to escape closure. In retrospect, though the closure of Central was regrettable it was probably a beneficial move, as it reduced the excessive number of major termini in Manchester, thus eliminating many cross-city jaunts for passengers. The South District line should not have closed, as with dieselisation, a regular service, and publicity it would have been a busy suburban line today. The demise of the Manchester-St. Pancras service is a pity, but with the Euston electrification, it was no use as a through service. But the loss of a decent service between Manchester and the East Midlands left a large gap in the railway network. The closure of the Chinley-Matlock section of the Midland line through the Peak was also a grave mistake, with the inadequate roads choked with tourists and heavy lorry traffic- even B.R. regret the closure as freight from the limestone quarries of the Buxton area had to detour via Chinley and the Hope Valley to reach the South. However the south to east curve avoiding reversal at Chinley was re-opened for freight traffic.

But even now there are moves afoot to re-open the line as a serious private preservation venture under the aegis of the Peak Railway Society, "the aim being to operate a regular passenger and freight service as well as steam trains". Originally they had their headquarters at Buxton, based on the Midland station site. However, the Buxton site was abandoned, and by 2015 they have succeeded in re-opening from Matlock to Rowsley as a predominantly steam hauled Heritage line conveying passengers. The closure of Woodhead to passengers in 1970 and freight in 1981, and concentration on the Hope Valley route was regrettable,
but in the circumstances, probably the best of a bad job - the Hope Valley route had to be retained anyway for its freight traffic and because permission to withdraw local services had several times been refused due to poor roads, often impassable in the winter, and difficulty in providing a replacement bus service. What is more closure of the Woodhead route allowed concentration of services via Sheffield at the Midland Station, thus giving much improved cross-country connections. The choice of New Mills instead of Marple as the lynch-pin of the remainder of the Midland line services was a strange one, but dictated by the fact that by 1972 only New Mills had stabling sidings for terminating trains, though other facilities at New Mills, particularly car parking, are much inferior to Marple.

The increasingly suburban nature of the services to Marple, and on the whole line, was further shown when in 1968 through ticketing facilities were withdrawn from all stations as an economy measure. Tickets henceforth could only be bought for stations directly served from the station in the case of Marple, stations Manchester to Sheffield inclusive. Before it had been possible to book a ticket to almost anywhere in Great Britain, calculating the fare on mileage. And thus the drastic cuts of the Beeching era, some justified, some in retrospect very regrettable, dismantled much of the once proud Midland system in the North West, and undid the work of the mid-19th Century Railway Pioneers. Marple in the process had lost almost every Main Line connection and become a purely suburban station - a process however which really began in 1902, when it was by-passed by 'New Line'. The net result has however been to make the Marple, Disley tunnel and Hope Valley route more important than ever before.

3. Freight Closures

While many lines in the district have remained open for freight traffic, the closure of goods stations has been almost total. The implementation of this part of the Beeching plan was very thorough, and went almost completely unnoticed, overshadowed by the more glamorous fights to save passenger lines. Within three years of the Beeching Report almost every goods depot in our area had closed down. Strines went first in August 1963, followed by Marple on 5th October 1964. With the closure of the goods yard, the track was promptly lifted. With the reduced services of the 1960's and the universal use of d.m.u.s, the Up loop and Down bay were no longer required, and were also removed. Marple was thus reduced to plain Up and Down lines with a crossover at the Southern end to enable terminating trains to turn back. The wooden goods shed was demolished soon after, and the former goods yard became an unofficial car park for rail users.

Rose Hill Goods Yard did not last much longer, and in March 1965 the last coal train left behind a Stanier 2-8-0 8F, the last steam train to call at Rose Hill. Bowden's the Coal Merchants maintained their business in Rose Hill Yard, receiving road borne supplies from a coal concentration depot set up at Woodley, until this too closed in 1972. Then coal had to come by road from Stockport or Ardwick West in Manchester, and is now totally dependent on road transport. General merchandise continued to be dealt with at New Mills East until 1968, when that too closed, and business transferred to Stockport Edgeley. This in its turn closed in 1972, and any goods coming by rail now had to be delivered by road from Ardwick West. Since the late 80's rail has abandoned general merchandise and wagon load traffic, though Company and Block trainload traffic to and from the Peak District Quarries remains buoyant.

At the same time parcels collection and delivery ceased when freight facilities were withdrawn, though parcels could still be consigned or collected by the public at the station. Eventually only Marple retained this facility in our district, and eventually all parcels and mail traffic was abandoned to road transport. And so the freight traffic dealt with at all such smaller goods depots was thrown onto the roads. To be fair, however, this was hardly B.R.'s fault, as the traffic lost was on the whole uneconomic in the face of road competition with its hidden subsidies, and the Government was adamant the Railways must pay their way.

4. The Closure of the Hayfield and Macclesfield Lines.

Every line and every station in the district was threatened in the 1960's. The Manchester-Marple-Hayfield and Macclesfield services were obvious targets, as they were heavy loss makers. In 1968, which saw the start of the system of grant-aid to be paid by

The last days of steam at Marple. The 15.30 Manchester Central-Sheffield Midland pauses at the up platform at Marple in May 1966 behind 'Black Five' 45404. Meanwhile at the Down platform a Derby Lightweight d.m.u. is leaving on a Hayfield-Manchester working. (I. R. Smith)

the Government to cover losses incurred on lines it was deemed socially desirable to keep open, these services required a subsidy of £344,000 p.a., and this figure continued to rise.

In 1966 B.R. therefore published proposals to withdraw all services between Manchester and Hayfield and Macclesfield, thus going further than even the Beeching report. This proposal was however turned down by the then Minister of Transport Barbara Castle, at least in so far as it related to the main line section between Piccadilly and New Mills because of its heavy use by commuters. She accepted however there was a case for the examination of the Macclesfield and Hayfield branches, and agreed to the re-publication of these parts of the proposals.

This is what B.R. did, and early in 1967 closure notices were posted for the New Mills-Hayfield and Marple Wharf-Macclesfield sections of line. T.U.C.C. public enquiries were held in March 1967 at Macclesfield and Hayfield. Many objections were raised, especially to the closure of the Macclesfield line, which would cut off any direct access between Marple and Macclesfield, as no alternative road service was feasible: in particular schoolboys travelling to the Kings School, Macclesfield would have no alternative public transport. While there were objections from the places, such as Higher Poynton, on the line, Macclesfield itself showed little interest. But the strongest protests came from Marple, where there was of course a very heavy commuter usage at Rose Hill. I myself was an objector to the closure, being a regular traveller between Rose Hill and Belle Vue, en route to Manchester Grammar School.

The outcome rested with the Minister for over two years after the enquiry, until on 12th June 1969 the Minister, by now Richard Marsh, announced that the Hayfield and Macclesfield Lines had to close, but that the Marple Wharf Junction-Rose Hill Section was to be spared. Evidently the strength of objections from Marple, with its vociferous Council and local organisations, must have impressed the Minister, so that Marple is left in the enviable position, in these post-Beeching days, of having two stations only a mile apart, one on the Main Line, the other on a branch terminating on the other side of the town - a generous provision, unparalleled now outside London. The salvation of Rose Hill was undoubtedly its commuter traffic, which would have transferred to the already congested roads, if the station had closed.

Events now moved quickly and the axe was inescapable, despite last minute pleas from Local Councils and M.P's to B.R., the Minister, and S.E.L.N.E.C. (the Passenger Transport Executive or P.T.E. set up under the 1968 Transport Act to control public transport in South East Lancashire and North East Cheshire). The official date of closure was Monday, 5th January 1970, and on the preceding Saturday an enthusiasts' excursion toured the two lines. The last train to run on the Macclesfield Line left Rose Hill late on the Saturday night to the accompaniment of detonators exploding and the glare or camera flashbulbs. The last trains on the Hayfield Branch ran the following day.

The Hayfield Branch was quickly lifted, and left derelict for some years. In 1975 however the station buildings and platform at Hayfield were demolished, and the site flattened to make a car park and bus station. The track-bed however remains in use as the Sett Valley Trail Bridleway, but in New Mills the course of the line has been eradicated by bulldozers and 'landscaped' into a footpath. Hayfield is now therefore dependent on buses for public transport, and lacks any through service by bus to Manchester - as sure a way as any to drive people into their cars.

The Macclesfield line however did not acquiesce to closure so easily. Early in 1970 a deputation headed by Dr. Michael Winstanley, Liberal M.P. for the Cheadle constituency, obtained an assurance from B.R. that the Macclesfield line would be left in situ until August to allow for the possibility of S.E.L.N.E.C. deciding to re-open the line. S.E.L.N.E.C. was not however very interested, as they were short of money, and half the line, beyond High Lane, was out of their area anyway.

However in May 1970 a group of railway enthusiasts and other interested people began making an attempt to save the line, and formed the 'Lyme Handley Railway Preservation Society', taking their name from the parish of Lyme Handley on the route. Their immediate aim was to prevent B.R. lifting the track, and then raise the £50-100,000 necessary to purchase the line and equipment to operate it. The eventual intention was to single the line, and run a regular diesel railcar service from Rose Hill to Macclesfied, with steam-hauled trains for enthusiasts at weekends. They proposed re-opening Middlewood High Level, and if B.R. would not allow them to run into Macclesfield Central, to build a separate station just to the north. The stations en route were to be unstaffed halts with the guard collecting fares; several new halts were also proposed.

Much detailed work was done on the feasibility of the scheme, and the valid point made that if B.R. had carried out the proposed economies of singling and unstaffing, closure might have been averted. A public meeting to drum up support was held in Marple Bridge in June 1970, and was attended by Dr. Michael Winstanley, Liberal M.P. for the Cheadle Constituency, as well as Local Councillors, members of the Dinting Railway Centre, and some railwaymen - about 80 in all. I too was present. There was some enthusiasm for the scheme, but one railwayman, a former driver on the line, said that in the 30 years he had worked on the line, he had seen more trains run empty than full. It was however decided to form a working party to negotiate with B.R. and report back to a public meeting in Hazel Grove in July. The working party certainly did work - they delivered 9,000 leaflets to the area and produced very detailed plans and costings for the re-opening and operation of the line. But at a meeting held with B.R. later in June it transpired that while B.R. was prepared to consider this scheme, and give access to the line for surveying etc., they required an immediate payment of £1,400 as compensation for not lifting the track in August - and this would only buy three months respite. B.R.'s argument was that they were losing interest charges on the capital tied up in the scrap value of the track, but as the scrap value was rising all the time, and the line was not lifted in the event for another six months, this was plainly a red herring. This was however the rock on which the scheme foundered, and though frantic attempts were made to raise the sum required, only about £300 was in hand by the crucial date. So the scheme was forced to fold up. It is possible that if B.R. had been more sympathetic, the scheme might have succeeded, though there would have been formidable difficulties; but now the line has gone for good.

Lifting of the line south of Rose Hill commenced late in 1970, well after the deadline given to the Lyme Handley society, and was completed by March 1971. The station at Higher Poynton was soon demolished, as was that at Bollington, where by 1973 industrial premises had risen on the site of the goods yard and main line, thus blocking any re-opening. The course of the line into Macclesfield Central is likewise blocked. High Lane Station however remained derelict for seven years after closure, until demolished in 1977. The land has been sold to the Local Authorities on the route, and was used as an unofficial footpath until the opening of the Middlewood Way in 1985.

At Rose Hill the main buildings on the Up platform were soon demolished, as they were no longer required now the station was a terminus. The station staff was reduced to one man on duty at any one time, with 2 men covering the 17 hours the station was open. A new booking office was provided on the Down platform by refitting the former ladies waiting room, with a ticket window facing the platform. The little lean-to wooden ticket office tacked onto the waiting room then became a store, and has now been removed.

The waiting room was redecorated and provided with a gas fire, while electric lighting was installed throughout to supersede gas lamps. Later, in September 1970, the signal box was closed and all signals at the station removed. The branch was thenceforth worked on a kind of 'one-engine in steam' principle, that is only one train is ever allowed on the branch at any one time. Despite this the track remained double, thus giving Rose Hill, quite unnecessarily, separate arrival and departure platforms. This arrangement, originally 'temporary', persisted because to single the line would require extensive signalling and track work changes at Marple Wharf Junction. For most of the 70's the line through Marple was about to be re-signalled at any time, so the work was put off. As a result the Rose Hill branch remained double track, an interim measure which lasted 10 years until the singling scheme was completed in July 1980.

In the early 1970's the single line head shunt did not even have a buffer stop and on one occasion the train coming in on the double line to reverse and form the 08.24 morning peak train to Manchester, which was 6 cars, ran off the end of the line! A buffer stop was soon then provided! I was late for school that day, though it sticks in my memory as cancellations of passenger trains were almost unheard of in those days, except in the industrial disputes of the early 1970's.

As a result of the closure of the Hayfield and Macclesfield lines, a revised service was Introduced to Rose Hill, Marple and New Mills. At long last Rose Hill, which had barely escaped doom, was given an even-interval hourly service, with most trains via the fastest Reddish route. On the debit side, however, there were fewer trains in the morning peak than before, and early morning and late evening services were withdrawn. The interval service was a great improvement, but the total number of trains remained the same as before - 17 to and 19 from Manchester. The service at Marple, however, went to pieces with the new timetable. Instead of a regular half-hourly service, the basis of the off-peak service became a train roughly every two hours each way between New Mills and Manchester (instead of hourly as before) routed the slow way via Guide Bridge. The gaps in this very irregular service were filled by hourly trains turning back at Marple, but again these were not quite regular. There were not many fewer trains than before: 32 to and 34 from Manchester In 1970, compared with 40 and 42 respectively in 1969, but the interval principle was lost. The whole effect was very messy, and really gave only an hourly service, as compared with half-hourly before, though peak-hour services remained good. Strines got a very poor service as a result. At the same time First Class accommodation was withdrawn from all services to Rose Hill, Marple and New Mills, as it was little used, and took up valuable space in the rush-hour.

And so in our district, the cold winds of change were blowing, but Marple escaped the Beaching Axe comparatively lightly, losing only its Midland line services, the Macclesfield branch, and one station at High Lane. Many a larger town or city, such as Gosport, Leigh (Lancs.) or Ripon lost their rail services altogether. Marple was very fortunate to retain two stations, as well as two lesser ones at Middlewood and Strines. In particular the survival of the Rose Hill branch was little short of miraculous, leaving Marple to join the select list of places to escape the Beeching Axe with two stations. The reason for this undoubtedly lies in the large number of peak-hour commuters, the inadequacy of the road system in the area, and not least due to the strength of opposition to the closure put up locally.

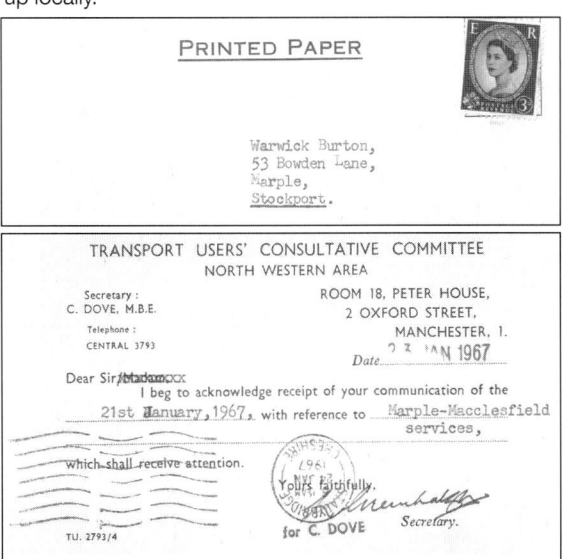

Marple station exterior 1964

My protest letter to the closure of the Rose Hill-Macclesfield line.

XI. Marple Rebuilt-1970

1. The Decision to Rebuild

With the rising costs of labour and materials of the 1960's, B.R. found itself no longer able to keep up with repair work on station buildings, and particularly canopies. This was nowhere more in evidence than at Marple. By the late 60's most of the fine canopies on both platforms had been allowed to get into such a state of disrepair that it was necessary to remove the glazing for safety, leaving the cast iron and timber skeleton giving little shelter. It is easy to criticise B.R. for this, but the station had been built for a Main Line use that had long since disappeared; and with short diesel trains most of the platform was not even used. Nor could B.R. really afford, with the annual deficit into 8 figures, to spend money on renewing the 3 miles of timbering and 1600 panes of glass necessary to put Marple's roof back in order. In addition the footbridge from Brabyns Brow to Up platform was an expensive white elephant now the loop line had gone.

What is more the buildings of the station were also expensive to maintain, and far too large for present needs. Staff had been greatly reduced in the 60's for economy, leaving one or at the most two porters and booking clerks on duty at any one time. There was no need for ticket collectors, shunters and foremen with the end of main line services and the general decline in traffic. The closure of the goods yard further reduced staff requirements. Marple had also lost its Station Master in the reorganisation of 1967, when Area Managers were introduced, each having several stations under his control. Marple at first came under an Area Manager at Chinley.

Soon in another reorganisation, control was transferred to Ardwick East, and then was under the Area Manager Guide Bridge, whose responsibility stretched to Ardwick, New Mills, Woodhead and Broadheath. Thus the station master's house stood empty. Parcels traffic had also declined, nor were Ladies rooms now considered necessary. In other words of the large range on the Down platform only a few rooms were still in use. On the Up, with the decline in passengers using the declining number of southward services, the waiting rooms had been boarded up out of use. Falling usage and facilities at the station, declining staff and spiralling costs contrived to make Marple an excessively large and ill-maintained station. It was indeed a sorry sight as I remember it, travelling to and from school - a vast range of half shut-up buildings, with an echoing, cavernous stair hall, and a gaunt skeleton of a roof on the platforms.

B.R. recognised the problem and realised something had to be done, as with the Ministerial refusal to even consider the closure of the line in 1966, the station's future seemed secure. Marple Council and various other local bodies put pressure on B.R., with the result that in 1967 they promised to reconstruct the station. However in March 1968 B.R. stated "as a result of the extremely serious financial position in which we find ourselves it has been found necessary to defer the start of the construction of Marple Station ... but this station remains high on our list of priorities". In February 1969, hopes were raised again that "in spite of pressure of commitments" work was likely to start that year. But nothing transpired. Later in the year B.R. regretted "that no date can be given for the scheme of improvements at Marple Station. The contract for the work has not yet been signed. The scheme is still on the priority list". Of course, the local press had a field day with all this delay, and there was criticism of B.R.'s plans especially as no canopies or public toilets were to be provided. Despite all this delay, B.R. did intend to rebuild, but were held up by shortage of capital; and it was in B.R.'s interest to build a new station as this would permit staff savings amounting to several thousand of pounds per annum. The cost of rebuilding was estimated at £39,000 including £7,000 for demolition of the old station. However, after so much delay, in January 1970 the work actually began.

2. The Plan for the New Station

B.R.'s plans were basically as follows: to remove all the existing buildings and ironwork as these were now superfluous to requirements. The footbridge was however to remain as it was quite sound, and would cost a 5-figure sum to replace, and the signal box was also to survive as there was as yet no plan to resignal the line. The old platforms were to be retained as the base for new platforms, but were to be shortened. Marple's platforms

Demolition of Marple's goods shed after closure on the 5th Oct 1964

were now too long, having been made to accommodate main line trains, and were not now called upon to handle more than an 8 car d.m.u. The platforms were however to be raised in height, as they were very low for modern coaches, having been built for the much lower and smaller stock of the 1860's and 70's. There was now no need for bays and loops, so the platforms need not be so broad as before, especially as the crowds for which they had been designed no longer occurred. The long footbridge between Brabyns Brow and Up platform had lost its purpose, now the lines it had straddled had gone, and was therefore to be removed.

On the other hand, there was a clear need for a car park, as people were already parking on the rough ground where the goods yard had been, and there was great potential for attracting car owners to use the station, if proper parking facilities were provided, as the roads out of Marple were jammed solid in the rush hour. There were also plans to revive the idea of connecting bus services, dead since the 1920s, by providing a bus turning circle at the station. The only way that all these facilities could be provided was to use the space left derelict by the closure of the goods yard. It was essential that the new station should require as few staff as possible, to economise on what was already a loss-making line.

With fewer passengers, the disappearance of most of the parcels traffic and simplified ticket issuing procedures, it was now practical for all the station work to be performed by one man for most of the day- except that is in the morning peak. But having only one member of staff would only be practicable if there was only one exit, as two exits would require two people to collect tickets. Also, if the person collecting tickets also had to issue tickets as well, it would be essential to have the Ticket Office and Entrance/Exit as close together as possible, so that they could book tickets up to the arrival of a train and then go out and collect tickets. In other words the sole entry and exit should be combined with the Ticket Office in one place. If it was anywhere on the Down platform, while being convenient for people coming from the Marple direction, it would be hopelessly inconvenient for those arriving by car or bus, or on foot from Marple Bridge; there could be no entry direct to the car park or Brabyns Brow to the Up platform if the sole entry was on the Down side. So the Ticket Office and entrance had to be on the Up side, convenient for the car park. This would also suit passengers walking to or from Marple Bridge. Things would not be so convenient for pedestrians from Marple, who would have to detour to reach the Down platform for Manchester, but this would be compensated for by having an easier exit when arriving from Manchester. Thus the basic outline of the station as rebuilt was pretty well determined by the need for economy of staff, and the plan adopted was probably the best compromise for all the station's users.

Therefore a combined ticket hall, waiting room and entrance/exit was to be sited near the footbridge, at the North end of the former goods yard, to give easy access to Up and Down platforms and the car park. To provide access to the station from Brabyns Brow from the Marple direction, a set of steps were necessary on the site of the old footbridge, while pedestrian access from Marple Bridge and all vehicular access was to be via the old goods yard gate. It was also decided to build two large and quite substantial waiting rooms on the Up platform for peak hour crowds; two were therefore erected, one on each side of the footbridge. This was however a mistake, as only a few trains were longer than two or at the most four coaches, and stopped opposite the footbridge and southern waiting room. Accordingly the northern waiting room was hardly ever used, and was now kept locked for most of the day, and was demolished in the mid 1980s.

On the other hand no canopies or shelters were to be provided on either platform, nor was the footbridge to retain any covering, so that passengers using the bridge and waiting for trains are exposed to the elements. What is more both waiting rooms were kept locked after 20.00 each evening due to vandalism. The money spent on the white elephant of a second waiting room could have been much better spent on providing a modest canopy on both platforms, and repairing the covering on the footbridge. It is a great pity that in the 60's and early 70's B.R. was so set against anything Victorian, as it would not have been difficult to retain several bays of the magnificent old roof, suitably refurbished to provide such cover in the vicinity of the footbridge on both platforms. A modern Ticket Office and waiting room could have been built under the canopies, and if suitably designed could have harmonised quite well. Even better, some of the handsome, solid Victorian buildings could have been retained instead of building new and miserable waiting rooms. But B.R. were philistines in those ultra modernist late 60's, and were determined to have rid of the old and replace it with the brutalistic modern architecture. Soon after the attitude changed, and when other stations In the area were rebuilt a few years later, efforts were made to retain some of the canopies and buildings as at Romiley and New Mills Central. The basic layout of the new Marple was sound but with a little more thought, better shelter and buildings could have been provided for a similar cost, and without total demolition.

3. Demolition and Rebuilding

The contract for rebuilding was let to a firm called 'Rata' of London early in 1970, and work began in late January. First of all a great ramp of scaffolding and planks was constructed behind the Down platform buildings to enable vehicles to bring in plant and materials, and remove demolition debris. The Down side waiting room was removed by burning it down, and then all the ironwork of the canopies was removed from the Down platform, leaving only the footbridge. This was done rapidly, and in February work started on removing the canopies on the Up side. The Up waiting room range was also demolished, with the exception of the gents toilet retained for use by the workmen.

Early in March, with demolition half completed, bricks and concrete were delivered for the construction of the new buildings and work started as soon as sites were cleared. The most dramatic part of the work was the demolition of the long footbridge at the south end of the Up platform. First the roof was removed, then the timber sides and floor stripped, and finally each span cut away from its supporting pillar and from each other. Each span was then in turn lifted bodily by a large hired crane, and the supporting pillars and steps demolished, All of the station ironwork went for scrap, with the exception of a few of the 'S.& M.' roundels, which were rescued and preserved in private hands.

During all this, the station never closed, and access to both platforms had to be maintained at all times. It can be imagined therefore what a difficult job demolition was, and it is remarkable how smoothly it all went. In April work began on raising the platforms about 9 inches up to the required height, while the new buildings were rising. Fencing at the rear of newly raised and narrowed platforms followed in May and soon after permanent electric light was installed; the gas lighting had been removed in January, and temporary electric lighting slung on wires draped about the station. By late August, the Up platform was substantially complete, and the Down nearly so, while the new buildings were ready for use. Accordingly, the staff were transferred to their new accommodation on the Up platform, and the old booking office on the Down closed. The old buildings were quickly gutted, and demolished by early September, the site being flattened by using the rubble to fill in the former Down bay, and subsequently sown with grass. As the Autumn progressed, the car park was laid-out, with flagged paths around the sides, while the centre was covered with rubble and cinder hardcore. A staircase, erected in July, now linked the footpath from the booking hall to Brabyns Brow, for the benefit of passengers walking to or from Marple. Tidying up continued throughout October, and the station was largely complete and tidy in time for the official opening. The whole reconstruction from start to finish cost £40,000, which was only £1,000 above the estimate.

4. The Official Opening

The station had of course never closed, but it was felt desirable to mark the reconstruction by a suitable ceremony. The

The Opening Ceremony for Marple's rebuilt station on Wednesday 28th October 1970. Councillor M. T. Burton, Chairman of Marple Urban District Council, himself a railwayman, and the author's father flags away the 12.33 to Manchester, which will break the tape across the line.

Marple from the North c.1895 (Hayday Publishing)

Marple in the early days of dieselisation c.1961 (Manchester Libraries)

station was not in fact quite ready by the day fixed for the Official Opening - 28th October 1970. The car park had not been surfaced, and the stairs up to Brabyns Brow still lacked banisters. The soon-to-be-removed heaters had not yet been fixed in the waiting room, while the unpainted signal box looked out of place in a new station. In fact, on the morning before the ceremony, workmen were clearing debris and equipment left in the car park, while station staff swept and cleaned the station.

A special off-peak bargain fare of 2/- (10p) for a Day Return to Manchester, instead of the usual 5/- (25p) was offered to mark the opening day, to tempt passengers to the new station; quite good use was made of this facility due to good publicity in the form of posters put up in Marple. The booking hall was filled with a fine display of plants, provided by the Marple Council. There were some minor hitches in the preparation such as the discovery that the white tape to be 'cut' by the first train to use the officially opened station was too short to stretch across the tracks; accordingly the lady relief clerk was despatched into Marple to buy needle, thread and more ribbon to lengthen the tape!

The opening ceremony was to be performed by Councillor M.T. Burton, Chairman of Marple Urban District Council for 1970-71. That he should perform the opening ceremony was doubly appropriate, as not only was he a long-serving railwayman, but had also worked at Marple on occasions whilst a District Relief Goods Clerk. The official parties began arriving shortly before midday. First to arrive was Councillor M.T. Burton, to be followed by various officials and councillors of the Marple Council. These were followed by a group of Railway Officers, including K.J. Davies, the Divisional Manager, Manchester, the Divisional Civil Engineer, P. Robb (who was responsible overall for the reconstruction), the Public Relations Officer, and a member of the local Area Management staff from Ardwick. As well as these two official parties, there were reporters from papers as diverse as the 'North Cheshire Herald' and 'Guardian', and a crowd of spectators, including some retired long-service railwaymen.

At about noon the ceremony began - under the footbridge on the Down platform - a small rostrum had been erected, surrounded by a floral display, and provided with a microphone. The Divisional Manager opened the proceedings with a speech, and was followed by Councillor M.T. Burton. He dwelt on the 'Golden Age of Railways', with a brief account of the history of the station, and the services it enjoyed in its heyday. He speculated on the millions of passengers and thousands of tons of freight which must have passed through the station; the new station was compared to the old; and finally he exhorted people to use the new station.

Meanwhile the 12.00 train from Manchester, formed by a two car d.m.u. had arrived at the Up platform, and crossed over to form the 12.33 to Manchester, which was to be the 'first' train to leave the officially opened station; the white tape was then stretched across the line between the pillars of the footbridge on either platform. Just before 12.33, Councillor Burton gave the 'right-away' to the 'first train' in approved railway manner by blowing a whistle and waving a green flag.

This was repeated several times for the benefit of reporters and photographers before the train actually drew forward, broke the tape, and so departed. The station was thus declared officially open, and it is gratifying to note that the 'first' train left on time at 12.33 precisely! After a short tour of inspection of the station, during which it was noticed that vandals had already carved their initials on the new teak waiting room seats, the official party departed in cars for a substantial buffet lunch, with sherry, served in the Marple Council Offices. The day was rounded off by a film show provided by B.R. at the Senior Citizens Hall (known then as 'The Old Folks Hall') that evening, which despite atrocious weather, attracted an audience of about 60.

5. Description of the New Station

The station as rebuilt has two platforms - the Up 442 feet long, the Down 485 feet, that is 105 and 65 feet respectively shorter than before. They are just capable of taking an 8-car d.m.u., and are more than ample for the normal two coach trains. The disused portion of the Up platform remains, albeit overgrown, and has on occasions been used to accommodate excursion trains of 10 coaches. The new platforms are much narrower than before, but quite ample for even the heaviest traffic encountered today. The Down platform is 11 feet wide throughout, while the Up is 15 feet wide at the North, broadening to 30 feet in the vicinity of the footbridge, and 11 feet for the lesser used Southern end. The tarmac-surfaced platforms are now about 3'6" high, which is almost level with the steps of modern carriages.

Linking the two platforms was the only piece of the 1875 station to remain - the footbridge. The timber decking and steps were modern, but the iron frame was as good as when built. The platforms are backed by a 6 foot high fence of vertical timbering, un-climbable except for the most acrobatic fare-dodger. The buildings on both platforms are of red brick throughout, with flat roofs and white painted timber fascia boards at cornice level. Such box-like, flat roofed buildings had been very popular for the last 20 or 25 years, though they went out of fashion - the newest stations at Brinnington and Hattersley have reverted to pitched roofs. The use of a white fascia board clearly marks the building as of the late 60's or 70's while the use of homely brick is a reaction against the monstrosities of post-war modernist concrete and plastic architecture. What is more, brick retains its appearance and durability much longer than concrete or plastic. The buildings of

Marple station opening ceremony 28th Oct 1970. The Divisional Manager gives a speech. The author looks on, amused (on the right)

the new Marple Station are clearly a run-of-the-mill product of the late 60's, and while they lack the grandeur and self-confidence of Victorian architecture, they are not without a simple elegance.

The Down waiting rooms were large - too large if anything - each being 52 feet long and 13 feet wide. They were not quite identical, but differ only in the arrangement of windows and doors. While moderately attractive from outside, they are extremely uninviting inside, the overwhelming impression being cold and dark. There is not enough light, due to a shortage of windows, and the dark red brick walls heighten the gloom, though later painted white. The tiled floor is dark, cold and hard, and there are not enough seats. The only heating provided is a pair of quite inadequate and tiny electric wall heaters in each room. For a space this size some better form of heating is required. So uninviting are the waiting rooms that even on cold and wet days most people prefer to wait outside or shelter under the footbridge. These modern rooms are gloomier, more cavernous and very much colder than the 'outdated' Victorian ones they replaced.

The Up building is more pleasant inside. It is entered from the car park by a set of double doors and one single door, all of the varnished teak, employed on much of the station woodwork. The doors are set back a few feet to provide a porch recess. There is a sliding door onto the platform, to permit the railman on duty to have only a narrow exit for ticket-checking. But ticket checks have been discontinued in recent years. The building consists of a ticket hall, office, staff mess room, staff toilet and two storage closets. The ticket hall is quite attractive, with good natural lighting from skylights in the roof, and the glass panelled doors. There is a space for posters and information board and leaflet racks on the wall. The hall also acts as a small waiting room for the Up platform, and has a couple of seats for this purpose.

A large plate glass window looks directly from the adjoining office to the ticket hall, and this contains the booking window. Certainly this is more inviting than the little porthole in Victorian Booking Offices, and it is now possible to see who you are talking to and book a ticket without crouching down. The office contained one relic from the old station - the booking office clock, which kept excellent time. Adjoining is the staff mess room, with cooker, sink etc., to enable staff to make tea and enjoy a proper meal, without getting steam and cooking smells in the office. On the other side of the office is the staff toilet, and an alcove housing the parcels weighing machine, which could be rolled out to weigh long or bulky parcels, While Marple retained certain parcels services, it was necessary for the public to carry the parcels to or from the station. Those requiring railway collection or delivery were dealt with at the parcels concentration depot at Manchester Mayfield - consequently few parcels passed through Marple. One major criticism of the Up building is that it is impossible to see out of the office to the platforms, due to the lack of windows. Thus the staff could not see when a train was coming so as to prepare to check tickets nor could they keep a watch for vandals. The argument was that if windows were provided, they would encourage burglars, but if the windows had been made long and narrow, it would be impossible to use them for break-ins, while giving the staff surveillance of the platforms.

Outside the Up building, laid out on the site of the goods yard, is the car park, which is capable of taking about 80 cars without undue congestion. Paved footpaths lead from the ticket office to the main car park exit, for Marple Bridge pedestrians, and to a set of steps up to Brabyns Brow for those living in Marple itself. These steps have the same entrance onto the road as the old footbridge over the Up loop had. Below are the huts which house the local gang of Permanent Way Department platelayers, and Signal Maintenance staff.

At the other end of the station, on the Up platform stood another relic of the old station, the signal box, still operating until 1980. It was of a standard Midland design, easily recognisable by the sturdy four-square timber frame. with horizontal boarding in between on the ground floor, and vertical boarding in smaller panels beneath the windows at first floor level. The windows with cut-off corners at the top, were distinctively Midland, as were the gothic finials gracing the apex of the hipped slate roof. Inside a standard. Midland lever frame was still in use until 1980, dating from 1905. Of the 33 levers, 20 were painted white, denoting they were out of use and were relics of when Marple was a busy layout. The 13 in use were painted variously red, yellow or black denoting that they controlled stop signals, distant signals, or points respectively. The only set of points still in use are at the South of the station, and are regularly used to turn back terminating trains. Above the lever frame was the 'block-shelf', which housed the signalling instruments. The line through Marple then being controlled by the 'Absolute Block' method of signalling (which in its essentials dates from the late 19th Century), electric bells were used for all communication with the boxes on either side - Strines, and Marple Wharf Junction. Trains were 'described' and emergency information conveyed by a laid-down set of bell signals, while 'Block Indicators' were used to give the signalman a visual reminder of the state of the line, i.e. whether the section of line between one box and the next was

    a) available for occupation by a train ('Line Blocked'), or
    b) clear for the imminent passage of a train ('Line Clear'), or
    c) occupied by a train or obstructed ('Train on Line').

When the station was rebuilt in 1970 the block bells and instruments in use dated from the 1900s and were of solid Midland Railway make. But these were replaced by modern B.R. standard combined bells and indicators in 1976. In 1980 semaphore signals still in use at Marple are of modern B.R. type, but stand on the exact site of their Midland predecessors.

Underneath the box on the 'ground floor', made a semi-basement by the rise in height of the platform, were the batteries for the electrical instruments in the box, and the mechanical 'interlocking' which was so arranged to physically prevent the signalman pulling a wrong lever. Here also were the mechanical devices of pulleys, chains and levers which converted the pull on a lever into a movement of a rod or wire to operate points & signals.

Marple signal box was closed on 27th July 1980 along with Marple Wharf Junction and Strines as part of the Romiley - New Mills Central resignalling and the line converted to 'Track Circuit Block' system by which the passage of trains operates the signals by means of low voltage electrical circuits running though the tracks. Semaphore signals were replaced by modern 3 aspect colour light signals. The line through Marple thus came under the control of Romiley signal box which also controlled the points and signals in Marple station and at Marple Wharf Junction.

The station in 1980 was largely as it was left when rebuilding was completed in October 1970, but there have been some subsequent improvements. As originally built the new booking office only had one booking window, quite insufficient for peak-hour business, when an additional booking clerk was brought to the station to cater for the demand, At first two clerks had to serve through one window, but this ludicrous situation was resolved later in the year by the installation of a second booking window.

The gap left by the demolition of the stair hall and entrance to the station on Brabyns Brow had left a large gap in the stone wall, which had originally been filled up with brick. This looked very unsightly and under pressure from Marple Council, B.R. replaced this by a proper stone wall, giving a much better aesthetic effect. The station car park had only been left half finished when the station opened, and the finishing touches followed slowly. First of all, early in 1971, the entrance was widened to permit two cars to pass, easing the congestion on Brabyns Brow, and making the gateway less of a blind corner. Crash barriers were erected round the car park early in 1972 to protect pedestrians, but it took another year before the car park was finally tarmacked, and a proper kerb provided. Originally a charge was made for the use of the car park, which discouraged use of the station, and many passengers drove to Romiley where there was a free car park next to the station. After a few years of local pressure, B.R. removed charges and usage of the station by car-owners leapt up. Finally, 6 years after rebuilding, the signal box was repainted to match the rest of the station-just in time to close 4 years later!.

Marple as rebuilt appears a totally modern station, but in fact the basic layout of the site, bounded by great stone retaining walls east and west, and the Brabyns Park and Brabyns Brow overbridges north and south, is that of 1875; the platforms are greatly altered, but are built on those of 1865 and 1875, while the footbridge had not moved at all. And for those who look closely, there are many traces of the former glories of the station to be found hidden in undergrowth. I was sorry to see the decline and demolition of the old station, but the new buildings serve the needs of Marple better and more economically than the old station could. It is a pity however that some of the magnificent canopy and station buildings could not have been preserved for the very practical purpose of sheltering passengers.

XII. The Turn Of the Tide. 1970 - 1980

1. Continuing Doubts- the early 70's

Despite hopeful signs like the re-building of Marple Station doubts about the future of the Railways continued. For one thing local Railways like the Marple line continued losing money; by 1970 the annual grant-aid for the Manchester - Marple, New Mills and Rose Hill services was in the region of £½m. Secondly, 1970 which had ended with the opening of the new Marple Station had begun with the draconian measures of the closure of the Hayfield, Macclesfield and Woodhead lines-the latter to passengers only in 1970 but to all traffic in 1981. Railway closures continued into the mid-70's and after the trauma of the Beeching era, few believed any Railways were safe from closure, or even had any future. The motorway-building boom was at its height, car ownership rising fast and petrol cheap. Who needed railways? B.R.'s losses continued to mount, despite the pruning of 'dead wood' in the 60's, and the pressure to economise increased. Having found that closing lines did not, in the long run pay off, efforts were concentrated on economising on the staffing and maintenance bill for those stations remaining open: the rebuilding of Marple had been directed to this aim. Accordingly in May 1973 work started on 'rationalising' Strines. Until then Strines had remained a charming old fashioned country station. Admittedly the goods yard and warehouse had gone, and the staff reduced to signalman and porter/clerk, but the solid stone buildings with hard Victorian benches, coal fires, and the deliberate tick of the old clock had little changed from the day the station had opened, while the whole place remained gas-lit. The last regular porter/clerk was Sid Cottrell, who was a character. Few passengers used the station after the morning peak, and in the early 70's the train service was sparse. Sid used to say that it was rare to take more than 30 'bob' (£1.50) after the morning 'rush', though on a Monday morning he could take well over £50 in season ticket revenue. People even brought parcels to the station now and again. His other station duties included turning the gas lights on and off, and filling the signal lamps with oil - a duty which had by then now virtually disappeared with the use of electrical lights even in semaphore signals. Like many railwaymen, Sid was a keen gardener, and grew some flowers on the station, though his duties were so light that he spent much of his time in summer gathering the blackberries which grew profusely on the embankments, and, between trains, cutting lawns for people living nearby to supplement his income.

This scene of bucolic tranquillity however came to an end when B.R. decided to reduce Strines to an unstaffed halt. It is in fact surprising that Strines survived the Beeching era at all, or retained staff as late as 1973. First of all small shelters were constructed on either platform out of stone salvaged from the demolition of the gentlemen's lavatory - which Strines had retained to the end, 3 years after Marple and Rose Hill had lost such facilities. Old station benches were placed in these shelters to provide elementary vandal-proof waiting accommodation. Later in the summer of 1973, electric lighting was installed, and the gas lights swept away. The electric lights worked off an automatic time switch, and no longer required a man to give them daily attention. This done, the station was unstaffed, and notices posted at the station reading: -

STRINES STATION

On and from Monday 10th September 1973, this station will become an UNSTAFFED HALT
Passengers requiring to purchase tickets may do so at their destination station, or at the station where they change trains.
Passengers alighting from trains are requested to deposit their tickets in the boxes provided near station exits.
Season tickets may be obtained by Postal Application to the Area Manager, Romiley Station, or purchased at destination station. There are NO Parcels facilities available.
Train enquiries may be made by telephoning Manchester Piccadilly.

There was no official ceremony to mark the reduction of Strines to an unstaffed halt, and only two spectators, one of whom was myself, when Strines Booking Office sold its last two tickets, which we kept as souvenirs. However regular users of the station

Strines from the north c.1962. Note the goods shed. (Mowat Collection)

did arrange among themselves a presentation of a cheque and testimonial to Sid Cottrell as a mark of their appreciation of his friendly service. This ceremony took place on the platform after the arrival of the evening commuter train in the week after the closure of the Booking Office.

The station buildings stood empty for some months, despite attempts by various people to buy them to convert into a house, and became a target for vandals. But it was not until a year after unstaffing that the buildings were finally razed. Finally in 1975, the platforms were resurfaced, and the footbridge removed and access to the Up platform was via the underbridge at the North of the station. By 1973 only the Signalman in his box was left to survey the station, but the signal box closed in 1980.

And so Strines was converted into an unstaffed halt with the minimum of facilities - two bare platforms, a stark shelter on each, and automatic electric light - a far cry from the 19th C. station with its own station master and diverse buildings. What has happened to Strines is typical of many of the small rural stations which escaped the Beeching axe. While such economies are unpalatable, and have in many cases been excessive, such reductions in facilities have increased the chance of survival of many small stations, by reducing B.R.'s deficit. Strines was in 1980 the only station in our area to have lost its staff, though Middlewood Low Level was staffed on a one-shift basis in the morning only in common with many stations on the Buxton LNW line. Marple and Rose Hill were by contrast still staffed during the whole period trains ran, i.e. 6 a.m. to midnight.

The early 70's were marked by alterations to the structure of nearly every station in the district. At some such as Belle Vue or Hyde North, buildings were completely demolished and temporary 'Portakabins' erected, followed by 'bus-stop' type shelters. But at others such as Reddish North or Romiley the old buildings were retained in part and adapted to modern requirements. No station in the area has escaped modernisation, having survived since the 19th C. with very little change. Even at New Mills, which had survived almost unaltered since 1867, the Up platform waiting room was replaced by an open fronted stone shelter. One thing in particular has become universal - electric light. In 1969 the only stations between Manchester Piccadilly and Sheffield Midland (exclusive) via Reddish not entirely gas lit were Ashburys and Chinley. Some stations such as High Lane and Middlewood were still oil lit, and Middlewood remained so until 1972. By 1975 all stations were electrically lit in our area, Woodley being the last to enter the 20th C. in this respect.

But the rationalisation of stations has been nowhere as severe as on some other lines, where all that has been left are 'bus - shelters' and no staff. Many stations are still staffed, except e.g. Strines and Fairfield, and have retained some buildings. Not all the modernisation has been retrograde as electric lighting is certainly better than gas, higher platforms as at Bredbury, Romiley and Marple a boon to the less agile passenger, and stations began to get painted more regularly than in the 60's, when, under the threat of Beeching cuts, maintenance almost ceased.

Meanwhile in the early 70's petrol prices began to rise sharply, and the general public voiced resentment at the damage

54

and pollution caused by road transport, as a result of a growing interest in environmental matters. There arose a considerable weight of public opinion that road and air, hailed as the answer to all transport problems in the 1960's, were not going to answer those of the late 20th C. Those in power took another look at the Railways, and decided that if road transport was not to overwhelm our lives, the Railways must not be allowed to decline any further, and in places must be improved, particularly in major conurbations. The spate of closures slowed down considerably after 1970, and died away altogether in 1975, since when lines and stations have been re-opened, or even built afresh. It was realised that the Beeching axe had been too severe but in most cases it was too late to repair the damage. If many lines had survived a few more years - say to 1972 - the turning tide would have probably prevented their closure - such as the Hayfield and Macclesfield Branches or the Midland Peak Line. But now they are gone, and only now are we seeing the effects of the folly of excessive closures, especially in the Peak District National Park.

2. S.E.L.N.E.C. and the 'Picc-Vic' Scheme

A need for better public transport in the great cities had been recognised in the 1968 Transport Act, which set-up Passenger Transport Executives (P.T.E.s) in the country's main conurbations. One of these was Manchester, where the P.T.E., set-up in 1969, embraced Manchester, Altrincham, Stockport, Oldham, Rochdale, Bury and Bolton and was entitled S.E.L.N.E.C. (South East Lancashire and North East Cheshire). The P.T.E.'s were set-up to co-ordinate all public transport in their area. They were to liaise with B.R. over the running of rail services, but their main activity was operating bus services, which they took over from the former municipal corporations. Consequently for the first few years, little real interest was shown in railways. But a detailed study of the transport needs of the Manchester area completed in 1970 concluded that an efficient public transport network was the only way to maintain the environment of the city and its suburbs. In particular it was essential to tempt car owners to use the Railway by improving the services. The most far reaching proposal was to construct an electrified underground link between Piccadilly and Victoria Stations - and thus nicknamed 'Picc-Vic' - to link up the systems North and South of the city, sundered since 1844. While the Picc-Vic Tunnel would not have directly benefited the Marple Lines, which would continue to run into the Main line platforms at Piccadilly (High Level), inter-change with the Picc-Vic would give better access to city-centre as well as Victoria Station and places North of Manchester. But the plan did propose up-grading the Manchester-Marple, New Mills and Rose Hill lines, with more frequent services, modernised stations and bus-rail Interchanges at key stations.

While this seemed to assure a rosy future for Marple, New Mills and also Rose Hill, which only escaped closure by the skin of its teeth, the S.E.L.N.E.C plan tended to categorise too many lines as 'hopeless cases' for closure - e.g. the Hyde loop. Another ludicrous idea was to close the Buxton LNW line beyond Hazel Grove, and convert the trackbed into a bus-way; largely one

L.N.E.R. A4 Pacific 'Sir Nigel Gresley' on a Manchester to Scarborough steam special south of Marple South Tunnel. 29th April 1978 (I.R. Smith)

suspects because the S.E.L.N.E.C area ended at Hazel Grove. A subsequent plan of 1972 proposed electrification to New Mills and Rose Hill, and the construction of a East-West tunnel to complement the Picc-Vic link. This was to be a deep level tube, called the Deansgate Tunnel, running from a deep level station at Piccadilly, under the Picc-Vic station to join up with the M.S.J.A. near Deansgate. The Marple and Glossop services were to be funnelled into the deep level Piccadilly by means of a dive-under at Ardwick, and run through the tunnel to Warrington and Altrincham - an ambitious scheme altogether. The Picc-Vic scheme obtained Parliamentary Assent in 1972, but in 1975 the Labour Government told Manchester there was no money for the Picc-Vic scheme. Since then the scheme has remained dormant, officially disowned by the Conservative Greater Manchester Council, and the scheme eventually faded away.

The scheme failed because S.E.L.N.E.C spent too much time in long term planning, and too little in actually getting the work started while the money was available. Liverpool or Newcastle got on with it and now have successful Underground and Metro networks respectively. From 1974 however the 'Centreline' high frequency mini-bus service operated between Piccadilly and Victoria, providing at least some form of cross-Manchester link. Since then in 1988 the 'Castlefield Curve' has opened to link the railways north and south of the Manchester. From 1992 the ever expanding Manchester Metrolink network has given both north-south running and access to the city centre.

3. Greater Manchester Transport (1974-79)

S.E.L.N.E.C. took over financial responsibility for running Manchester's local rail services on New Year's Day 1972. Incidentally the amount of support for the Manchester-New Mills/Rose Hill service was £475,000 in 1973. Then in the Local Government re-organisation of 1974 Marple ceased to be an Urban District Council in Cheshire for administrative purposes, being subsumed into Stockport, within Greater Manchester, though many still regard Marple as being geographically still within Cheshire. S.E.L.N.E.C. became Greater Manchester Transport Passenger Executive (G.M.P.T.E.). Like S.E.L.N.E.C. before it, the G.M.P.T.E. does not run the Railway services, but paid B.R. to do so, and had a large say in the planning of services. This has been of great benefit to all the lines in our district. The threat of closure at Marple and Rose Hill is now a dream, and lines such as the Buxton L.N.W. Line and Hyde Loop seem secure. Some improvements were made by S.E.L.N.E.C. and G.M.T.P.E. to the Marple and Rose Hill services. The main one was the introduction of one extra Rose Hill - Manchester morning peak train, as Rose Hill had been left with a very poor morning service ever since the closure of the Macclesfield line. Marple also gained an extra Down morning and Up evening commuter train. But under G.M.P.T.E even more dramatic changes were made. From 2nd May 1977, a half hourly service was introduced between Piccadilly and New Mills Central, calling at all stations via Bredbury. Instead of the erratic services via Hyde which had existed since 1970 when the Hayfield Branch closed. Thus the service to New Mills- and Strines - was increased nearly fourfold, from every two hours to half hourly; this gave New Mills its best ever service, especially with the Sheffield expresses calling, excelling even the post 1955 'modernisation plan' service; and Strines had an almost half hourly service.

Additional peak hour trains terminated at Marple, giving a much improved morning and evening commuter service; no off-peak trains however now terminated at Marple, thus removing the operating nuisance of having terminated trains reversing, and standing for periods in the station, causing delay to through express passenger and goods trains.

A novel feature of the May 1977 timetable was the re-appearance of express services calling at Marple, in the form of stopping the 17.24 express from Piccadilly to Sheffield and Doncaster at Marple. This was basically to give a fast evening commuter service to Marple. Arriving, non-stop from Manchester, in 16 minutes at 17.40, this is undoubtedly the fastest ever Manchester to Marple timing since 1880, when the Midland transferred its express services from London Road to Central: the 1875 timetable for instance shows several trains performing the London Road-Marple run in 15 minutes, e.g. the 16.50 London Road - St. Pancras reaching Marple at 17.05- such is progress! Even more surprises were in store in May 1979 when the 17.24

Rose Hill Station from the north. 11th September 1978. (Author)

ex Manchester, still non-stop to Marple, was extended beyond Doncaster to Cleethorpes, giving Marple through services to such places as Scunthorpe and Grimsby, which it has certainly never had before, not even in its pre-grouping heyday.

Until 1977, with the decline of Midland main line services, only one Up and one Down main line train called at Marple each week: a semi-fast Sunday Liverpool-Sheffield train, and a return train, mainly for the benefit of hikers to the Hope Valley, giving Marple a once-weekly service to Liverpool and Sheffield! But from 1980 the Down service started at Hull, giving Marple a Sundays only service from such places as Brough and Goole. These were however faint shadows of former main line glories. The May 1977 timetable gave Marple 44 Up and 42 Down trains, the best ever service between Marple and Piccadilly or its predecessor London Road; though the total of 86 trains is well below the station's main line heyday of the late 19th C., or the 1950's or 60's when Midland line trains still called. While the number of services to and from Piccadilly was higher than ever before, there had been more trains to and from Manchester in the past, though they had been distributed among two or three termini. So while the timetable of 1980 was a good one, it did in fact only restore the service to its pre-1970 level. Apart from the very occasional main line services, Marple was now a completely suburban station, though the process towards this began as long ago as 1898 when the Midland decided to build the Disley cut-off. But the May 1977 timetable also brought great improvements at Rose Hill.

In 1970 with the closure of the Macclesfield line, Rose Hill had gained an hourly off-peak service, but a much worse peak-hour service, and lost its early morning and late evening services altogether. In May 1977 the morning peak service was doubled from 4 to 8 trains between 07.00 and 09.00, and the hourly interval service extended late into the evening, giving Rose Hill 24 Up and 26 Down services, which was undoubtedly the best ever service up till then. But the fastest timing of 27 minutes compared unfavourably with 18 minutes achieved fn 1875! One unfortunate feature of the 1977 timetable however was the routing of all off-peak services via Guide Bridge, though these ran non-stop between Piccadilly and Guide Bridge to give a timing only slightly slower than via Bredbury. A better plan would have been to run all Rose Hill services via Bredbury, and alternate New Mills services via Guide Bridge, the other New Mills service each hour routed via Bredbury. The co-operation between B.R. and G.M.P.T.E. did not however stop at an improved train service. For the first time for many years extensive publicity for the line was mounted, and connections between rail and bus services advertised: at Rose Hill for Hawk Green, and at Marple for Hawk Green, Mellor and Glossop Road, thus reviving an idea dead since bus and rail services parted company in the 1920's. There has however been no move to bring buses directly into Marple's forecourt, where a bus turning circle was proposed in re-building - and anyway there is now no room in the forecourt for buses, with
the heavy usage by private cars. In 1976 the G.M.P.T.E. introduced the 'Saver Seven' scheme. Previously a weekly zoned bus pass for the Greater Manchester Area had been available. Now its use was extended to include train services as well, the pass now gave unlimited travel on all bus services in the Area, and in addition on all rail services within a specified zone, there being a choice of four rail zones, with different prices for each. The scheme was very successful and made through bus-rail journeys much easier, through 'Saver Seven' the need for a weekly season ticket largely disappeared, though there was still a demand for seasons for a month or more. An unfortunate aspect of the scheme when first started was that Romiley was included in Zone 2, while Marple and Rose Hill were in Zone 4, involving a jump in price of the pass from £3 to £4 per week. As a result of this many passengers drove to Romiley, to the detriment of Marple and Rose Rill. After pressure however from the Marple Community Council (a body formed to represent Marple's interests after the merger of the former Marple Urban District Council into Greater Manchester in 1974), the zoning system was altered, so that the jump in price between Romiley and Marple or Rose Hill, now in Zone 3, was not so steep. G.M.P.T.E.'s overall control of services was now also to be seen on the Passenger coaches of trains, where the GMT symbol of a stylised 'M' could be seen painted on the coach sides. In addition to providing a better service at Rose Hill, the G.M.P.T.E. decided to improve facilities at the station. The work was carried out on their behalf by B.R., and involved converting the former goods yard into a car park and bus turning area. As the goods yard was occupied by Bowden & Son, Coal Merchants, who had stayed on in the yard after the withdrawal of goods trains, it was necessary to provide alternative accommodation. Work began in March 1977 to provide such accommodation in the triangle of land at the South end of the former goods yard. This involved removing some trees, which brought protests from residents nearby, and a rap on B. R.'s knuckles from the Stockport Borough Planning Committee for starting work before planning permission had been granted. However work proceeded, and slowly a car park was created in the centre of the former goods yard, and a bus turning area provided beside the South end of the Down platform; work was delayed until Bowden's were finally installed in their new coal yard, which was incidentally only a fraction of the size of the old yard, showing how much the demand for coal had dropped in the previous 20 years. Meanwhile the Down platform was raised to the standard modern height and a new set of entrances and exits made, giving access to the new car park and bus stop from the Down platform.

No work was however done on the Up platform, which remained very low, except providing a red ticket collecting booth. Passengers were faced with a long roundabout walk to the bus stop and car park. The work was eventually completed in the Autumn of 1978, with access to the car park and bus stop by the lane formerly leading to the Council depot, instead of direct onto Stockport Road via the old exit, which was now quite unsuitable with a blind bend on the hump of the bridge. The Rose Hill branch was singled from Sunday 27th July 1980 and the Down platform taken out of use. This was a big improvement making the station accessible to all including the disabled, elderly and infirm and gave better access to the car park. Thus refurbished Rose Hill had good road/rail interchange, and superior to those at Marple, but the car park was not so well patronised, and connecting bus services did not run into the yard, as Marple had a better train service

Even more dramatic has been the opening of completely new stations, something which would have seemed inconceivable in the Beeching era so few years before. Work started late in 1976 at Brinnington, between Reddish and Bredbury, on a station to serve the estate which has grown up in post-war years. It was officially opened by the Lord Lieutenant of Greater Manchester on 12th December 1977 (though it was nowhere near complete) in a tape-breaking ceremony derived directly from the opening of Marple. Hard on its heels followed a new station on the Glossop line at Hattersley, just east of Godley Junction to serve another modern estate. In addition a complete and lavish reconstruction of Bredbury was completed in 1978. At Hattersley and Bredbury the schemes included large new car parks, and in all cases bus-rail links were an integral part of the scheme. Marple was thus the prototype new station for our area, and the success of Marple, particularly the car park gave impetus to these other schemes. These three new stations include platform canopies - obviously the lesson of Marple has also been learned here.

The result of these improvements has been to enable the railways to retain their passengers in an era of rising car ownership and even attract new custom, when otherwise usage would have

56

continued to dwindle away. It is amazing how the tide turned in the years to 1980. In 1969, closure was the watchword; no line seemed safe, and it seemed only a matter of time before Marple went the way of many other stations. Even the Rose Hill branch had a secure future - a line which escaped the axe by a hair's breadth, and all the talk was of improvements not closure: such has been the reaction to the folly of mass Railway closures, and the unacceptable demands of road transport on the environment.

4. Future Prospects

The lines in our area now had an assured future - of that there is no doubt. In 1980 the main line through Marple was particularly secure, in that it carried the three basic types of Railway traffic - express passenger, suburban and freight. With the closure of the Woodhead and Midland Disley Tunnel/Peak District lines to passengers, the route through Marple was now the only Inter-City passenger route eastward from Manchester. The express service was hourly between Manchester and Sheffield with alternate trains calling at New Mills. Since May 1979 the whole Manchester-Sheffield service was re-organised, as part of a general improvement to Trans - Pennine services. The Manchester-Hull service was concentrated on the Hope Valley Line, instead of the LNW Standedge route, and additional services provided between Manchester and Grimsby and Cleethorpes. This was basically done by linking up the existing Manchester-Sheffield expresses with existing, but improved, services east of Sheffield and providing better coaches in the form of 'cross-country' d.m.u.s displaced from services elsewhere in the country. These were soon to be replaced by loco-hauled main line trains.

Most of the trains, which were hourly, now extended to Doncaster, and beyond there three each way ran daily between Manchester and Grimsby and Cleethorpes, and then later to and from Hull. The principal express train passing through was however the daily service each way between Manchester and Harwich Parkeston Quay, where it connected with Continental boat sailings. This was the only regular loco-hauled weekday passenger train to use the line, unless you count the 02.10 (a .m.!) from Manchester to Lincoln, which is basically a newspaper train bound for Grimsby. Summer Saturdays however saw a great variety of holiday trains passing through, including services to Skegness and Yarmouth, and between Sheffield or the Midlands and Blackpool or Llandudno. On Sundays however ran the last vestige of the Midland service, in the form of two trains each way between Manchester and St. Pancras. These called at all stations of any importance, including a reversal at Sheffield, and took between 5 and 6 hours- a far cry from the 3 hours 35 minutes of 1904 or the 3 hours 10 minutes of the 'Midland Pullman' of the 60's! The local service has already been described, and with the express service gave a line density off-peak of 3 passenger trains an hour South of Marple Wharf, and 4 an hour North thereof. Into this had to be slotted a heavy freight service.

Most of the freight traffic consisted of limestone aggregate from the Buxton area passing in 'company trains', which are block train loads of private wagons run specifically for one customer. The largest such flow was from I.C.I. Tunstead with 11 trips weekly to distribution depots at Miles Platting and 16 to Dean Lane, Newton Heath. There were also lesser flows from Dove Holes Quarry and Topley Pike to Salford and Pendleton respectively. An oil train also ran once-weekly from Port Clarence on Teesside to the Quarries at Hindlow.

There were in addition conventional mixed 'wagonload' freight services. Each night a through service left Peak Forest Yard for Healey Mills Yard in Yorkshire using the Marple route; and six times a day trips ran each way between Peak Forest Yard and Dewsnap Yard, Guide Bridge, moving miscellaneous traffic such as coal and general merchandise for Buxton, and lesser flows of limestone and lime products for use in chemical and construction industries. In all about 25 freight trains used the Marple route daily, and in 1980 1½m tonnes of freight passed through Marple Station (or including empty workings and taking the gross laden weight- 3½ m tonnes) with virtually no environmental damage. Finally the route was used by parcels services from Manchester Mayfield to St. Pancras and Sheffield, and by overnight newspaper services to Sheffield and Cleethorpes. All in all, the line carried a very diverse flow of traffic, giving it a secure future as an essential freight and passenger route. There was also a heavy flow of traffic of about 14 company trains each way daily from the Buxton area to the I.C.I. works on the Cheshire Plain, via the Disley Tunnel route.

The 1970's have also seen the re-appearance of steam hauled specials on the Marple route This is because the Guide Bridge-Sheffield route is 'passed' for use by privately owned preserved steam locos, usually originating from the Steam Centre at Dinting, Carnforth, or the National Railway Museum, York. Each summer this brings a number of steam locos through Marple, including locos such as the A4 Pacific 'Sir Nigel Gresley', never before seen on the route. Undoubtedly the most celebrated visitor was 'Flying Scotsman' in 1973 en route from exile in America to Derby for overhaul, when about 1,000 people crowded on and around Marple Station to see it pass through. It was pleasant to see steam hauled trains on the line particularly behind Dinting's 'Scots Guardsman', 'Bahamas' or 'Leander', which represent the types of locomotives once common on the L.M.S.

In 1980 the future of the Woodhead route, open for freight only since 1970, was in doubt, as the electrical equipment was life-expired. With the decline in the coal traffic From South Yorkshire to Fiddler's Ferry Power Station on which the line depended, the Woodhead route closed in 1981, as it was the least viable of the remaining four Trans-Pennine lines, and carried no passenger service. The closure of Woodhead diverted more freight traffic onto the Hope Valley/Marple/Disley routes, and thus further strengthening their viability. The closure of Woodhead also led to the closure of the Godley- Woodley- Stockport route and dashed hopes of a re-instated Marple - Stockport route.

A major constraint on operating a dense service of mixed traffic over the line is the signalling system. The old arrangement of irregularly spaced mechanical signal boxes, and 'Absolute Block' regulations with semaphore signals is not conducive to a rapid flow of traffic. By contrast the modern 'Track Circuit Block' system allows trains to run at much closer headways, with colour light signals controlling the trains automatically wherever possible, with a consequent improvement in speed of operation. This form of signalling has been introduced piecemeal into the Manchester area, and in 1973 was extended from Ashburys to just short of Romiley, with the aim of extending onto New Mills. Seven years later, the Romiley- New Mills Resignalling was implemented on Sunday 27th July 1980. Under this scheme, the Signal boxes at Marple, Marple Wharf Junction, and Strines were closed, and signalling centralised at a new control panel at Romiley This links up with the previous resignalling from Ashburys, while Woodley and New Mills Junction (at the Central station) - remain as manually-worked 'fringe' boxes to the scheme. The line from Romiley to New Mills has been track-circuited throughout, and three aspect colour light signals, many in totally new positions, so as to maximise line capacity have replaced the old semaphores. The Rose Hill branch has also been singled. It was originally intended that the single line should start at Marple Wharf Junction, but it was found that there was not room between the Viaduct and junction for the requisite point work. So a double line junction was retained at Marple Wharf, with the two tracks continuing round the curve far enough to allow a train to stand clear of the junction on each line. Thus in theory it was possible for 3 trains to stand simultaneously on the Rose Hill branch, due to the new signalling and layout. This is a great improvement on the previous situation, when only one train could be on the branch at once despite the double track. The Peak Railway Society purchased Marple and Marple Wharf Signalboxes intact for preservation on the Matlock Rowsley section of the Peak Line. Marple Wharf Junction signal box was dismantled in February 1981, though in the event only parts of these signal boxes were able to be re-used.

This marked yet another stage in the massive modernisation of the Railways in our area in the last quarter of the 20th C. In 1955, before the modernisation plan, B.R. were operating a basically 19th C. system relying on coal, iron and gas. The diesels arrived in 1955, but 10 years later steam was still common. Early in 1970, despite the demise of steam, the appearance of our railway was still basically 19th C., with frequent mechanical signal boxes, manually operated, and basically Victorian in design and equipment. The signals were all semaphores, lit by oil lamps at night. The lineside equipment largely pre-dated the Grouping and telegraph wires strode alongside the tracks. The stations were pure Victorian, with a profusion of cast iron, coal fires, gas or even oil lighting.

An up train of empties for the Peak District passes Marple Wharf Junction 1978, from the south. (Author)

By 1980 the vast 19th C. station buildings had largely disappeared, along with much of the iron work. Modern concrete and wire replace the picturesque wooden fences; gas lighting and coal fires are a thing of the past. The old fashioned permanent way, with wooden sleepers, 'bull-headed' rail with joints every 60 feet giving the distinctive 'clickety click' was rapidly being replaced by modern continuously welded rail on concrete sleepers. The forests of telegraph wires and semaphore signals have disappeared, replaced by modern cables and prosaic colour light signals. The signal boxes too have gone, as control is centralised: but this is nothing new - remember how the present Marple box replaced three old boxes when it opened in 1905. The physical appearance of our railway has probably changed more rapidly in the last 15 years up to 1980 years than at any other time. Now only the permanent structure - the bridges and tunnels, and the actual alignment serve to remind us of the 19thC., along with such features as mileposts and gradient boards, though these too may disappear with metrication. Little however can be done to alter the alignment, and it is unlikely that the present speed restrictions on the line through Marple will be eased to allow higher speed, due to the sinuous nature of the route. There is a blanket speed restriction of 60 m.p.h. from New Mills to Romiley, with lower speeds of 45 m.p.h. in the sharply curved Marple South Tunnel and 50 m.p.h. at Marple Wharf.

For some years it appeared likely that the Disley Tunnel route, which has remained open solely for 'company trains' plying between the Peak District and the Cheshire Plain, would close if the formation was required for a motorway in the vicinity of Hazel Grove. If this had occurred traffic would have been diverted via Marple and the 'Marple Curve' at Romiley. The curve had therefore been left largely in situ since closure in 1967, in case this happened. When in 1975 the motorway scheme was abandoned, it became obvious that the 'Marple Curve' would not be required in the foreseeable future, and the track was removed; though it was possible that if the expense of retaining Disley Tunnel became too onerous, the 'Marple Curve' might have re-opened in the 1970's. Traffic on the road between Marple and Stockport has in recent years reached saturation point. As a result early in 1979 a suggestion was put forward to either widen the existing road or build a completely new route. The Marple Community Council however objected on the grounds that either scheme would ruin the rural approach to Marple and only generate more traffic. They therefore put a counter proposal to re-open the 'Marple Curve' as a single track, and run a regular train service between Marple and Rose Hill and Stockport. The terminus in Stockport would be a re-opened Tiviot Dale Station, which was now very close to the Merseyway shopping precinct, and would have been even closer when the precinct was extended. With free car parks at Marple and Rose Hill, and bus-rail interchange facilities at the latter, it should be possible to attract sufficient commuters and shoppers to the service to reduce the level of traffic on the road, and such a scheme would be a fraction of the cost of a new or widened road, would cause no environmental damage, and be of great benefit to those without cars. The G.M.P.T.E. felt the scheme could not be justified at the time, but agreed to attempt to safeguard the track

Marple Wharf Junction Signal Box interior, July 1980. (author)

bed from development for the time being, and asked the M.C.C. to undertake further studies into the feasibility of re-opening.

The Marple Community Council was pressing B.R. to stop some of the Sheffield expresses at Marple, as it has better car parking facilities than New Mills, though it was unlikely B.R. would heed the suggestion. The Community Council was also pressing for improved booking facilities at Marple. Romiley and New Mills both had the facility of booking tickets to main line destinations, but at Marple it was impossible to get a ticket for anywhere beyond Manchester or Sheffield - despite having regular, albeit limited, services to places such as Liverpool, Cleethorpes and Doncaster. This caused the passenger using these services considerable inconvenience in obtaining a ticket on the trains or at destination, and provides ample scope for fare evasion. What is more passengers travelling via Manchester Piccadilly to e.g. London had to leave the platforms to re-book. A station of the importance of Marple ought, like Romiley or Guide Bridge, to have had the facility of booking tickets to principal destinations, and certainly to places - such as Doncaster- which could be reached by through train. However, in 2015 it is now possible to book tickets to any destination in the country at Marple and Rose Hill.

In the long term, the G.M.P.T.E. favoured electrification to New Mills and Rose Hill, which made sense in view of the increasing cost and scarcity of diesel fuel. What is more the d.m.u.s providing the services on our line were in 1980 in some cases nearly 20 years old, though only designed for 10 to 15 years of life. They were becoming increasingly difficult to maintain and unreliable. Internally they gave a very bad impression to the passenger, though some refurbished units were now appearing. It looked as though we were stuck with the d.m.u.s for the foreseeable future, but they could not last forever, and electrification may be the only sensible answer for a suburban line like ours.

In conclusion, the last 60 years have seen our Railways at last emerge out of their 19th C. form. They have passed through an era of retrenchment, of closure, threat of closure, of demolition and reduction in services. The 70's however have seen a miraculous change, with the Railways passing out of an era of despondency. The last few years have seen a continuous improvement of services and facilities. Now, in 1980 after 15 years of doubt, it seemed that our Railways had an assured future into the 21st Century.

The Royal Train conveying King Edward VII and Queen Alexandra, passing Bredbury Station (extreme Right) on 12th July, 1905. The King and Queen were paying a state visit to Sheffield, and the Royal Train is en route from London St. Pancras, via Sheffield and the Dore and Chinley Line, to Manchester Victoria, where the L.N.W took over for the final leg to Huyton, near Liverpool. The Royal Party de-trained here to spend the night at Knowsley Hall as guests of Lord Derby. The L.N.W. Royal Coaches are double-headed by two Midland Railway 4-4-0 express locomotives built at Derby, designed by S.W. Johnson. This train would have passed through Marple Station a few minutes before the photograph was taken (J.N. Wood).

Demolition of Marple Station Footbridge, March 1970. A mobile road crane removes the first span of the 1875 footbridge linking the Up platform to Brabyns Brow (North Cheshire Herald).

XIII. The Railways of Marple. 1980-2015

This final chapter was written in the spring of 2015 to update the book from 1980 to the present and to commemorate the 150th anniversary of Marple station. When writing this section it soon became apparent that there have been a lot of changes, some of which have not been recorded. To quote Alan Bennett in 'The History Boys' "there is no period so remote as the recent past". As a lot of research was needed on my part, I would welcome any corrections or further information.

1. Abbreviations since 1980 for Chapter XIII

ACoRP -	The Association of Community Rail Partnerships	ROSCO -	Rolling Stock Leasing Company
BR -	British Rail/Railways	SEMCoRP -	South East Manchester Community Rail Partnership
BRBR -	British Rail Board Residuary	SMBC -	Stockport Metropolitan Borough Council
DfT -	Department for Transport	SX -	Saturdays excepted
FoMS -	Friends of Marple station	SO -	Saturdays only
FoRHS -	Friends of Rose Hill Station	TfGM -	Transport for Greater Manchester
FoSS -	Friends of Strines Station	TOC -	Train Operating Companies
ORR -	Office of Rail Regulation/Rail & Road	WTT -	Working Timetable

Marple signal box exterior 12th September 1978 (author).

Marple signal box interior 12th September 1978 (author).

2. Marple Station

The 'new' station of 1970 remained much the same, except for the demise of the signalbox in 1980, until the opening of the new footbridge in 2012. The Down platform waiting rooms were often kept locked due to vandalism and minimal staffing, and the northern one was demolished in the mid 1980's. The station was not continuously staffed by the mid 80's, and not at all on a Sunday. So a gate was made in the fence from the car park to the up platform so passengers could access the station when the ticket office had no staff and buy tickets on the train. Eventually guards on trains were issued with new ticket machines which could sell tickets to a range of destinations, removing the need to re-book, and in recent years the station has received a state-of-the-art Ticket Machine on the Up platform. A disabled toilet, bike lockers and train information displays have also been provided.

Signalboxes

When Marple Wharf Junction and Marple Station signalboxes were taken out of use on Sunday 27th July 1980, they were donated to the Peak Railway Society which was and still is trying to re-open the Matlock-Buxton line. The signalboxes went in part or whole to Buxton. Marple Wharf Junction was dismantled early in 1981. However in the event Peak Rail vacated the Buxton site and decided to concentrate on re-opening northwards from Matlock. In the event the Marple signalboxes were not used as a whole but parts re-used in other signalboxes on Peak Rail, especially the window sections from Marple. Incidentally the Hayfield line tunnel at New Mills was retained for many years to stable trains turning back at New Mills but is now no longer used for that purpose. This probably dates from 2007 when New Mills was re-signalled, allowing trains from Manchester to depart from the Up platform, they had just arrived at, back to Manchester. Track Circuit Block and colour light signalling was extended to New Mills Central, which remains a manual box at the time of writing. From New Mills Central to New Mills South Junction, where the Marple line joins the Disley Tunnel route, remains an outpost of Absolute Block signalling. Eventually all Signalling in the Marple area, now controlled from Romiley and New Mills Central signalboxes, will be controlled from the new Network Rail's North West Rail Operating Centre at Ashburys, which is opened in 2014. It is currently taking over of the Crewe-Carlisle line bit by bit. The aim is that the whole of the Rail Network will be controlled from twelve signalling centres by 2019; six are already in operation. In the last four years a GSM-R (Global System for Mobile Communications - Railways) Mast has been erected at the north end of Marple station. This gives real-time location of trains - like a SatNav. In the long term it will control radio signalling in the area.

Car Park

The former cattle market area across the road from Marple station became an unofficial car park from the 1970's onwards but was adopted and surfaced, albeit with crushed stone, by Network Rail, though owned by Stockport Council, in the early 1990's. It is currently full to capacity after 8.30 am and further car parking space at Marple station is an urgent issue.

New Footbridge

The origin of the new footbridge with a lift arose from the campaigning of the indefatigable late Marple resident, Paul Rice. As he grew older he found it increasingly difficult to cross the bridge at Marple with luggage. On occasions he took a train to New Mills and returned to Manchester on the same train. He was taken to task by the authorities for this. Thus began his campaign to get a new footbridge with lift at the station. This fitted in with the Department for Transport (DfT) of improvements on high usage stations as part of the 'Access For All' programme. Cheadle Hulme also got a similar footbridge, as did Hazel Grove. Some people opposed the demolition of the footbridge as it was the only bit of the old station left standing, (except of course the platforms!); but if objections had dragged on too long, the funding for the new footbridge may have been lost and the money spent elsewhere. When the new footbridge/lift was mooted there was talk of retaining the old footbridge, but Network Rail felt there was not enough space for two footbridges, which would also add to maintenance costs. Network Rail did however offer to move the old footbridge to a new location. One idea was a footbridge over the canal but it was felt this would be out of place and British Waterways would have rejected the idea as the canal is a Conservation Area. At the same time the idea of a canopy to shelter passengers from the rain was mooted for those passengers who dislike the dismal 'new' waiting room.

When the old Marple station footbridge was about to be removed Network Rail drilled out the original iron rivets and replaced them with steel bolts to make dismantling easier. Work started in mid February 2012 with contractors, Spencer, preparing the foundations for the two new footbridge piers and lift shaft, the work taking place with diggers excavating behind the existing or temporary fencing on each platform. The new reinforced concrete foundations were laid in late February and early March. The concrete towers for the lifts were erected by early April and soon clad in stone. The old footbridge remained in use until mid April, but not for much longer, as on the 15th April the new footbridge span was delivered by road by C&G haulage in the dead of night; the lorry carrying the span backed with some careful manoeuvring into the station yard from Brabyns Brow. Work then commenced on adding the staircases to the new bridge and working on the lifts. The old footbridge was then shorn of its staircases which were stored in the station yard. The old Footbridge was finally dismantled the on the night of 17th June 2012 and lifted on the 18th June 2012 at about 2am in the morning and work was competed by about 3.30am. The new footbridge then came into use but the lifts took a little longer.

The old dismantled footbridge taken on three lorries provided by C&G Transport, Spencer and Ainscough and was delivered at Network Rail expense to Peak Rail at Rowsley South Station. There it now rests, awaiting use as a footbridge to a second platform at Rowsley South when Peak Rail expands to Rowsley Village. Peak Rail have reopened the Matlock–Rowsley section of the Midland Railway Peak Main Line and intend to press further towards Buxton.

The new footbridge and lift finally opened on 24th August 2012 attended by representatives of Network Rail, Northern Rail, the bridge project team, our local MP for Hazel Grove Andrew Stunell and local councillors. The first person to use the lift was Paul Rice! The new footbridge is a great improvement and the lift is a boon to the disabled and those with heavy pushchairs or luggage, though the lift is only available when the station is staffed i.e. 06.15-20.40 Mondays to Fridays, 07.10-21.30 Saturdays but not on Sundays at all. Stone cladding was incorporated to harmonize with existing station and did add to cost but is aesthetically most pleasing. The cost of the Marple footbridge was approximately £1.5 million. The opportunity was taken during the project to install new station toilets for the disabled, install a lower level, diasabled-friendly, ticket office window, tidy up the platform layout and repaint the waiting room exterior.

Friends of Marple Station (FoMS)

The seed that grew into the Friends of Marple Station group derived from a meeting with Craig Wright, formerly a Stockport Councillor, of the Friends of Rose Hill Station group. Craig had been approached by the rail operator about the condition of the waiting room at Marple and was asked whether FoRHS might be able to come up with a few ideas to improve this environment. A meeting was held on 28th February 2013 at 'The Railway' pub next to Rose Hill station with Craig, another local councillor and three members of Marple Civic Society. At this meeting Chris Taylor was given the task of developing some ideas and on 11th April 2013 an on-site meeting was held at the waiting room at Marple station. After this on site meeting it was agreed that the building was in a poor state of disrepair, bleak and was not a welcoming place. If anything it was felt that the condition of the waiting room let the overall ambience of the station down, especially after the investment made in the new footbridge.

In late November 2013, Chris Taylor was commuting to work in Manchester and was sat in the waiting room on a cold and wet winter morning. Whilst reading a free newspaper a big drip from the leaking roof landed on his head. May be it was the so called 'eureka' moment but nonetheless it gave Chris the impetus to say to himself that something needed to be done. Chris became acquainted with Peter Black through the Marple Civic Society and knew of his professional expertise as a town planner specialising in railway projects. So Chris made contact with Peter through the Marple Civic Society and the concept of adopting the station as part of a friends group gathered pace. Peter and Chris had an early morning meeting with the station manager, Theo McLauchlan, on the day the new glass was installed in the ticket office to discuss a Friends of Marple Station group.

Also after going across to Glossop station to get inspiration from an established 'Friends Group' there, Peter and Chris organised the first meeting to gauge the interest in forming a group for Marple station. Chris produced a poster and started a Twitter account and Peter appeared on local radio highlighting the forthcoming meeting. On 30th April 2014, Peter and Chris held their first meeting upstairs at the 'Navigation' pub in Marple. 14 people attended and all were supportive of the idea. Over the following months further meetings followed and membership has grown. The group try to meet on the last Sunday of every month to carry out general maintenance and jobs. They have been given use of the space at the end of the waiting room and welcome new members in their efforts towards making Marple a station that we can all be proud of once more. The group adopted a painting of a tiger that was sited on the cabins at the bottom of the stairs down from Brabyns Brow. They have also installed flower tubs on the platform, and have plans for planters with 'pick your own' edible produce. Ideas to improve the station environment include proposals for various items of artwork, including work by local schools and colleges, the Tiger motif, the history of Marple station and its 150th anniversary, Marple attractions and Miss Marple. The waiting room benches have been refurbished and a waiting room library and even refreshment facilities are planned. The Waitrose 'Community Matters' devoted one of its three token collection boxes for deserving causes at Waitrose Piccadilly over the winter of 2014-15 and this will yield funds to the FoMS. The station waiting room was decked with Christmas decorations in December 2014. Some of the decorations were donated by the author and had belonged to his late father, 'Monty Burton', who opened the new station in 1970! I am sure he would have been 'right chuffed' to know they had been used this way. So all in all Marple station is certainly being improved and brightened up!

The Marple Station Tiger

The FoMS have adopted a brilliant icon of a Tiger for their publicity. It was the work of an up-and-coming Marple art student Dan Lighten and is partly inspired by the work of 'Banksy' who spray-paints art works onto walls all over the world. Dan stencilled the tiger onto a large board about six feet square and sprayed "If removed return to Jungle – or alternative" on the back. He was wondering what to do with it when he got off the train at Marple and saw the Permanent Way cabins in the car park. That was just the place to put the Tiger! He then went in the dead of night with a friend with the tiger on the roof rack of the car. He then screwed the board onto the cabin hoping nobody would see it but it stayed there 4 or 5 years until discovered by the FoMS and embraced as their icon. Posters with the Tiger now adorn the station and Piccadilly and there are plans to hang the original in the waiting room and using a jungle theme. Dan is still pursuing a career in art and some of his canvasses hang for sale in the Cloudberry café in Marple to raise money for his volunteering project in 2015.

Seven Stiles

As a result of local pressure the Seven Stiles footpath was resurfaced and improved between the Peak Forest Canal and Marple station. It has, for as long as I can remember, been narrow and muddy, partly due to seepage of water from the canal. It forms of course an increasingly useful short cut from the growing Ley Hey Park and Winnngton Road housing estates and Marple station. At its other end of course it is a short cut to Rose Hill station. As a boy I regularly used Seven Stiles footpath between Bowden Lane and Marple on my way to school in Manchester via Marple station when the Rose Hill service was less frequent than now-and I do remember four of the original seven stiles surviving as actual stiles into the early 1970's!

Miss Marple

The character of Miss Marple is based on Christie's step grandmother, or her Aunt (Margaret West), and her cronies. Agatha Christie attributed the inspiration for the character of Miss Marple to a number of sources, stating that Miss Marple was "the sort of old lady who would have been rather like some of my step grandmother's Ealing cronies – old ladies whom I have met in so many villages where I have gone to stay as a girl". Christie also used material from her fictional creation, spinster Caroline Sheppard, who appeared in The Murder of Roger Ackroyd.

When Michael Morton adapted the novel for the stage, he replaced the character of Caroline with a young girl. This change saddened Christie and she determined to give old maids a voice so Miss Marple was born. She was to be "a white haired old lady with a gentle appealing manner". From research on the internet, the first known appearance of Miss Jane Marple was from issue 350 of 'The Royal Magazine', December 1927. This contained the first printing of a short story 'The Tuesday Night Club' which later became the first chapter of 'The Thirteen Problems', in 1932. 'The Thirteen Problems' book is sometimes called 'The Tuesday Club Murders' as its name was changed for the USA market when it was published the following year. However Miss Marple's first appearance in a full-length novel was in 'The Murder at the Vicarage' in 1930. There is no definitive source for the derivation of the name 'Marple'. The most common explanation is that the name was taken from Marple railway station, through which Christie passed, or alternatively she stumbled across it when thumbing through the Bradshaw timetable on visits to her sister Madge's home at Abney Hall, Cheadle. Another explanation is that at the time when Agatha Christie was thinking up the name Henry Bradshaw-Isherwood was in residence at Marple Hall and put the majority of the Hall's furniture and contents up for sale at auction. It is believed that Agatha Christie bought a pair of Jacobean chairs from the Marple Hall auction, which is said she kept throughout her life at her home in Torquay. It is hoped that a plaque to Agatha Christie and Miss Marple will be unveiled at Marple station later in 2015. This will make the link between Marple Station and Hall-with Miss Marple. Other ideas for commemorating Miss Marple include artwork featuring the book covers of Agatha Christie's novels featuring Miss Marple along the station fence and silhouette drawings of Miss Marple's head.

3. Strines Station

It is a miracle that Strines survived the Beeching axe and in 1980 had a very good service basically half hourly and formed by the New Mills turnbacks. Since then the service has got worse and more erratic. However usage of the station has increased in leaps and bounds in the last 20 years, increasing sixfold since 1997. And this growth seems set to continue with the recent building of nearly 100 houses on 'Mill Green'-the site of the former Strines Print Works (see Ch XIII. 6) on Train Services 1980-2015. Usage increased nearly 3% in 2013-14 compared with the previous year.

The Friends of Strines Station (FoSS)

FoSS was founded in June 2013, with help and encouragement from the successful Friends of Rose Hill Station. It has been responsible for considerable improvements to the station and car park, making it more attractive to users. At the request of FoSS, Northern Rail installed extra benches on both platforms and these were complemented by metal herb planters, made and donated by Cardiem, a Strines company, and filled with compost donated and delivered by Stewart Milne, the Mill Green developers. The car park was also vastly improved. Old rails had been left to rust in the former station goods yard for years, despite their scrap value, as well as redundant concrete sleepers; this encouraged and helped conceal fly tipping. The scrap rail and rubbish were removed by Network Rail from the carpark area and work began. FoSS requested that some of the Housing Developers' £130,000 Section 106 grant money for local improvements be spent on providing a better surface for the car park, drainage and lighting around the station – the station itself is well lit but the approaches and car park are badly lit if at all. Plans for these improvements are in development with Stockport Council. With the rubbish removed from the car park the FoSS set to work to construct large wooden planters filled with flowers many donated by local residents. A vegetable and herb bed was also created and tomatoes, cucumbers and herbs were harvested in the summer of 2014. Hundreds of flowering bulbs were also planted in the woodland areas by the station and bird boxes installed. Invasive Himalayan Balsam was cleared from the station approach and primroses planted on the banks. With all this voluntary work the environs are now almost a rustic paradise. But more remains to be done, and the FoSS meets several times a year and has regular litter picking and working parties.

Passenger Survey

The FoSS also commissioned a passenger survey of the station from DJS Research Ltd, who have their headquarters in Strines. Some of the key findings emerged were very interesting:

-Half the respondents used the train to get to work, particularly in Manchester, and there are a number of businesses in the Strines area who use the station for links with the wider rail network. Off peak leisure use was however equally important, and some used the station to get to places of education.

-Two fifths of respondents were non-Strines residents, suggesting that some drive to Strines deliberately, perhaps because of its large car parking space. Strines residents were far more likely to use the station for leisure, particularly at weekends.

-Most wanted to see a more frequent service especially in the peak hours; also better trains, improved punctuality and faster journey times.

-The single biggest desired change to the station and its environs was better lighting on the walk up to the station and in the underbridge giving access to and from the up platform, which of course is the one you alight at arriving from Manchester in the evening. This lack of lighting was currently seen as intimidating, particularly for female passengers.

- Other improvements that would be welcomed are electronic timetable displays and CCTV in the car park. These deficiencies were discouraging usage of Strines station, forcing them to use other stations in the area, when Strines was more convenient, or discouraging use of rail altogether.

On the basis of this FoSS plans to continue to work towards long term improvements in trains services and the station environment both by their 'hands-on' approach and engaging with the franchise operator, currently Northern Rail.

'The Railway Children'

There is an Edith Nesbit connection with the station, many locals believing that the station was a source of inspiration for 'The Railway Children'. Some of the descriptions of the landscape in the book are similar to areas near to Strines station. Nesbit's half sister lived at Paradise Farm on Cobden Edge for a time, towards the end of the nineteenth century and Edith visited her there on more than one occasion. Very close to Paradise Farm there is a cottage called 'Three Chimneys' which is the name of the cottage where the family in the 'Railway Children' lived. Passages in the book which describe the view from the cottage and the way down from it to the station are very similar to what you can see from this point on Cobden Edge even today and to the route down to Strines station. E. Nesbit's nephew is the first entry in the baptism register at St. Paul's Church in Strines on 11th November 1880, the church having opened in August of that year.

New Mills Local History Society has published in its notes No. 29 'New Mills and the Edith Nesbit Connection' by Barbara Matthews. This publication includes a Nesbit Trail which can be walked using New Mills and Strines stations. The trail includes locations connected with Nesbit's visits to family and friends in the local area and places which also appear to have inspired some of her other writing (not just 'The Railway Children').

4. Rose Hill Station

After singling of the line in 1980 things chugged along with little change at Rose Hill, with the service much as in 1980. Staffing at the station was progressively reduced so that the ticket office was only staffed for about 3 hours in the morning peak with the clerk leaving by train mid morning to take up a day turn at Romiley. Fortunately this trend has now been reversed. The station car park formed out of the derelict goods yard in the 1970's has on various occasions played host to bus services coming into the station yard to provide road/rail interchange. At present bus services do not come into the station yard and road /rail interchange is at the main Stockport Road bus stops. If re-regulation of bus services takes place it is possible that Rose Hill station yard may again become a road/rail interchange point

The Friends of Rose Hill Station (FoRHS) was formed in on 29th June 2009 to improve the facilities and services at Rose Hill, with six aims featured in its constitution. The Friends regularly meet in the adjacent 'Railway' pub and have work parties on improving and maintaining the station. The founders of the FoRHS were David Sumner, now chairperson, and Craig Wright, until recently Stockport MBC Councillor for the local ward. Membership now stands at 30 with an active core of 10-12 members. Volunteers at Rose Hill have put in over 1,200 man-hours in five years to significantly improve the station environment- and this excludes admin and meetings. The success of the Friends of Rose Hill station has inspired similar groups – the Friends of Marple Station and a similar one for Strines.

FoRHS
Friends of ROSE HILL station

The aims and achievements of the FoRHS to date include:-

1. The promotion of practical environmental enhancement works, especially by volunteers, for the benefit of the community and passengers.

Station gardens have been created and maintained and hanging baskets and platform flower tubs have been installed. A Community Orchard has also been created by the car park with nine trees, which includes two Stockport raised varieties of apple. Six bat/insect/bird nesting boxes have also been specially placed on the station to encourage wild life. Work is also in hand to tidy up and replant the overgrown derelict former up platform, particularly removing the forest of ash saplings on the embankment which have the potential for spreading the 'ash dieback virus'. The station buildings have been spruced up and the canopy repainted. The waiting room, which had been locked for many years and used as a train crew mess room, was refurbished by Northern Rail in about 2007. The Friends have been give permission to adorn it, within reason, and also keys for access to the waiting room and to the store room which has been created by partitioning off a bit of the room, at the end where the ticket window used to be. There the Friends store their high-visibility jackets (supplied by Northern) garden tools, hosepipe etc. There is a book swap in a book case fixed in the alcove next to the old chimney breast. The books are labelled as being part of the FoRHS book swap. People are invited to borrow any number and either pass them on or bring them back; or to donate any of their own. It has been so successful that the bookcase with bookshelves on both sides of the chimney breast are going to have to be replaced. An old GMPTE 'Rose Hill' station sign and one of the Cheshire Best Kept Stations awards were recently been put on display on the wall. There is also now a replica early British Railways style maroon 'totem' station sign on the gable end. The heater in the waiting room is effective, unlike the one at Marple, and people use the room regularly whilst waiting for trains. Having said that, because trains turn back at Rose Hill and are half hourly for much of the day, nobody has to wait long for a train, so some passengers sit on the train, rather than in the waiting room. In recognition of these enhancement works the Friends have received four Cheshire Best Kept Station awards and a Marple Civic Society award.

2. To publicise and raise awareness of the benefits of "green transport plans" and the attractions of the station area and its environs to increase station usage.

The Friends have carried out three passenger number surveys and questionnaires. For the results see page 65.

To raise the profile of the station there has been an imaginative innovation - the introduction of Santa Specials and a Story train to encourage travel for children. The Friends also maintain a website and notice board at the station. A high quality glossy Guide to Five Walks from the Station has been produced in the autumn of 2014 to encourage Green Tourism. Cycle usage to and from the station has also been encouraged; Rose Hill is at an advantage, being on more level terrain than Marple and having no footbridge to negotiate should you wish to take your cycle by train. Rose Hill is on the National Cycle Network Route 55 and in June 2014 a cycle storage shelter in the car park was opened by the Stockport Civic authorities.

3. To encourage community involvement, particularly by young people and schools and colleges in conservation, educational artworks and other creative works.

Two local schools that use the station - Marple Hall School and Rose Hill Primary School - are involved with these community initiatives. Marple Hall School produced an 8 metre long and 1.5 metre high 'Holiday Destinations by Rail' mural for the platform which was unveiled in 2014 by the Mayor of Stockport, our local MP and their Headmaster. Rose Hill Primary School provides a changing art exhibition in the waiting room and has planted roses and trees including a specially named Rosa 'Rose Hill' Hybrid rose. This school's involvement was recognised by another award last year by Cheshire Best Kept Stations. Rose Hill Primary School regularly supplies the waiting room with new paintings by children (usually by years 1, 2 or 3) for the picture frames.

4. To encourage local businesses to improve their own properties and to sponsor environmental enhancements at the station area.

The Vernon Building Society and Manchester Airport Group have grant-aided the community orchard and major garden works. Donations in kind from a local paint supplier, builders' merchant and garden centre have been received and one of our next projects will be to produce another mural, in conjunction with Marple Hall High School, on a blank concrete panel fence in the station car park in partnership with Josh Robinson Civil Engineers (the owner of the panel fence).

5. To Campaign for improved train services and infrastructure facilities.

An outstanding achievement was the diversion of one of the three Marple services to Rose Hill from 12th December 2010, giving Rose Hill a half hourly service during the day and giving a better spread of services between the two stations. This has resulted in a substantial increase in passenger usage which continues year on year (for figures see 5. 'Train Services 1980-2015'). The bulk of Rose Hill's passenger growth has been off peak-the car park is about one third full at 8.30 am but filling up as the morning progresses. One of the anomalies of privatisation is that various bits of land which are not operational or leased out by Network Rail can fall into limbo or be sold off inappropriately. One such piece of land was a piece bounded by Stockport Road, 'The Railway' pub, the station and the station car park, which had become and remains an overgrown eyesore. This was sold in December 2007 to a potential developer when it could have been used to extend the station car park.

The Friends attended meetings with Northern Rail and Transport for Greater Manchester (TfGM) to press the case for a Sunday service and better evening service. One improvement resulting has been the installation of CCTV, passenger information screens, a new accessible booking office facility and a member of staff who opens the office from 06.00 until 12.50 Monday to Friday. These improvements, aided by an enthusiastic and welcoming 'stationmaster' (Tony Tweedie) have contributed to the big increase in passenger numbers. Many other comparable stations are totally unstaffed. Though strictly speaking employed to man the ticket office, Tony carries out many duties beyond the norm, such as tidying the station in the morning and has a foliage plant that he looks after in the waiting room. Regular cleaning however at Rose Hill, as at Marple, is carried out by contractors, the cleaning company ISS.

6. To work in partnership with ALL stakeholders to achieve these aims.

The Friends are in regular contact with the Northern Rail Station Manager and Client & Stakeholder Manager, Network Rail, Stockport Metropolitan Borough Council's rail officer, the Goyt Valley Rail Users Association, the South East Manchester Community Rail Partnership (SEMCoRP) and other 'Friends' groups in and around Greater Manchester. Local groups including schools, Civic Society, Marple Festivals and businesses all support efforts to improve the station facilities and train service. The Friends also participate in Marple Carnival's Car Boot sales in the Station car park to raise funds.

However there is much that could still be done to improve the station in addition to those mentioned above These include better trains than the hated 'Pacers' and more capacity at peak times, and trains that do not discharge toilets when standing at the station. Now that there is CCTV coverage the unsightly concrete barriers at the car park entrance and exits could be removed. The station should also be made more visible from the main road with a notice board at the top of the ramp. On the station platform there is a high step and gap that needs to be rectified. The white line platform edging is also in need of renovation. The franchise parameters for prospective bidders for the Northern franchise set out in March 2015 by Rail North do not specify a Sunday service for Rose Hill nor any detail of enhanced evening services. So there is still much for the FoRHS to do!

5. Privatisation and Franchises GMPTE and TfGM

Greater Manchester Passenger Transport Executive (GMPTE) was formed in 1974 and lasted as the operational arm of transport authority in the Greater Manchester area, GMPTA, until 1 April 2011. From that date it became Transport for Greater Manchester (TfGM), the operational arm of the new Greater Manchester Combined Authority through its joint transport committee, TfGMC. This continues to co-ordinate transport for Greater Manchester including the Marple and Rose Hill lines.

Divisions and Regions

Up to the mid 1980s British Rail had been operated and managed geographically, with the Marple area in the Manchester Division of the London Midland Region. But from 1982 to the mid-1990s the geographical structure of BR was gradually abolished, with the Divisions going quite quickly between 1982 and 1985 and the Regions lingered on until the early 1990s. The system was 'sectorised' into business sectors. The passenger sectors were Inter-City (express services), Network South East (London commuter services) and Regional Railways (regional services). Trainload Freight took trainload freight, Railfreight Distribution took wagon load freight, Freightliner took intermodal traffic and Rail Express Systems took parcels traffic. Passenger services in the Manchester area became part of the Regional Railways sector with the local brand 'Network North West'. Things began to look up and had sectorisation been allowed to continue under the nationalized British Rail umbrella, it would have perhaps been more successful and less bureaucratic than privatisation. The Hazel Grove chord and the vastly improved Manchester –Sheffield express service and through Hope Valley local service via Marple were results of sectorisation.

Privatisation

Even the controversial Margaret Thatcher, divisive in life, divisive in death, the architect of privatisation of public services, did not attempt the to move the railways out of public ownership, though many peripheral activities, such as hotels and shipping services, were sold off in the mid 1980's. Her ill-judged quasi state funeral in 2014 was a waste of public money in a time of recession and an insult to the North of England, Wales, Scotland and Ireland. It was left to another Tory Prime Minister, John Major, who despite his other positive achievements and other affairs, to decide on the folly of privatising the railways which came into effect on All Fools Day-1st April 1994, to take over British Rail's entire operational infrastructure. (In case the reader accuses the author of political bias the Labour Minister of Transport Barbara Castle sanctioned the closure of about 2,500 miles of railway including the Stockport Tiviot Dale line and the Chinley-Matlock line, and the closure of the Hayfield and Macclesfield lines were sanctioned by another Labour Minister, Richard Marsh).

Unlike the pre 1948 private railway companies. which were geographical and integrated ownership, the new system was different. The physical assets such as track, stations, structures and land were vested in a private company 'Railtrack'. Any land deemed surplus to requirements was placed in a body known as British Rail Board Residuary (BRBR) with the remit to dispose of all such land. One piece of land placed with BRBR was the former entrance to the goods yard at Rose Hill station-see the Rose Hill section. BRBR has now ceased to exist, its assets going to Network Rail. However its demise left some land and structures in limbo, unclear who owns or is responsible for them. Railtrack got into financial difficulties and went into voluntary liquidation on 18th October 2002. As a result a government body, Network Rail, was formed to take over its functions; Network Rail is a Government body so the Railways have been partially re-nationalised after a fashion. Network Rail leases the station to the Train Operators for the duration of their franchise, but not the land; so at Rose Hill Network Rail lease the station and its buildings to Northern Rail but not Pearson's Coal Yard in the former goods yard.

Regulation

The Rail Regulator, the statutory officer at the head of the Office of the Rail Regulator (ORR), was established to regulate the railway industry, to prevent monopoly, and to enforce consumer protection conditions of operators' licences. He did this through his powers to supervise and control the usage of capacity of railway facilities such as railway routes and stations. His approval was needed before an access contract for the use of track, stations or certain maintenance facilities could be valid. He was to enforce domestic competition law, to issue, modify and enforce operating licences and to supervise the development of certain industry-wide codes, the most important of which is the network code. Probably the Rail Regulator's most significant power was the establishment, usually every five years, of the financial framework in which Railtrack (now Network Rail) operates, through the carrying out reviews of access charges. This settled the structure and level of access charges which the infrastructure provider is entitled to charge train operators for the operation, maintenance, renewal and enhancement of the national railway network. ORR's role only covered economic regulation; safety regulation remained the responsibility of the Health and Safety Executive, but that position changed in 2005 when safety regulation was transferred to ORR. The ORR became the Office of Rail & Road from the 1st April 2015. All British Rail's passenger coaches, locomotives, and multiple units were allocated to three Rolling Stock Leasing Companies (ROSCOs)-Porterbrook, Angel Trains and Eversholt Rail Group. Freight locomotives and wagons were owned by the freight train operators. British Rail Infrastructure Services (BRIS) took responsibility for the engineering requirements of the railway. BRIS was subsequently organised for privatisation on the basis of seven Infrastructure Maintenance Units, which maintained the railway tracks, and six Track Renewal Units, which undertook track renewals, both organised geographically. In 2004 infrastructure maintenance (Track, Signalling, and Electric Overhead wires), was taken back 'in-house' by Network Rail, but track renewal remains contracted out to the private sector.

Franchises

Train operating is subsidised by the Government via the Department for Transport. The 25 initial actual Franchises for operating of trains and stations were awarded to train operating companies (TOCs) between February 1996 and March 1997 by the Director of Passenger Rail Franchising. The franchises were generally for a set period but there has been a kaleidoscopic situation with franchises frequently changing hands and the areas and lines covered by a franchise also changing. Very few of the original 1990's franchises still operate what was originally allocated in the 90s. Some franchises have been awarded to competitors with railways including bus operators such as Stagecoach and National Express, and some franchises have gone to the wall or have been abandoned due to financial difficulties. Others have been awarded to foreign or multi-national companies.

A more Byzantine and labyrinthine system would be hard to devise, which is not helped by an unsympathetic London–centric Civil Service. While there have been many improvements and greater emphasis on customer care and commercially viable operating in some areas. Passenger usage of rail travel nationally has also grown a massive 62% between 1998 and 2011-much higher than in other European countries. In fact rail travel has more than doubled nationally since 1980. Northern Rail has seen a 47% increase in passenger usage in the last ten years, though growth on other services in the Manchester area has been higher. But on the other hand that growth may have happened any way with the increase in road congestion and fuel prices and in many ways the nationalized British Rail was moving rapidly in a positive direction in the 80's and early 90's. Critics of privatisation have pointed out that passenger numbers started rising 18 months before the privatisation process began, as the economy started recovering from the recession of the early 1990s.

On the negative side there has been a fragmentation of the network and lack of co-operation between franchises; and the sometimes frequent changes of franchise and franchises getting into financial difficulty has led to instability and an understandable reluctance for long term investment and planning in some areas. On the East Coast Main Line the franchise was for some years held by GNER (Great North Eastern Railway) which had to pull out, despite offering an excellent service to the public and being increasingly profitable, due to its parent company, Sea Containers, getting into financial difficulty. It then passed to National Express which also lost the franchise due to financial difficulties. The franchise was then passed to East Coast and effectively temporarily re-nationalized and run by the Government.

East Coast currently ran a good and profitable service which actually contributed to Treasury funds. Despite this the Tory Government was hell-bent on returning the franchise to private hands, and the franchise passed out of state hands in March 2015 into a consortium headed by Virgin but with the bulk in the hands of Stagecoach. As one of the alleged benefits of privatisation is competition, it seems a little perverse that Virgin, who operate the Anglo-Scottish West Coast Main Line and airlines will also be operating the rival East Coast Main Line!

Also one of the results of privatisation is that in places the system has been set in stone, with a reluctance to close little used stations or lines-so called 'grandfather' services, so called because they have been inherited from the past. A bizarre local example of this is the Stockport – Stalybridge service which has one train a week (one-way) on a Friday! On the other hand there is a commendable reluctance to close anything as it might be needed in the future.

Franchises in the Marple Area

Under the 1994 privatisation plans for Britain's railways Network North West was let as a single franchise from 2nd March 1997 to Great Western Holdings who marketed the services under the brand name 'North Western Trains'(NWT). The trains were painted dark blue with large gold stars at the ends of each carriage. On 2nd March 1998 First Group bought out the other shareholders in Great Western Holdings and NWT was re-branded First North Western.

In 2000 the Strategic Rail Authority decided on a re-shaping of the franchise map for Northern England. First North Western and Arriva Trains Northern were to be combined. A new Trans Pennine Express franchise was created to run fast inter-urban services and any services into Wales were transferred to the Wales & Borders franchise. The new combined franchise, known as Northern Rail, was awarded to a consortium of Serco and Abellio (NS - Dutch State Railways) from 12 December 2004.

The seven-year Northern Rail franchise was due to end in September 2011 but in May 2010 Department for Transport (DfT) announced that, as Northern had met performance targets in the previous year their franchise would be extended by two years to Sept 2013. Following the franchising hiatus in 2012 after DfT mishandled the West Coast Main Line re-franchising, costing the taxpayer many millions of pounds, Northern Rail was given a further six month extension until 31 Mar 2014. The revised DfT re-franchise programme then moved the end of the Northern franchise once again, this time to 1st April 2016, thus turning the original seven-year franchise into a 12-year franchise. The Invitation to Tender for the new franchise was issued in March 2015. In September 2014 it was announced that the three shortlisted bidders would be Abellio (Dutch State Railways), Arriva (Deutsche Bahn) and Govia (in which the French SNCF have a stake).

The new franchise will be awarded before the end of 2015, to commence on 1st April 2016 for 9 years, with the option to extend by one year. A new body, Rail North, has issued a prescriptive paper for bidders which sets out exactly what they must do to win the franchise. This includes replacement of all the pacers by 2020, a fund for significant station improvements and many train service improvements. But not included is an improved evening service for either line or a Sunday service for Rose Hill or the Hyde Loop.

Consultation was invited from interested parties for the re-franchising process. Feedback has included the following points

-The peak hour service needs a comprehensive review. Peak time gaps in the service discourage commuters from using rail. A late evening service needs reviving, for commuters working late or travelling back from a distance.

-A better evening and Sunday service is required especially at Rose Hill, which has no Sunday service at all.

-Strines station has shown remarkable passenger growth and needs a better service; it is suggested it should have an hourly off peak service and a better morning and evening peak hour service.

-The trains in use are life expired, sub standard and uncomfortable. A passenger survey conducted in May 2014 noted a surprising percentage in favour of higher fares in return for improved or new rolling stock (38% yes, 47% no, 8% unsure). The public are content with the half hourly off peak service (82%) and speed of service (62%).

-Reducing calls at the presently lightly used stations will not lead to any significant improvement in journey times. Passengers value a reliable, punctual, clean comfortable service rather than faster journey times.

-The maintenance of a staffed ticket office and waiting room at least at present levels is essential and Strines needs a better train service and facilities, particularly lighting in and on the approaches to the station.

-The new franchisee should make small annual grants up to £1,000 available to Friends groups to encourage the sprucing up of new and existing stations.

- Revenue protection on trains is poor. Too many passengers on short journeys evade paying, particularly on short journeys e.g. between Brinnington and Reddish. It is necessary for the Train Operator to improve revenue collection which would also reduce the deficit on the service. Northern has recently extended higher peak hour fares to the afternoon period. If they were to collect the revenue that is lost by ticketless travel, they might not have to introduce this unpopular measure which has actually led to a decline in travel. The Department for Transport recently published a report to put a figure on 'Ticketless Travel'. This showed that it is much larger than had been previously thought. Despite a lack of co-operation by guards, the comprehensive survey found that, over the whole of Northern Rail, ticketless travel amounted to between 6.6% and 11.5% of revenue, equating to between £16.5m and £30.4m loss of revenue. Worse were the findings in the South Manchester area, which includes the Marple and Rose Hill lines and it is the worst area on Northern for this problem, where ticketless travel is estimated at between 11.1% (=£4.3m) and 19.1% (=£8.1m) of revenue. This has resulted in franchise bidders being asked to put forward proposals for Driver Control Operation (DCO) in which the driver controls door opening and closing, at present done by the guard, leaving the guards to spend all their time checking and issuing tickets and on passenger welfare duties. This system works well on Glasgow suburban trains. Not only is revenue protection superior but station dwell times are reduced as passengers no longer have to wait for the guard to release the doors leading to improved punctuality. Guards are certain to resist this change, but the railways cannot continue to lose millions because guards are unwilling or unable, due to overcrowding, to check and issue tickets. The problem is compounded by the lack of ticket collection or checks at most stations except erratically at Piccadilly.

This reminds me of my time as a management trainee in the North East in the late 1970's. There was a dispute over the introduction of Paytrains which involved the guard collecting fares at stations where ticket office staff had been withdrawn. The dispute dragged on for some time but when resolved a guard asked a lady in the Hartlepool area to pay the fare. She indignantly refused at first saying "Don't be ridiculous-these trains are free!" Northern Rail please note!

6. Train Services 1980-2015

The early 1980s

The late 1970's Timetable serving Marple and Rose Hill is described in Chapter XII and this basic pattern was of, roughly, one off-peak train to and from Rose Hill via Guide Bridge (Mondays to Saturdays), with an evening but no Sunday service. The Rose Hill evening service was whittled away so that by 1982 the last but one train from Manchester was 19.30 followed by an odd final working at 23.02 from Manchester Oxford Road to Rose Hill, presumably for late night revellers! This late night service was discontinued from October 1991with the last departure from Manchester for Rose Hill was at 18.53 and even earlier on a Saturday.

Marple was served by 2 trains an hour off peak via Bredbury and terminating at New Mills Central. The occasional peak hour train went via Guide Bridge or turned back at Marple. Passing through Marple hourly were the Manchester-Sheffield fast trains, some stopping at New Mills Central to connect with rather infrequent Hope Valley stoppers. Most of the fast Sheffield trains continued to Hull with a few serving Cleethorpes. One or two peak hour fast trains continued to call at Marple until the opening of the Hazel Grove Chord. From 1983 the Manchester-Harwich Parkeston Quay, still loco hauled, was extended to start back from Edinburgh and Glasgow instead of Manchester Piccadilly, via the West Coast Main Line, Manchester Victoria, the Midland Junction line from Miles Platting to Ashburys and via Marple. There was also a train from Barrow in Furness and another from Glasgow/Edinburgh to Nottingham, both via the same route, and with balancing workings.

The Hazel Grove Chord

The Disley Tunnel route had been threatened with closure to make for a motorway in the late 1970's but by the early 1980's rail traffic was increasing and British Rail, with its new 'sectorised' structure wanted to introduce new services, one route being the Manchester-Sheffield route. Such has been the growth on this route that the Hope Valley line is now in 2015 running almost at full capacity with the existing signalling. The route through Marple, as in the late 19th C, was congested and slow, due to the heavy engineering works and sinuous route between Romiley and New Mills South Junction. The Buxton line had been electrified from Stockport to Hazel Grove 1st June 1981. It was then decided to build a single track high speed link between the LNW Stockport-Buxton line to the Midland Railway 'New Line' just east of Hazel Grove station from Hazel Grove East Junction on the Buxton line to Hazel Grove High Level Junction on the Midland route. This meant that express trains could avoid the Marple route, going instead straight onto the Midland New Line and through Disley Tunnel and Hazel Grove to Stockport Edgeley. This also meant the new Liverpool-East Anglia service could enter the through platforms at Manchester Piccadilly without crossing all the approach line to Piccadilly which they would have to have done if they had used the Marple route. The new services could also serve Stockport and open up new connectional opportunities. The Hazel Grove Chord was opened on 29 April 1986 by the Bishop of Chester, Michael Baughen. The first train to cut the ribbon was the short-lived Sprinter 151 002.

With the opening of the Chord the Manchester–Sheffield service was recast from Monday 12th May 1986 with the hourly express trains on the Manchester-Sheffield route diverted away from the Marple route to call at Stockport Edgeley and run via Hazel Grove, the new Chord and Disley tunnel to rejoin the route via Marple at New Mills South Junction, thus avoiding Marple. One Liverpool-Sheffield evening peak train continued to call at Marple replaced in the late 1980s by a 17.35 Oxford Road to Chinley semi-fast calling at Marple. The service was hourly for most of the day with alternate trains running on a completely new axis from Liverpool Lime Street to East Anglia and on the Manchester-Hull/Cleethorpes axis, both services being roughly once every two hours, to give an hourly Manchester –Sheffield express service. The new services were to East Anglia were mainly operated by the new class 150 and 151 'Sprinters', while the services to Hull and Cleethorpes were operated by class 31/4 diesel locos hauling rakes of Mark 2 coaches with the odd Mark I thrown in. By the early 90's the fast service was concentrated on the Livepool-East Anglia axis, with some workings to the new 1991 Stanstead Airport station. But in 1992 some of the Hope Valley stoppers were extended to Doncaster and Cleethorpes; this became a fast Manchester-Cleethorpes service via the Hazel Grove Chord in 1993. There were some even more exotic through services which had previously passed through Marple, These included: 'The European' from Edinburgh and Glasgow via the West Coast main line, Manchester Victoria, Stockport, Sheffield and Nottingham to Harwich Parkeston Quay, the 'North West Dane' from Blackpool North to Harwich, and a service from Glasgow and Edinburgh to Nottingham, both following the same route as 'The European'. There was also a service from Manchester Piccadilly to Norwich.

All of these of these had balancing return workings. Other named trains using the route in the late 80s included the 'Rhinelander' between Manchester and Harwich, and 'The Loreley' between Liverpool and Harwich. These too were loco-hauled with air conditioned Mark 2 coaches with a Mark 1 buffet car. Gradually however the naming of trains on this cross country axis went out of fashion, as class 156 Super Sprinters replaced loco hauled trains from May 1988 onwards. These in turn were replaced by the new class 158 Sprinters. Prior to the opening of the Hazel Grove Chord workings such as these had passed through Marple. Later with the opening of Manchester Airport station in 1993 further journey opportunities have been created with an hourly Manchester Airport-Cleethorpes service currently operating, reversing at Manchester Piccadilly and using the Hazel Grove Chord. All the services via the Hazel Grove Chord, which also include some freight trains, pass through the southern end of the Marple area via Disley Tunnel.

At the same time from May 1986 the Manchester –Sheffield Hope Valley stopping service was recast with the previous arrangement of two separate services operating in and out of New Mills from Manchester and Sheffield replaced by a through stopping train between Manchester and Sheffield calling at all stations via Bredbury and Marple except Ardwick every two hours, with an hourly service in the peak hours, thus finally recreating direct services from Marple to the Hope Valley and Sheffield. Gradually these Hope Valley trains have started running non stop to Reddish and began to omit Strines. So Marple from 1996 was still basically served by 2 trains an hour to New Mills Central with one every two hours going on to Sheffield. One oddity remained in the evening peak when the 17.38 from Liverpool Lime Street to Sheffield called at Romiley, Marple (17.58), New Mills, Chinley and Hathersage to give these places a fast commuter service. In the morning a similar working, the 05.23 Hull to Liverpool called at the same places including Marple at 07.51 to give a Manchester arrival of 08.10.

Manchester Victoria

During the West Coast Main Line upgrade of 1998-9 Marple trains were diverted in late 1998 to Manchester Victoria via Ashburys, the 'Midland Junction' line and Miles Platting to relieve congestion at Manchester Piccadilly. It took 25 minutes from Ashburys to Victoria plus the time from Marple to Ashburys, giving an overall journey time of about 45 minutes. However some commuters preferred Victoria as a terminal as being more central to the business district of Manchester compared to Piccadilly. But a far cry from the pre First World War 20 minutes non stop timings to Victoria! There has been talk of diverting Marple trains permanently into Manchester Victoria as Manchester Piccadilly and its approaches are running at nearly full capacity, and if HS2 is ever built, platform space will be at a premium, even with adding two extra through platforms next to platforms 13 & 14 and proposed new ones north of the present station on the site of the old goods depot, an area now occupied by huts. While some might welcome services to Victoria, being nearer the business and shopping districts of Manchester, others would not and main line connections would be lost and journey times extended.

The Marple 'Fast' Service and Rose Hill Improvements

When North Western Trains won the Regional Railways NW franchise in 1997, they bid to run about 4 trains a day from Rochdale to Euston via Victoria & Newton-le-Willows and from Manchester Airport to Euston via Crewe. These services were introduced in May 1998, and were promoted on high levels of customer service and low fares. Journey time was slow because they had poor paths on the West Coast Main Line. Consequently passenger usage was poor. After First Group took over, they quickly realised these trains were a financial black hole and negotiated their way out of running them with GMPTE. Because these were franchise commitments they had to offer something else in return, and the hourly fast trains to Marple were part of the deal - I suspect at the behest of GMPTE who had an aspiration to run four trains per hour to Marple. In May 2000 the Euston services were discontinued and were replaced by an additional off peak fast service to Marple via Bredbury and calling only at Romiley; some took as little as 17 minutes from Manchester. But the return service was usually semi-fast calling at all stations to Reddish and taking correspondingly longer. During this period when Marple had three trains an hour and Rose Hill only one. A sample taken from the winter timetable of 2006-7 was as follows: Marple had 47 services to and from Manchester Mondays to Fridays and 42 on Saturdays, all via Bredbury.

The fastest time on the 'fast' trains was 22 minutes to Manchester, only running non stop from Reddish. From Manchester the 'fast' trains were first stop Romiley and taking a creditable 20 minutes. The fastest peak hour train to Manchester was the 08.10 from Marple calling only at Romiley, but taking 23 minutes! The fastest train from Manchester was the 17.45 which stopped only at Bredbury and Romiley and took a very creditable 17 minutes. The Sunday service was roughly two hourly, formed of Hope Valley stoppers, with 7 to and 8 from Manchester. However the total of 94 services calling Marple, while an improvement on what had gone before, was still below the high water mark of 109 in August 1898, but higher than 87 in 1910. To be fair though this was the best ever service to Manchester Piccadilly. The service consisted of one train an hour being formed by a New Mills/Sheffield train on alternate hours and the rest turning back at Marple - never would one of the bay platforms have been more useful! Strines had a relatively sparse service outside the peaks with one train each way every two hours. This high level of service to Marple only lasted a few years however with the diversion of one train an hour to Rose Hill in 2010.

In 2006-07 Rose Hill had 19 services to Manchester Mondays-Fridays and 14 Saturdays, and 17 services from Manchester Monday to Fridays and 13 Saturdays. The imbalance between services to and from Manchester is because some early morning services ran empty to Rose Hill for the early morning trains. The last train from Manchester was 20.27 and all were routed via Guide Bridge. There was no Sunday service to Rose Hill. However from 12th December 2010 the fast train to Marple was diverted to Rose Hill, under pressure on Northern from the Friends of Rose Hill station, formed in June 2009. This gave a much better spread of services and both Marple and Rose Hill a half hourly service. At first these Rose Hill trains alternated via the Guide Bridge route taking about 32 minutes to Manchester and semi fast via Bredbury taking only 24 minutes; from Manchester alternate trains ran via Guide Bridge taking about 29 minutes to Rose Hill and the other non stop via Bredbury and taking only 20 minutes. Marple was left with a fast train (to Sheffield) via Bredbury taking about 21 minutes from Manchester and a stopping train via Bredbury taking about 24 minutes. The same pattern operated to Manchester with similar timings. This service pattern however soon began to disintegrate with timetable changes leaving the very messy service currently operating.

Marple Timetables as at 17th May 2015

Currently the Fast Manchester – Sheffield services operate via Stockport Edgeley, the Hazel Grove chord and Disley Tunnel, thus avoiding Marple. The service is basically half hourly with one train operated by First Trans Pennine Express between Manchester Airport and Cleethorpes, and the other operated by East Midlands Trains on the Liverpool to Norwich axis, though the evening trains only operate as far as Nottingham. The Sunday service of course is not so frequent.

Currently the services serving Marple and Rose Hill are all operated by Northern. The fastest trains serving Marple are generally the Hope Valley stopping trains to and from Sheffield which are non stop to and from Reddish and then all stations; Monday to Friday they omit Strines but alternate trains call on Saturdays -the first of the many anomalies between the Monday-Friday and Saturday services on the line!

Marple has 39 trains from and 38 to Manchester Piccadilly Monday to Friday. The first service from Manchester is at 06.21 and the last at 23.24. Off peak the trains are at 14 and 49 minutes past the hour giving a roughly half hourly service-the train at 49 minutes past the hour is the semi-fast to Sheffield. All trains Monday to Friday are routed via Bredbury and alternate ones off peak terminate at New Mills Central. This is supplemented in the peak by 6 Marple turn backs. This pattern is repeated in the reverse direction to Manchester. The fastest trains at around 21 minutes are the Sheffield trains, matched by the 17.17 from Manchester. Paradoxically THE fastest train of the day is against the predominant commuter flow being the 07.54 Manchester-Marple calling at Romiley only and taking 16 minutes. To Manchester Monday to Friday the first train is at 06.17 and the last at 23.36 again all via Bredbury. Trains from Marple are generally at 09 (the Sheffield semi fast) and 36 minutes past the hour, again giving a roughly half hourly service. The fastest times to Manchester are slightly slower than from Manchester with the Sheffield trains taking about 25 minutes such as the 08.10 (train from Sheffield calling at Romiley only) from Marple. However customer research indicates that fast journey time and number of stops is in fact less important to many passengers than punctuality, reliability and getting a seat.

On Saturdays the pattern is completely different with 30 trains each way, due to the lower demand for peak hour commuter trains. The Sheffield trains run hourly semi-fast via Bredbury and take 20-25 minutes There are no New Mills turnbacks on Saturdays, with alternate trains from Manchester being routed via Guide Bridge and turning back at Marple. Bizarrely these trains return via Bredbury giving a completely imbalanced service. The Sunday service is much more limited with 12 trains from and 11 to Manchester in summer – roughly hourly-but only 8 to and 9 from Manchester in winter, all semi fast via Bredbury and all calling at Strines. These are Hope Valley stoppers and the summer/winter imbalance reflects the fact that they serve leisure users such as ramblers and hikers. In the period leading up to Christmas 2014 Northern operated three extra trains for shoppers from Marple to Manchester via Bredbury and five return trains. This was necessary as overcrowding was so severe on trains into Manchester that passengers boarding after Bredbury could not physically get on the trains. This augurs well for a general improvement in Sunday services. But the Marple line has a very poor Sunday service compared with the half hourly Hadfield/Glossop service. Hazel Grove has a half hourly Sunday service with one train an hour continuing to Buxton; of these, nine each way call at Middlewood giving this remote station the best Sunday service in the area!

Rose Hill now has in many ways the best service ever, with 27 trains *to* and 26 *from* Manchester Mondays to Fridays and 26 *to* and 25 *from* Manchester on Saturdays. The imbalance is due to some trains running empty to Rose Hill in the morning peak. But there is no Sunday service and very little service after the evening peak with the last train from Manchester at 20.35 returning at 21.11. There is however a good morning service with the first train (which comes in empty stock) at 06.30 to Manchester Monday to Friday. There is even inbound commuter traffic at Rose Hill with students arriving by train to colleges in Marple.

All Monday to Friday trains are routed via Guide Bridge and consequently take longer than those from Marple with timings varying, depending on stops, from 27 to 34 minutes from Manchester. The fastest train from Manchester again, against the commuter flow, is the 08.07 from Manchester which takes only 25 minutes via Guide Bridge. It then forms the 08.35 to Manchester via Bredbury also taking only 25 minutes. Off peak trains from Manchester are at 05 and 34 minutes past the hour again roughly half hourly. To Manchester off peak trains are exactly half hourly at 23 and 53 minutes past the hour from Rose Hill and take 31-33 minutes. On Saturdays however the Rose Hill trains are routed via Guide Bridge to Manchester but via Bredbury from Manchester, though they are only slightly quicker via Bredbury at 27 minutes due to stops. This imbalance of course reflects the unbalanced nature of the Marple service on a Saturday and is equally bizarre!

Strines is served mainly by the New Mills turnbacks Monday to Friday but because these do not operate on Saturdays, it is served on Saturdays by the Sheffield trains, giving a faster service. Strines has 14 trains to and 13 from Manchester Monday to Friday. On Saturdays it has 11 to and 10 from Manchester. Strines has quite a good commuter peak service but only every 2 hours off peak, except paradoxically in the very late evening with 3 trains each way-far better than Rose Hill for late night revellers! Strines has a Sunday service identical to that provided to Marple.

Marple is staffed with a ticket office 06.15-20.40 Mondays to Fridays, 07.10-21.30 Saturdays and Rose Hill is staffed 06.00-

The figures are:-

Station	population	population
	0 to 0.8 km from station	0.8 to 2 km from station
Marple	3547	19185
Rose Hill	6758	17641
Strines	176	1286

12.50 Monday to Friday; Strines and Middlewwood are unstaffed. In recent years ticket collection has ceased but it is possible to book tickets to anywhere in the country.

British trains, unlike their continental counterparts, do tend to have slightly differing Weekday and Saturday services but this is taken to rather ridiculous extremes on the current Marple, Strines and Rose Hill services! Northern has not really got to grips with equalizing the routing of the Monday to Friday and Saturday services to Marple and Rose Hill leading to the ridiculous imbalances described. There are unlikely to be any major recast of the Marple and Rose Hill timetable until the new franchise is awarded in April 2016. However the Marple route needs constant maintenance and major repairs were undertaken to Marple Goyt Viaduct near the Roman Lakes in 2014-15.

Passenger Usage and Population Figures

2013 -14 figures produced for the ORR (Office of Rail Regulation) show usage figures as follows with percentage increase since 2012-13. Marple with 475,192 passengers - an amazing 8.5% increase. This compares with 221,306 in 1997-8. The main growth has taken place in the first years of the 21st century from 253,476 in 2002-3 (the last year of the First North

Western franchise) to 426,684 in 2008-9. There have been fluctuations in that period but the trend has been inexorably upwards, with passenger numbers all but doubling in the last fifteen years. Train services at Marple are generally more regular and frequent to Manchester Piccadilly (formerly London Road) than in the pre war years. With a total Monday to Friday service of 77 trains calling in August 2014 this compares favourably with the LNER 63 services to and from London Road in July 1938, but that was of course supplemented by 32 LMS services, giving 95 in total, And neither of these compare with the pre First World War figures of a total of 87 in 1910 and 109 in 1898.

Marple is no longer served by main line trains to London and other long distance destinations as it was in the past, nor has the luxury of services to three different Manchester termini-London Road, Central and Victoria. Nor does the volume of freight pass through as in the past. But Marple has emerged from the Beeching era with a relatively heavily used station, a secure future and a more regular service throughout the day to Manchester. If only the Stockport line had not been closed though!

The picture at Rose Hill is equally buoyant rising from 60,187 passengers a year in 1997-8 to 97,780 in 2008-9 (the year the Friends of Rose Hill Station were formed), up again to 136,116 in 2012-13 and up a staggering 16.2% to 158,066 in 2013-4. Usage has therefore more than doubled in the last fifteen years partly due to the half hourly off peak service introduced in December 2010. The Rose Hill service has increased by leaps and bounds - only 18 services calling each way in 1910; 34 in 1938 and now 53 in August 2014! This of course reflects the enormous increase in suburban development in the vicinity and also the doubling of the off peak service to half hourly due to pressure from the Friends of Rose Hill Station. In fact in the five years since the FoRHS were formed in 2009 passenger usage has increased by 75% - the future here appears rosy!

Strines has rarely had a frequent a service and its service today compares favourably with the past, and given its remote location, Strines was lucky to survive. Given the recent housing developments in the area its future too seems secure. Strines has shown even more dramatic growth from 3,431 passengers in 1997-8 to 6,284 in 2006-07, 10,604 in 2010-11 and doubling again in just two years to 21,728 in 2013-14- 2.9% growth since 2012-13. So usage at Strines has increased approximately six-fold in the last 15 years. The twofold increase in the last two years or so is undoubtedly due to the building of nearly 100 houses on the former Strines Mill site, 'Mill Green', which is very near the station.

The actual figures for all stations are probably higher due to 'ticketless travel'. If this were taken into account and growth continues, usage at Marple seems set to break the half million mark soon! There are 2537 stations in 2013-14 operated by the mainline (Network Rail) railway and therefore does not include stations on London Underground and on Heritage Railways. With regards rankings in station usage (based on total entries and exits in 2013-14) Marple, and Rose Hill (Marple) and Strines are ranked 886th, 1,460th and 2,167th respectively. Middlewood has also shown a dramatic increase in passengers, despite its remote location, from 9,923 in 1998-9 to 25,572 in 2012-13. Romiley had 318,916 passengers in 2013-14 up 7.8% and New Mills Central 213,648, up 4.4%.

This means Marple is in the top third busiest stations in Great Britain! This compares with Manchester Piccadilly with 24,476,181-the 12th busiest station in Great Britain behind Birmingham New St at over 34 million, Leeds at nearly 28 million and Glasgow Central over 27 million and the busiest in the country, London Waterloo with 98,442,724 passengers. The least busy in our area with just 26 passengers a year was Reddish South (3rd from bottom) and Denton with only 110 (10th from bottom); but this is nothing short of miraculous as only one train a week calls at Reddish South and Denton on a Friday in one direction only from Stockport to Stalybridge! At least they are ahead of the quietest station in the country – Teesside Airport with 8 passengers in the whole year!

The growth of rail usage is very encouraging and is partly due to the increase in new housing in the area - Strines is a case in point. But it is also due to increasing road congestion and rising petrol prices, making rail travel more attractive. Much of the growth is in off-peak travel; is to be hoped that Northern's recent change in ticketing by which journeys made after 16.00 are no longer at the cheaper off peak fares does not discourage this growth. This foolhardy move also means that if you set off from e.g. Bolton and have to change onto a train leaving after 16.00 you are stung for the full fare!

There are more stations now between Marple and Manchester than there ever were in the heyday of railways. Brinnington opened in 1977 and Ryder Brow was opened in November 1985. It is just south of Belle Vue station, which was re-sited at the extreme northern end of its formerly very large layout. However the inner-city stations of Ardwick and Ashburys are little used compared with bygone years. Many Marple and Rose Hill trains omit stations nearer Manchester to speed up journey times and because usage of these stations does not justify as intense a service as those further out.

Population densities are given by the Transport for Greater Manchester report for 2011 and indicates that the catchment areas of Marple, Rose Hill and Strines have a high proportions of 'wealthy achievers', 'urban prosperity' and 'comfortably off' compared to other stations on the line. Marple and Rose Hill show a high level of train usage compared to population. So it can be seen that Rose Hill actually has a higher population living near the station than Marple.

Passenger numbers on the network nationally have grown almost annually for many years now from just over 1.1 billion in 2007-8 to 1,612 billion in the year ending 30th September 2014. Marple, Rose Hill and Strines are in line with the national trend. In fact the railways are now carrying more passengers at any time since just after the First World War! It is estimated that the next 5 years passenger numbers will exceed 2 billion. If only Northern would collect all its fares and clamp down on ticketless travel and the figure would be even higher!

7. Rolling stock

First generation post 1955 Modernisation Plan d.m.u.s (diesel multiple units), including the 3-car class 108 and 2-car class 101, continued to be used on both the Marple and Rose Hill trains until the end of 2003. The last five of the class 101, including 101 685 in BR green and affectionately known as 'Daisy', were finally withdrawn on 24 Dec 2003. Newer generation d.m.u.s had started to be introduced in the late 90's – mainly class 142 Pacers, less frequently class 150 'Sprinters' and the occasional class 156 'Super Sprinters'. These classes of d.m.u. continue to provide the stock on the lines in 2014. The 'Pacers', having a wheelbase with just four wheels and a very lightweight bus body: they give a rough and uncomfortable ride. One particular negative nickname for them is 'nodding donkeys'!

The long wheelbase class 142's cause a particular problem with flange squeal on the sharp curve at the start of the Rose Hill branch at Marple Wharf Junction. I travelled on one to Rose Hill in January 2015 and can say it is the worst train I have I have ever used on the Marple lines since I started travelling on the line in 1958. Having being a professional railway man for thirteen years can honestly say it was the worst ride I have ever had in my life bar one - in the brake van on an empty unfitted coal train from South Hetton Colliery to Hartlepool in 1977. 4 wheel carriages were disappearing in the late 19th C and yet they reappeared in the 1980's and undoubtedly helped the economics of many marginal branch lines, but are now hopelessly inadequate.

They are mainly confined to the South West and North of England-but the Pacers there are of better quality and better maintained. The class 142 Pacers are owned by Angel trains and the class 144 by Porterbrook and leased to Northern Rail. In October 2014 Patrick McLouglin, the Secretary of State for Transport, stated that they may be refurbished and remain in traffic beyond 2020. Much of this view derives from the fact the Northern franchise requires the biggest 'subsidy' in the country, and so comes low in the pecking order for new rolling stock and investment, though with a general election looming there are hints from the Government that perhaps better rolling stock is a possibility, but will be probably hand-me-downs from services being electrified.

There is also a proposal to refurbish 30 year old London Underground 'D' stock for use on diesel operated lines. Another problem is that there is nobody prepared to build new diesel trains. The counter argument is that the relatively poorer quality of services and rolling stock in the North is hampering economic growth, hindering further growth in passenger usage and leading to even worse road congestion-and the roads like the railways in the North are at bursting point and statistically more dangerous for accidents and deaths than rail-no rail passengers have been killed on the railways of Britain in the last 8 years. On November 5th 2014 Northern Rail Managing Director Alex Hynes at the National Rail Conference made a call for more and better trains and preferably electrification; "people arrive on a sleek Pendolino train at Manchester Piccadilly and then we put them on a Pacer to Marple". There is an increasing pressure to replace these 'tin cans on wheels' at the highest levels; the most likely outcome is that the electrification process which has now started rolling again after a hiatus of nearly quarter of a century will cascade better rolling stock onto the Marple lines. In February 2015 the invitation to Tender for the new Northern franchise to start on 1st April 2016 decreed that the Pacers must be gone by 2020 at the latest and the new bidders (Abellio, Arriva and Govia) must be prepared to provide at least 120 new diesel 'carriages' for the non- electrified lines in the North and the Sprinter class 150, 153 155 and 156 and any cascaded rolling stock must be refurbished 'as new'. All of these improvements are long overdue.

The bidders must submit their bids by late June 2015; Department for Transport (DfT) and Rail North (representing a consortium of Northern Transport Authorities but dominated by Greater Manchester and West Yorkshire) will then consider the bids. It is hoped that the winning bidder will be announced in late autumn but certainly before the end of the year. The new franchise will be for nine years with an option to extend it by one year. After two previous franchises that specified 'no growth', there is much optimism in the North that the new franchise will bring the long-overdue improvements that we have all been calling-for for years. Goyt Valley Rail Users' Association have made submissions during the consultation period (Summer 2014) and have made further representations to the short-listed bidders about the aspirations of users of our lines, for improved trains, services, station amenities etc. during the new franchise. Craig Wright, chairman of the Association said "We are optimistic that the new franchisee, whoever it is, will implement genuine improvements. We are pleased that the franchise will be overseen by Rail North but we must all remain vigilant to ensure that we don't get more of the same." The continued use of Pacers on the Marple and similar lines in the North West and other regional areas is certainly a political hot potato at the moment! But it seems that the hated Pacers will be with us for some years yet, though the government has promised they will be gone by 2020. But that was in the run up to the May 2015 General Election! So we shall see!

DB Schencker limestone train from the Peak District just after 9am 21st November 2014 (Arthur Procter).

Freight Trains through Marple mid February 2015

Pass Marple Wharf Jn	Depart	From	To	Arrive	Days Run
00.11	21.05	Lostock Works	Tunstead (near Buxton)	00.55	TTHO
00.13	23.03	Peak Forest	Bletchley Yard	05.24	WO
01.32	23.43	West Burton Power Station	Guide Bridge Yard	02.04	FSX
01.42	01.12	Guide Bridge Yard	Tunstead	02.23	MSX
02.39	01.56/9	Tunstead	Bredbury Tilcon or Pendleton	03.28/42	MSX
02.49	02.29	Guide Bridge Yard	Tunstead	04.07	MSX
03.04	03.01	Tunstead	Leeds Hunslet	06.25	MSX
03.47	02.21	Tunstead	Bredbury Tilcon or Pendleton	03.53/04.05	SO
04.32	03.52	Tunstead	Fiddlers Ferry Power Station	07.20	MSX
04.53	03.44	Peak Forest	Hope St Salford Cemex	05.28	SO
06.50	14.45	Cwmbargoed (S.Wales) FO	Earles Sidings (Hope)	07.48	SO
07.58	07.04	Bredbury Tilcon	Tunstead	08.41	SX
08.25	07.37	Bredbury Tilcon	Tunstead	09.23	SO
09.00	07.46	Pendleton	Tunstead	09.58	SX
09.13	07.37	Pendleton	Tunstead	10.32	SO
09.49	09.06	Hope St Salford Cemex	Peak Forest	10.48	SO
11.00	09.54	Peak Forest	Hope St Salford Cemex	11.47	SX
11.44	09.25	Dowlow Sidings Buxton	Ashburys	12.18	SO
14.45	13.05	Dowlow Sidings Buxton	Ashburys	15.20	SX
16.03	15.25	Hope St Salford Cemex	Peak Forest	17.08	SX
16.29	15.51	Tunstead	Bredbury Tilcon	17.18	SX
21.21	20.33	Bredbury Tilcon	Tunstead	22.01	SX
22.42	21.30	Peak Forest	Acton Yard near London	04.33	WTHO

FO = Fridays only
SO = Saturdays only
FSX = Monday-Thursday
WO = Wednesday Only
TTHO = Tuesday and Thursday Only
SX = Saturday excepted
MSX = Tuesday-Friday
WTHO = Wednesday and Thursday Only
None of above abbreviations include Sundays

8. Freight Trains

The days of pick up goods trains, local goods stations, coal depots, parcels and newspaper trains has now long since gone. But in the 21st Century Marple station continues to see a regular flow of freight trains, mainly conveying stone from the Peak District to various depots mainly in the Manchester area but some to destinations further afield. Freight trains were, until recently, mainly operated by the former EWS (English, Welsh and Scottish) but are now owned by the German DB Schenker (Deutshe Bahn - the German State Railways). However the Guide Bridge, West Burton and Fiddlers Ferry services are operated by Freightliner Heavy Haul. A snapshot supplied by Network Rail in February 2015 showed a great variety of freight trains passing through Marple. There were also several Light Engine movements each way - engines returning without a load to Guide Bridge or to the quarries/stone terminals. In the October 2014 Working Timetable there were also a number of Mondays Only freights to and from the Peak District, presumably because the terminals were shut on a Sunday. There were also a Mondays only Empty Passenger Train from Nottingham to Liverpool Lime Street and one daily from Manchester Piccadilly to Nottingham, presumably to position trains on the Liverpool - East Anglia axis. The October 2014 snapshot also shows flows from Earles Sidings near Hope and destinations as near as Salford and Weaste and as far afield as New Cumnock in the Scottish borders plus a flow between Bredbury Greater Manchester Waste Disposal Site and Roxby Landfill Site Waste Management Scunthorpe. Clearly freight flows are an ever changing kaleidoscope! There are also other flows avoiding Marple through Disley Tunnel.

9. Marple - Stockport

Marple badly requires a regular rail service to Stockport, The Manchester Central - Tiviot Dale - Romiley - Marple passenger service was closed in 1967, though the trackbed of the 'Marple Curve' from Romiley to Bredbury on the Woodley - Heaton Mersey freight route was left in situ until 1975 in case the Disley Tunnel route was closed to make way for a motorway, and freight trains from the Peak District were diverted via Marple. The Marple Community Council tried to keep the Marple Curve intact and re-instate the Marple-Stockport service but to no avail. The freight only route from Godley, Woodley and Stockport Tiviot Dale to Heaton Mersey remained open until 1980 but lost its reason for existence with the closure of the Woodhead route to freight in 1981 with the demise of coal traffic from Yorkshire to Fiddlers Ferry Power Station.

The section from Godley Junction to Woodley and from Portwood to Heaton Mersey West Junction closed in 1980 leaving a stub from Woodley to Portwood Public Delivery Siding. This in its turn succumbed by 1987, leaving just a stub from Woodley to the Bredbury Waste Disposal Unit and Tilcon Stone Centre, just east of the Romiley-Ashburys line, which remains open to this day. The trackbed was rapidly built on to accommodate motorways; the Manchester Outer Ring Motorway from the M62 reached Denton by the late 1980's and the M63 -now the M60 -cut through Stockport via Portwood on the course of the Tiviot Dale line in April 1989 severing any chance of the re-opening of the Marple – Stockport direct line. Since then a massive supermarket, originally Safeways, but currently Morrisons, has been built on the site of the line and the cutting from Romiley towards Bredbury has been filled in, making it well nigh impossible to re-open the line. A short section of tunnel survives near Brinnington but the possibility of re-opening this line appears remote in the extreme.

It is difficult to imagine that when I was a boy in the mid 60's it was possible to get from Marple station to Stockport Tiviot Dale in about 12 minutes from Marple (e.g. depart Marple 08.35 and 8.29 from Rose Hill -change at Romiley) arrive Tiviot Dale 08.47 (Bradshaw April 1961). Today so speedy a journey would only be accomplished in the dead of night or in a helicopter such has been progress! Before the First World War the fastest trains from Marple to Stockport had taken as little as 7 minutes!

Tiviot Dale was at closure seen as out of the town centre and lacking onward main line connections, but would now be well placed for the main shopping centre. Since the closure of the Manchester Central South District via Tiviot Dale to Marple in 1967 it has become apparent that this closure was a major blunder; more remote lines like the Hope Valley survived, thankfully because of the difficulty of providing a reliable all year round bus service but relatively busy but 'uneconomic' services such as the Tiviot Dale line with apparently adequate alternative bus services fell prey to closure - and under a Labour Government it has to be said. With increasing petrol prices and gridlock congestion the folly of such closures is now apparent.

There have been various proposals to link Marple with Stockport by rail based public transport ever since closure. In the mid 80s there was a proposal to run a Marple - Stockport service via Woodley but the four minutes reversal time necessary at Woodley would have made the service very slow. There still exists a rail route from Marple to Stockport Edgeley via Guide Bridge but the journey time via this devious route would be uncompetitive. Another possibility is restoring the Stockport-Manchester Victoria route with street running as far as Reddish and a possible link to Marple. It would not be beyond the wit of man to create a Stockport facing link between the Marple-Manchester and Stockport-Victoria lines north of Reddish Viaduct or even use some of the abandoned and built on Romiley - Stockport link near Bredbury though these schemes would be prohibitively expensive. Another more devious route would be to re-open the Macclesfield line to near Middlewood and build a curve to the Buxton line but this would not give a very attractive journey time to Stockport, though it would link with the main line at Edgeley. But with growing road traffic and congestion drastic solutions may be needed.

The most likely solution seems to be the proposals produced in early 2015 by Stockport MBC and Transport for Greater Manchester envisaging a number of options for Metrolink extensions in to Stockport via conversions of existing passenger and freight lines to tram-train. The East Didsbury-Stockport town centre route would offer the potential to continue via Brinnington to join the projected Marple-Manchester tram-train route at Bredbury, thus restoring a Marple-Stockport line. This is however likely to be at least ten years away as things stand! If only Barbara Castle had not consented to the closure of the Tiviot Dale Line!

10. Tourism

The trackbed of the closed Rose-Hill Macclesfield line was sold to the Local Authorities on the route and has been converted into a footpath, bridleway and cycle track, and follows the former trackbed except for the last section into Macclesfield which has been built on, and the trail has to deviate via the River Bollin to reach the centre of Macclesfield and the station. 'Tewiffic!' enthused Dr David Bellamy, jumping for joy at the opening the new walkway at the official opening of the Middlewood Way on May 30th 1985 at Higher Poynton station, now a beautifully landscaped picnic area. David, as the botanic man insisted on being called, unveiled a plaque there, further marked his presence with a tree planting ceremony and delighted onlookers and councillors alike by removing his shoes and socks and wading through a mucky pond. Bubbling over with approbation, bearded Bellamy was clearly impressed with the Middlewood Way and lavished praise on the Stockport and Macclesfield councils who, with the Department of Environment's grants of £1.3 million have done such a fine job reclaiming the derelict railway track and turning it into a nature treasure trail.

The trackbed of the Hayfield line was purchased from British Rail by Derbyshire County Council in 1973, (except for New Mills Tunnel) and turned into the Sett Valley Trail. The station buildings at Hayfield were demolished in 1975, and an information centre, picnic area, car park and toilets built on the site. The Pennine Bridleway follows the section of the Trail between Hayfield and Birch Vale.

An interesting leisure feature offered in recent years and again in 2015 were the Folk trains on the line. The High Peak & Hope Valley Community Partnership is a co-operative venture of Local Authorities, Northern Rail and Community groups which share in the aim of enhancing rail services in the Peak District and Hope Valley. The Partnership offers Folk Music trains and guided walks on some Glossop and Hope Valley services from Manchester to Hathersage via Marple. Selected weekend services both at lunch time and in the evening carry folk music groups and are in some cases linked in with food and drink events. The local timetables also include details of station to station guided walks on selected Saturdays throughout the year.

Events in the spring of 2015 included a Hope Valley Folk train on St. Valentines Day 14th February. The train was the 11.49 from Manchester to Hathersage (and Sheffield) calling at Marple. The return trip was the 14.33 from Hathersage allowing time for lunch. The entertainment is provided by the 'Full Circle Folk Club' which plays a varied mix of Blues, Folk Irish and Country music. These are however a little frustrating for Strines users as they call on the way out but not on the way back! On March 7th there is a 'Peak Forest Canal Winter Stroll' starting from Marple station and ending up 6½ miles later at Whaley Bridge station. The Marple line also sees occasional steam hauled chartered trains passing through.

The South East Manchester Community Rail Partnership supports leisure travel and encourages green travel to the area. Marple, Rose Hill and Strines are gateways to areas of natural beauty with access to the Peak Forest and Macclesfield canals, the Peak District, the Middlewood Way and other footpaths and country parks. Improvements are needed to exploit the leisure and tourist potential of the area served by the stations and reduce traffic congestion. Better Sunday and evening services would help encourage green travel.

The tourist potential of Marple has never been fully exploited, despite the efforts of the Marple Local History Society, the Mellor Archaeological Dig, the Marple Locks and other Festivals. The area abounds in opportunities for walkers and cyclists and has the attractions of the magnificent Canal heritage plus the Roman Lakes and the excavations at the Mellor Mill site and Shaw Cairn. Before the First World War Marple was a major destination for day trippers from Manchester and beyond by train. Ann Hearle's book 'Marple and Mellor a New History' records that on just two days in late May 1877 2,700 Sunday School children came by train from Manchester to Marple. With an improved and better marketed rail service, especially on Sundays and integrated with local buses, it could once again a thriving tourist destination. The Mellor Archaeological Trust in 2009 published a very comprehensive booklet and map with heritage walks around Mellor, Ludworth and Marple Bridge, with details of public transport access. The Friends of Rose Hill Station have encouraged green tourism in their recently published attractive leaflet giving details of five easy to moderate walks based on Rose Hill Station and taking in many of the main sights of Marple and district. So things are moving in a positive direction. But it may be some years before we see the crowds flocking to Marple by train as occurred in the late 19th C or to the Roman Lakes in the early 20thC, and queues of people stretching along Brabyns Brow for trains!

11. The Future

In the event, the Picc-Vic underground link never materialized in central Manchester. But the opening in 1988 of the Castlefield curve, between Deansgate and the L.N.W. Liverpool and Manchester line the route utilised the old freight only 'Manchester South Junction' section of the M.S.J.A. Line to Ordsall Lane Junction. Thence a new line was constructed to join the L. & Y. Manchester Victoria - Bolton/Wigan line at a new station at Salford Crescent. This allowed north - south running and services were put on from stations such as Buxton, Hazel Grove and Stockport to Southport and Blackpool, and now the link is used as well for long distance services from Manchester Airport to Scotland. Though linking up the networks north and south of Manchester, unlike the Picc-Vic scheme, it did not give rail access to the city centre. The opening of the curve led to the gradual run down of Manchester Victoria with for instance the Trans Pennine services transferred to the route into Manchester Piccadilly via Stalybridge and Guide Bridge in October 1989. This has put added strain on Piccadilly, especially the through platforms 13 and 14. However in May 2014 an additional new Newcastle - Liverpool service has started running via Manchester Victoria, as Piccadilly is at saturation point.

In 1992 the Manchester Metrolink network opened, taking over the former 'heavy rail' lines to Bury and Altrincham with trams and street running through central Manchester. The system was opened by the Queen on 17th July 1992 and the final link to the undercroft of Manchester Piccadilly on 20th July. Thus at last the north-south divide of Manchester has been bridged. The system is very successful and soon extended. However so great is the strain on Piccadilly that there is currently talk of two additional through platforms. In March 2015 the Ordsall Chord was approved from Castlefield running eastward to Victoria allowing trains from east of Manchester to Manchester Airport to go direct, via the Midland Junction line at Ashburys, Victoria, Oxford Road and the through platforms at Piccadilly without reversal at Piccadilly and vice-versa.

The Chancellor, George Osborne, in his 'Northern Powerhouse' speech in Manchester on 23rd June 2014 proposed a new High Speed link, dubbed 'HS3', to link Manchester and Leeds partly using existing lines but speeded up with new infrastructure and tunnels. One possibility is re-opening the New 1954 Woodhead tunnel, closed in 1981, or boring new tunnels through Standedge, though this was rejected by the Transport Minister, Baroness Kramer, early in 2015, preferring instead the Northern Hub project which would increase capacity on the Hope Valley route. This is just as well as that line is operating at almost full capacity at the moment.

There is also talk of re-opening the Midland route through the Peak, though it is not clear how this would dovetail with the cycle track and pathway along much of the line and the section already re-opened by Peak Rail from Matlock to Rowsley. All these proposals would affect the Trans-Pennine services using the Disley tunnel. But at the same time the Department of Transport issued a consultation paper on the future of franchising in the North West. This basically seeks to concentrate resources on a railway which gives the best economic benefits and is affordable 'with focused and targeted use of resources'. The danger is that less heavily used lines and stations could be cut or starved of resources in favour of more profitable potentially High Speed inter urban lines. This is a particular worry for the Marple lines as the Northern franchise generally is subsidised to the tune of 53p for every passenger mile, which is by far the highest figure for any franchise, comparing unfavourably with 16p per mile subsidy for each passenger on the more profitable Trans Pennine Routes. Another snag with HS2 and HS3 is that of 'connectivity' in that the High Speed stations in Leeds and Birmingham will not be at the present stations, which like Manchester Piccadilly are at bursting point. This would make onward connections difficult and negate some of the advantages of the higher speed services.

In 2015 Stockport MBC and Transport for Greater Manchester (TfGM) jointly produced a report on the long term future of rail in the area. It talks about a number of options for Metrolink extensions in to Stockport by means of conversions of existing passenger and freight lines to tram-train. The lines listed for possible conversion to tram-train include Manchester-Rose Hill via Bredbury, East Didsbury-Hazel Grove (along the Midland's 'New Line') and East Didsbury-Stockport town centre, via Cheadle Heath and the Stockport-Altrincham line. The Route to East Didsbury will be to a new station and not the existing one on the Styal loop line; it will utilize part of the Midland South District line which used to link Marple to Manchester Central. It is proposing conversion of the Rose Hill - Manchester service to tramway operation to link in with the rest of the Metrolink network which has recently been extended to Oldham, Manchester Airport and Ashton. They are awaiting evaluation of a Tram/Train pilot scheme in the Sheffield and Rotherham area in which trams and freight & passenger services share the same tracks.

If this is successful it is proposed to convert the Rose Hill service via Reddish to tramway operation at 750 Volts DC with overhead wires. The service would dive down at Ashburys to run at street level to join the rest of the Metrolink Network in the undercroft of Manchester Piccadilly. The proposal is for trams at up to 6 minute headways linking Rose Hill and central Manchester, thus giving Rose Hill by far the most frequent service in Marple. There is also a longer term suggestion to extend the tram-train along the course of the Rose Hill-Macclesfield line to High Lane where a Park and Ride facility could intercept potential passengers coming in on the congested A6. The conventional Sheffield/ Hope Valley semi fast trains and 'heavy rail' services to Marple & New Mills along with the freight trains conveying limestone would all run via Guide Bridge and Hyde. The section from Romiley to Marple Wharf Junction would operate under the Sheffield model with trams and conventional freight and passenger trains sharing this busy section of track. Tram-train investment in UK awaits the successful operation of the planned Sheffield - Rotherham pilot scheme. As this is not expected to open until 2018 it is likely to be 2020 before firm plans for tram-train schemes in Stockport are developed. In early 2015 the Electrification Task Force placed the Manchester - Marple - Hope Valley and Rose Hill lines in 'Tier Two' for priorities in the North. So, who knows? The Marple and Rose Hill lines could be electrified as conventional heavy rail like the adjacent Glossop/Hadfield and Hazel Grove lines!

Marple Railway photo album
Additional items of great historical interest.

YOU are sure to like the new Diesel passenger trains which, for local services, have so many advantages over their steam train predecessors. For the traveller, the principal of these are the comfort of the new coaches, their neat and attractive design, their cleanliness and their speed.

The coaches, which have been designed in the modern open style, are light, airy and easy to keep clean and the seats are very comfortable.

They are operated in units of two or multiples thereof, which can be driven from either end (with obvious advantages when reversing at the end of a journey) and the two coaches are connected by a corridor. First and second class accommodation for about 125 passengers is provided and there are toilet facilities and ample space for luggage.

The units are powered by two horizontal engines of at least 150 h.p. each slung beneath one of the coaches between the two sets of wheels. Where steep gradients occur it may be necessary for both vehicles to be powered. Diesel trains, like electric trains, can accelerate and decelerate very quickly, an important factor in the operation of local services.

These trains have proved very popular indeed wherever they have been introduced and more and more will be brought into use in various parts of the London Midland Region as part of the British Railways Modernisation Plan.

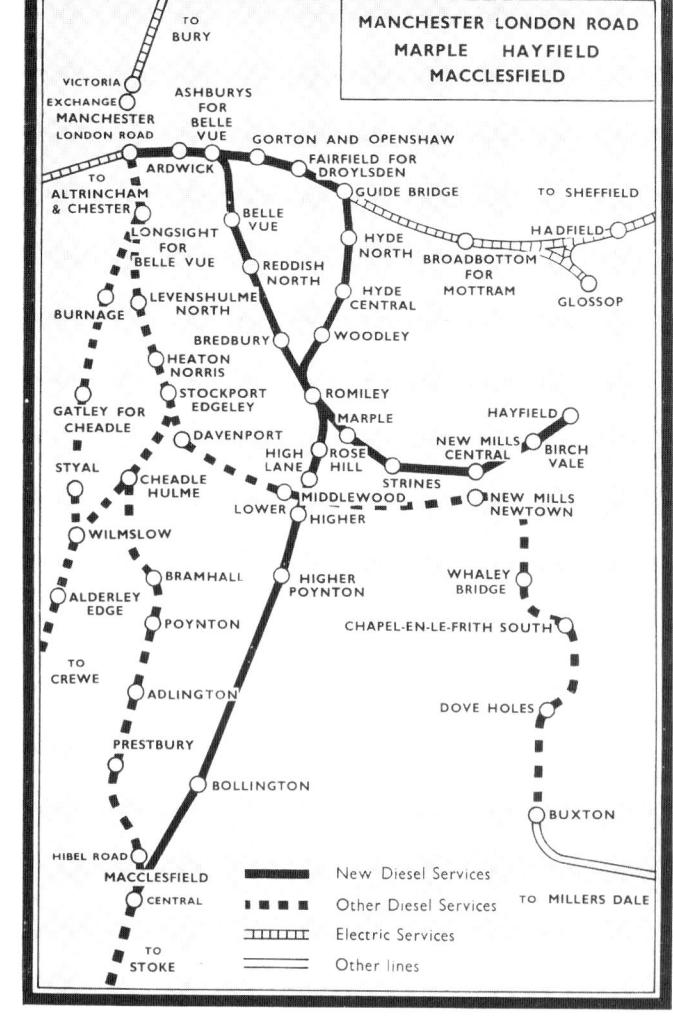

Dieselisation leaflet 1957

Sheffield & Midland Joint Railway.

Notice to Enginedrivers, Guards, Signalmen, Platelayers, and others, respecting Single Line Working in the Marple Cutting between Marple Tunnel and the Goyt Viaduct.

In consequence of a land slip Single Line Working by Pilotman is at present in operation on the down main line between Strines Station and Marple South Box.

A new Signal Box and two main line connections are being provided in the Marple Cutting, which will be brought into use as soon as they are completed.

Single Line Working by Pilotman and Fixed Signals will be adopted past the slip. The signals worked from the new Signal Box will be:—

A distant signal and a home signal to regulate the running of up trains and engines;
A distant signal and a home signal to regulate the running of down trains and engines;

The positions for the signals have not yet been decided upon, but they will indicate by their positions the lines to which they apply.

The new Signal Box will be open continuously.

The Pilotman must wear the Regulation Badge prescribed in Rule 70 in the Company's Book of Rules and Regulations.

Drivers and Guards must carry out the instructions given by the Pilotman, and no train or engine must enter upon the single line unless the Pilotman is present and personally orders the Train or Engine to start.

The Pilotman must accompany every train or engine over the single line.

Goyt Viaduct:—

The Goyt Viaduct Signal Box between Marple and Strines which is now closed will to-day (Monday, December 25th) be again brought into use as an intermediate Block Telegraph Signal Box.

The signals which are now out of use will again be brought into use, but the position of the up distant signal will be slightly altered.

This Signal Box will be open continuously.

Strines:—

Until further notice this Signal Box will be open continuously.

Marple South Box:—

The position of the down main line distant signal will be slightly altered.

R. HAIG BROWN,
M. S. & L. Railway.

W. L. HUGLISTON,
Midland Railway.

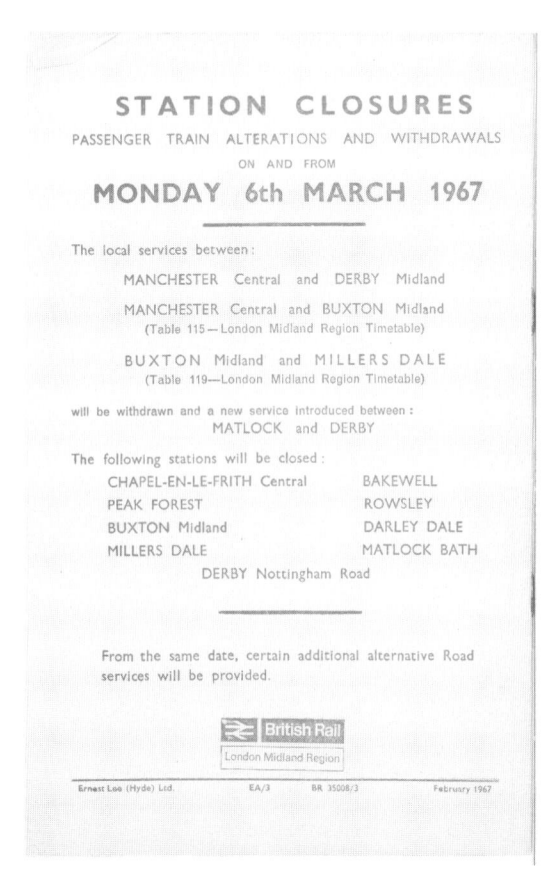

December 25th, 1893.

Marple landslip notice, Christmas Day 1893!

STATION CLOSURES
PASSENGER TRAIN ALTERATIONS AND WITHDRAWALS
ON AND FROM

MONDAY 6th MARCH 1967

The local services between:

MANCHESTER Central and DERBY Midland

MANCHESTER Central and BUXTON Midland
(Table 115 — London Midland Region Timetable)

BUXTON Midland and MILLERS DALE
(Table 119 — London Midland Region Timetable)

will be withdrawn and a new service introduced between:
MATLOCK and DERBY

The following stations will be closed:

CHAPEL-EN-LE-FRITH Central	BAKEWELL
PEAK FOREST	ROWSLEY
BUXTON Midland	DARLEY DALE
MILLERS DALE	MATLOCK BATH
DERBY Nottingham Road	

From the same date, certain additional alternative Road services will be provided.

British Rail
London Midland Region

Ernest Lee (Hyde) Ltd.   EA/3   BR 35008/3   February 1967

Closure notice 1967

72

Marple Aqueduct and narrowboat plus steam train on viaduct, mock-up by Arthur Procter, 2015.

April to June 2015

Guided Walks and Folk Trains in The Hope Valley and High Peak

www.hvhptp.org.uk

FRIENDS OF ROSE HILL STATION Marple

The friendly station

FIVE WALKS FROM ROSE HILL STATION MARPLE

Detailed itineraries can be downloaded from our website.

SPONSORS

Transport for Greater Manchester

STOCKPORT Metropolitan Borough Council

northern

ACoRP

Rose Hill inauguration of bike shelter, 18th July 2014

Friends of Strines Station carpark work party. September 2014

Marple Wharf signal box demolition for Peak Rail, March 1983.

Middlewood Way, 2015.

MARPLE RAIL TRAILS

L.M.S. Black Five on the 15:30 Manchester Central to Sheffield crossing Marple Goyt Viaduct in June 1966 (I. R. Smith)

Bradshaw August 1910

Addendum - The Horseboat 'Maria'

Another topic not mentioned in the original Railways of Marple book is the preserved horse drawn narrow boat 'Maria'. She was built at Jinks boatyard at Top Lock Marple in 1854 and the oldest narowboat still operating in country. She was used by the M.S.L. to convey limestone from Bugsworth to Guide Bridge for use as railway ballast. 'Maria' has no motor and is operated as a horse-drawn boat by the Horseboating society which aims to keep the tradition of Horse drawn boats alive. 'Maria' was restored in 1978-9 and is owned by the Ashton Packet Boat Company. She was operated as a Horse Drawn passenger boat between 1978 and 1999 from Guide Bridge to Marple bottom lock. In 2004-5 Maria celebrated her 150th anniversary and was restored to her late 19thC cargo-carrying state when operated by the M.S.L. which owned the Peak Forest, Ashton and Macclesfield canals.

In 2005 Maria was loaded with 16 tons of limestone at Bugsworth Basin, re-creating her role of 150 years ago, and pulled by 'Queenie' the 8 miles to Marple. In 2006 'Queenie' pulled 16 tons from Bugsworth to Guide Bridge, 16 miles and 16 locks! In August 2005 the boat, loaded with 10 tons of limestone, was towed by 'Queenie' for 80 miles to the Inland Waterways Association National Festival at Preston Brook. The journey was given the IWA award for the most enterprising and meritorious journey to the Festival. 'Maria' has been horseboated to Huddersfield and back several times, including being legged through Standedge Tunnel twice in the Tunnel's bicentenary year 2011, with the author assisting in legging! In 2008 a new boathorse 'Bilbo Baggins' was trained on the Ashton Canal by Sue Day, then made journeys to Bugsworth and horseboated from Marple Top Lock to Guide Bridge for the Marple Locks Festival in July 2011, again with the author helping crew 'Maria' as a member of the Horseboating Society. 'Maria' and Bilbo also passed through Marple in July 2014 whilst completing the Cheshire Ring of canals clockwise. 'Maria' is a real link with the railway past of the Peak Forest Canal.

'Bilbo' hauling ex-M.S.L. horseboat 'Maria' on Peak Forest Canal, 3rd July 2011 (author).

Ex-M.S.L. horseboat 'Maria' on Peak Forest Canal, 3rd July 2011 (author).

INDEX

A
Ancoats (Goods Depot) 18, 34
Aqueduct (Marple) 7-9
Architect of Marple Station 11
Ardwick 7, 8, 16, 47, 50, 52, 55, 68
Area Management 50-52
Arkwright's Bridge 11, 25
Ashburys 8, 16, 54, 57, 60, 65, 68, 70

B
Beeching Report 45-49, 54-55
'Beechwood' 12
Belle Vue 12, 38, 45, 48
Blackburn (services to) 6, 25-26, 32-34, 36-37
"Black Fives" 37, 45
Blackpool (services to) 6, 25-26, 32-34, 36-37,57, 71
Bollington 20--24, 37, 49
Bowdens Coal Merchants 47, 56
Brabyns Hall 10-11, 31
Bradshaw's Guide 9, 11, 17, 24, 34, 62
Bredbury 16-18, 45, 54-56, 58, 66-67, 70
Brickworks (Middlewood) 20-24
   (Rose Hill) 20-24
Brinnington (Junction) 16
   (Station) 52, 56, 68
Bristol (services to) 17-18, 19, 25-26. 32-33
British Railways Board 38-39
British Transport Commission 38-39
Bugsworth 7-10, 44
Bus Competition 33-35, 43, 50
Bus/Rail Interchange 50-53, 56, 58, 62
Buxton:
Proposed/opened lines to 8, 13-14
Macclesfield service 20-24
Services 25-29, 32, 35-8, 44-47, 57, 71
Turntable 28

C
Car Competition 33-35, 43, 46
Car Parks (Marple) 50-55, 60
   (Rose Hill) 62, 64
Carriages 13, 17-18. 36, 44, 58, 66, 68-69
Castlefield Curve 55, 71
Chapel-en-le-Frith 7, 11, 16
Cheadle Heath 31-34, 46
Cheshire Midland Railway 15
Chinley 24-25, 29, 31-36, 43, 46-47, 54
Chorlton-cum-Hardy ....
C.L.C 15, 31-32, 35, 44
Cleethorpes (services to) 47, 56-58, 65-66
Closures 44, 47-49, 54
Colliery Tramways 7, 20
Commuters 12
Compounds, Midland 37, 45
'Compstall' Station 9-11
Cromford & High Peak Railway ... 7-9, 14

D
Deansgate Tube 55
Deficits 45-48, 54
Derby (services to) ....
13, 14 17-18, 25-29, 32, 35-36, 38, 44
Didsbury 32
Dinting 8
Dieselisation 43-45
Disley 9, 12, 29, 32
D.M.U.'s 43-46,
Doncaster (services to) 47, 55
Doubling of Lines 14-15

E
Eastern Region 43
Electrification 43, 46-47, 58
Excursions 24, 29, 37, 70-71

F
Fairfield 8, 54
Fares 8, 17-18
First Class (abolition of) 49
'Flying Scotsman' 57
Franchises 63-65, 69
Friends of Marple Station 60-61
Friends of Rose Hill Station 60, 62-64, 68
Friends of Strines Station 60, 62

G
Gas Lighting 12, 54
G.C. & Mid. Joint Committee 27
G.C. & N.S. Joint Committee 27
Glossop 7-8, 39. 61, 71
G.M.P.T.E. 55-56, 58
Godley Junction 7, 8, 15, 56, 70
Goods Depots (Marple/Rose Hill) 15, 21-23, 28-29
Goods Trains 5, 18, 19, 28-29, 35, 46-47, 56-57, 64, 69-70
Gorton 13, 26, 37
Gowholes Yard 31-32
Grand Junction Railway 7, 8, 13
Great Central Railway 8, 25
Great Northern Railway 9, 11, 13-16
Grouping (1923) 34-35
Guide Bridge .... 8-10, 16-18, 26-28, 45, 49-50, 56, 65 , 67, 70-71

H
Hadfield 67, 71
'Harwich Boat Train' 46, 57, 65-66
Hayfield 8, 9 11, 13, 15-17, 26-29, 35, 38-39, 44-49, 55, 70
Hazel Grove (South) 32
   (Chord) 65-66
Heaton Mersey 31, 44, 70
Higher Poynton 20- 24, 36, 48
High Lane 22, 37, 44, 48, 54, 71
Hope Valley Line 7, 24-25, 31, 46-47, 57, 65-66, 70
Hudson Family (Brabyns Hall) 10-11, 31
Hyde (Central) 8-12, 37, 71
Hyde Junction (now North) 8-12, 15-16, 54
Hyde Loop 8-12, 55, 71

J
Johnson 'Spinners' 27, 37

K
King's Cross (London) 9, 14, 45

L
Lancashire & Yorkshire Ry (L. & Y.) 13-14, 19, 32-32, 34-35, 71
Landslip, Marple 24-25
Liverpool (services to) 16, 18, 25-26, 31-32, 36, 44, 46, 56, 58, 66
Liverpool and Manchester Rly (L. & M.) 7-8, 12
Liveries (Locos and Coaches) 13, 26, 44-45
Livestock 15, 45
L.M.S./L.N.E.R. Formation of 35
London and North Western
Railway (L.N.W.) .... 8-35 throughout
London Midland Region 38, 44, 64
Lowestoft (services to) 32
Lyme Handley Railway Society ... 48-49

M
Macclesfield 8, 20-24, 35, 37, 44-9, 54-55
Macclesfield, Bollington and
Marple Railway (M.B.M.) 20-24
Macclesfield Canal 7, 8
Mail 12, 15, 47

76

Manchester
  Central 18-19, 25-26, 32-33, 35- 39,
                                           44, 55, 68, 70
  Cornbrook 16, 18
  Division 64
  Liverpool Road 2, 7
  London Road........................ 8, 9 11, 14, 17-18, 25-26,
                                           29, 32-33, 36-39, 44, 55, 68
  Mayfield............................... 7, 39, 53
  Piccadilly 39, 46, 54-56, 58, 65-69, 71
  Store Street 7-8
  Victoria................................. 7-9, 25-26, 32-32-8, 43, 55,
                                           66, 68, 71
Manchester and Birmingham Rly 7-8, 13
Manchester, Buxton, Matlock and Midlands
Junction Railway (M.B.M. & M.J.) 8, 13
Manchester and Leeds Rly (L.& M.) 7
Manchester, Sheffield and
Lincolnshire Railway (M.S.L.)....... 8-25 throughout
Manchester South Junction and
Altrincham Railway (M.S.J.A.) 7, 15-16, 43
Manchester and Stockport Railway 16
Marple Curve............................. 16, 46, 58, 70
Marple Community Council (M.C.C.) 56, 58
Marple, New Mills and Hayfield
Junction Railway (M.N.M. & H.J.) 9-14
'Marple Tiger'............................61
Marple Wharf Jn 2, 9-11, 21-24, 334-35, 46,
                                           48, 55, 57, 60
Matlock...................................... 26,
Middlewood Curve 21-23, 35, 37, 44
Middlewood Station 20-24, 29, 44, 48, 54, 68
Middlewood Way........................63, 70-71
Midland Hotel (Marple) 6,7, 12
Midland Junction Line 19, 32, 66
Mileposts................................... 28, 58
Miss Marple...............................61
Modernization Plan.....................39-40
M.U.D.C....................................50, 52, 55-56
M.U.D.C. Depot (Rose Hill).......... 21-22, 56

N
Nameboards (at stations) 43
Nationalization............................ 38, 43-44
Navvies...................................... 9, 31-32
Network Rail...............................60
'New Line' (Disley cut-off) 31-33, 46-47, 56-58, 60, 66
New Mills................................... 7-2, 15-16, 26, 31, 36-37, 44-
                                           47, 49-50, 55-58, 60, 65-68
New Mills East (Goods Depot) 15
New Mills South Junction............ 60
Newton (for Hyde) 7-8
Northern Rail.............................63-71
North Staffordshire Railway (N.S.) 20-24, 35

O
Oakwood.................................... 34, 37
Office of Rail Regulation (O.R.R). 64, 67

P
Parcels....................................... 12, 53
Park and Paterson's Siding 22
Packet Boats (on Canal).............. 8
Peak Forest Canal Tramway (Marple) 7, 10
Peak Forest Canal Tramway (Bugsworth) 7-9
Peak Railway Society 47, 57, 60
'Picc-Vic' 55, 71
Population Figures.....................67-68
Portwood................................... 15, 70
Poynton Collieries 20
Privatisation..............................63-65
Pullmans................................... 16, 18-19, 26,43

R
Railcars..................................... 36-37
'Railway Children'......................62
Railway Executive...................... 38, 43
Railway Hotel/Inn (Marple) 7, 12
Railway Hotel/Inn (Rose Hill).......7, 12, 24, 62

'Rattlesnake'............................... 2, 10
Reddish (North) 17, 19, 29, 44-46, 54, 70
Reddish Junction 16
Resignalling................................33, 37, 55, 57, 60
Road Haulage Competition 35, 38
Romiley...................................... 8, 9, 11, 16, 31, 33, 37, 45-
                                           46, 54, 56-58, 60, 66, 70
Ross, Edward 12
Rowsley 7, 13, 14, 47, 57, 61, 71

S
St. Martin's Church, Marple......... 11, 15, 16, 28
St. Pancras (services to).............
14, 16-17, 25-28, 35-36, 46-47, 55
Saver Seven Tickets................... 50, 56
School children........................... 37,
S.E.L.N.E.C............................... 48, 55
Seven Stiles..............................10, 16-17.61
Sheffield..................................... 7-9, 15, 25-26, 32-33, 36-39,
                                           46-47, 54-55, 57-58, 65-67
Sheffield, Ashton-u-Lyne &
Manchester Railway (S .A. & M.)..7, 8
Sheffield and Midland
Joint Committee (S. & M.) 14-17
Signal boxes (Marple).................. 15-17, 28, 33, 37, 55
Sleeping Cars 16-19
South District Line...................... 18-19
Southport (services to) 19, 26, 36, 71
Staff at Marple........................... 28, 34-35, 44, 50
Station Masters at Marple 17, 28, 35, 50
Station Road (Marple)................. 12
Steam Specials 57
Stephenson, George 7
Stockport................................... 7, 8, 12, 15,16, 18, 21, 25-
                                           26, 31-32, 35, 44, 46, 55,
                                           58, 66, 70-71
Stockport, Disley and Whaley
Bridge Railway (S.D. & W.B.)........ 8, 9, 13, 14
Stockport and Woodley Railway . 15
Stockport, Timperley and
Altrincham Railway..................... 15
Strines 11-12, 15, 25, 29, 30, 49,
                                           54-55, 67, 71

T
Train Services
Marple
1862: 9. *1865*: 13. *1868*: 16.
1875: 17-18. *1880/7*:19. *1898*: 25-26. *1910*: 32-33
1918: 35. *1927*: 36. *1938*: 35-36. *1939/45*: 38.
1952: 44. *1958*: 44-45. *1969/70*: 49. *1977*: 55-56.
1979: 50·51. *1980*: 65-66. *1997*: 67. *2015*: 67
(Rose Hill). *1875/1910*: 24. *1918/1938*: 37
Post *1938* see services for Marple.
'Tram Train'...............................70-71
T.U.C.C 46, 48
Tunnels
  Bugsworth 32
  Cowburn................................. 24-25
  Disley..................................... 31-33, 46
  Marple North 9, 11
  South 9. 11, 16, 58
  New Mills................................ 3, 9, 60
  Totley..................................... 24-25
  Woodhead 7, 9-10
Turntables (Marple).................... 16-17, 26-27, 31,

V
Viaducts
  Marple 7-10
  Marple Goyt............................ 11,
  Stockport................................ 7

W
Water Columns (at Marple).......... 17
Watkin, Sir Edward 15,-16, 20
Whaley Bridge Branch - proposed 7-8
Withington 35,44
Woodhead Route........................ 7-8, 39, 46-47, 50, 57, 71
Woodley 11, 14-16, 28, 70

77

Bibliography

There are references to the Railways of our area in most of the standard railway histories of the Pre-Grouping Companies which served the district; in addition the railway press has included more specific articles relating to our district, which also cover the post 1923 period which is largely unchronicled in books.

Of the standard railway histories, the one with the most information on our area is GEORGE DOW: "GREAT CENTRAL" (3 Vols.) a very thorough and readable work. With such a book on the G.C. and its antecedents there is little need for any further references.

For the Midland Railway there is no one standard history. F.S. WILLIAMS "THE MIDLAND RAILWAY- ITS RISE AND PROGRESS" only goes up to 1875 (when it was written) but nonetheless gives the best account of the Midland's drive for Manchester. C. HAMILTON ELLIS "THE MID LAND RAILWAY" is very readable and the best general history up to 1923, but of necessity short. E.G. BARNES· "THE RISE OF THE MIDLAND RAILWAY" and "THE MIDLAND MAIN LINE" are rather fuller, but in some respects unbalanced.

Turning now to articles, J.P. WILSON and E.N.C. HAYWOOD'S "THE ROUTE THROUGH THE PEAK - DERBY TO MANCHESTER" (Trains Illustrated March and April 1960) is the best all - round account of the Midland's Peak Line from its inception to recent times, and includes much of interest about the operation of the line in the 50's. P.E. BAUGHAM "BUXTON CENTENARY - THE APPROACH FROM DERBY AND BURTON-ON-TRENT" (Railway Magazine October 1963) also gives an account of the Midland's approach to Manchester as well as of the LNW's re-use of the C.& H .P .R. The Dalesman Paperback "RAILWAYS IN THE PEAK DISTRICT" by C.P. NICHOLSON & P. BARNES has some interesting illustrations and has information on the C.& H.P.R ., the Midland Line through the Peak, the Hope Valley and Woodhead routes, but is very sketchy in places and contains some shocking errors of fact (e.g. on p.55).

The Macclesfield Line is referred to in "THE NORTH STAFFORDSHIRE RAILWAY" by A. CHRISTIANSEN and R.W. MILLER, (well worth reading anyway) and is dealt with specifically in an article in Railway World Feb 1971 by I.R. SMITH. The LNW Buxton Line is best dealt with in J.W. SUTHERLAND and W.J. SKILLEN'S article "BUXTON CENTENARY- THE APPROACH FROM STOCKPORT" in Railway Magazine June 1963. The "CHESHIRE LINES RAILWAY" by R.P. GRIFFITHS (Oakwood Press) is a good book on the C.L.C., supplementing Dows "Great Central". An excellent article, "THE HOPE VALLEY LINE" by R. KEELEY, appeared in Railway World Annual 1980. The same author has published ''MEMORIES OF L.N.E.R. STEAM" containing numerous fine steam age shots of Marple and District.

For the historical framework, M.D. GREVILLE'S booklets "THE CHRONOLOGY OF THE RAILWAYS OF LANCASHIRE" and "THE CHRONOLOGY OF THE RAILWAYS OF CHESHIRE" are essential reference. M.D. GREVILLE and G.O. HOLT'S "RAILWAY DEVELOPMENT IN MANCHESTER" (Railway Magazine Sept., Oct., and Nov. 1957) is the best general account of the Railways of Manchester, while a modern reprint of W. HARRISON'S 1882 booklet "HISTORY OF MANCHESTER RAILWAYS" is a fascinating insight into a 19th C. view of Railway History. G. FREEMAN ALLEN'S "THE TRAFFIC DIVISIONS OF B.R No.9- MANCHESTER" in Modern Railways Nov. and Dec. 1966, is a brilliant Beaching era view of the then state of Manchester's railways.

For those who like railway timetables, David and Charles publish reprints of BRADSHAW'S GUIDE for August 1887, April 1910 and July 1938. Middleton Press recently produced a BRADSHAW reprint for December 1895. The Manchester Central Library possess a near-complete set of Bradshaw's from the earliest days of the railways. Ian Allan some years ago published reprints of the G.C.R. and Midland Timetables both for July-September 1903, and these contain much fascinating information apart from the timetables, about how the railways operated in their heyday.

For more details on the Marple Canal Tramways, see D. RIPLEY: "THE PEAK FOREST TRAMWAY" Appendix 4

Finally for those who enjoy looking at photographs, there are several excellent albums published which include a good number of pictures of the area. These include A.C. GILBERT and M.A. KNIGHT'S "RAILWAYS AROUND MANCHESTER", J.R. HILLIER'S "L.M. STEAM IN THE PEAK DISTRICT", B. STEPHENSON'S "L.M.S. ALBUM No.3" and C.P. NICHOLSON'S "MAIN LINES IN THE PEAK DISTRICT".

Published since 1980
-Basil Jeuda 'The Macclesfield, Bollington & Marple Railway (1983).
-Basil Jeuda 'Memories of the North Staffordshire Railway (1986)
-Basil Jeuda 'The Knotty' (1996)
-Basil Jeuda 'North Staffordshire Railway in L.M.S. days' (2010-14)
-Paul Harrison 'Striking a Chord with Electric' - 20 years of the Hazel Grove Chord (2006). History of and train services using the Chord.
-Grahame Boyes and Brian Lamb 'The Peak Forest Canal and Railway' is a magisterial work covering not just the canal but also the temporary Marple tramway of 1797-c.1807 and the Marple Wharf branch (Railway Canal & Historical Society 2012)
-The RCHS journal No. 193 November 2005 has an article by Brian Lamb 'A shooting at Marple Wharf Junction Signal Box-a possible terrorist attack in 1921'.
-The temporary Marple Tramway is also dealt with in more depth in an article. in the RCHS journal No. 168 of November 1997.
-The British Railway Journal No. 53 March 1994 has an article 'Marple - a one-time centre for traffic of the Midland Railway' by the author.

The Marple Local History society continues to publish excellent books on Marple:-
-Ann Hearle 'Marple & Mellor A New History' (2012) has a short section on railways and some very interesting details of 19th C. excursionists to the area.
-Ann Hearle 'Brabyns Hall and Park' also touches on railways.
-Anthony Jones 'From fields to flowerbeds The Growth of Marple' (2013) charts the residential development of Marple encouraged by the railways.

And finally my own 'Marple Rail Trails' (1982) contains 30 photographs of great historic interest and additional railway information - see my biography at the end of the book for details of how to obtain it.

Steam Special through Marple 30th May, 2015 (Arthur Procter).